International Strategic Marketing

As Europe moves towards becoming a truly single European market, its contribution to global marketing grows. *International Strategic Marketing: A European Perspective* is a topical text that expands upon existing international marketing theory and synthesizes it with colourful examples of relevant international marketing practice.

With a strong theoretical framework this text draws out the key issues within the developing European Union (EU) and the role it plays in marketing around the globe. With cases such as the banana, grain and steel trade disputes with the US and World Trade Organization (WTO), the authors examine and evaluate the real contribution the EU makes to world trade, while also considering the challenges of global cultural diversity as marketers learn to work across cultural borders.

Other topics covered include international aspects of:

- Marketing Information Systems
- Marketing research
- Product development
- Pricing issues
- Promotion
- Distribution channels
- Planning.

With an engaging and highly practical approach, *International Strategic Marketing: A European Perspective* is a must-read text for all students seeking to understand how international marketing really works.

Additional resources for students and lecturers can be found at our textbook support site, www.routledge.com/textbooks/0415314178.

International Strategic Marketing

A European perspective

Marilyn A. Stone and J.B. McCall

Routledge
Taylor & Francis Group

LONDON AND NEW YORK

First published 2004
by Routledge
11 New Fetter Lane, London EC4P 4EE

Simultaneously published in the USA and Canada
by Routledge
29 West 35th Street, New York, NY 10001

Routledge is an imprint of the Taylor & Francis Group

© 2004 Marilyn A. Stone and J.B. McCall

Typeset in Perpetua and Bell Gothic by Florence Production Ltd, Stoodleigh, Devon
Printed and bound in Great Britain by TJ International Ltd, Padstow, Cornwall

British Library Cataloguing in Publication Data
A catalogue record for this book is available from the British Library

Library of Congress Cataloging in Publication Data
A catalog record for this book has been requested

ISBN 0–415–31416–X (hbk)
ISBN 0–415–31417–8 (pbk)

Marilyn Stone dedicates her contribution in this work to her family, Phil, Juliette and Anthony, and to her parents, Nuala and Robert, in recognition of all the unstinting support they have all given her in pursuit of an appreciation of international marketing.

J.B. McCall dedicates his contribution in this work to his wife, Brenda, Tim, Robert, Mhairi and their family who have encouraged and questioned his involvement in international marketing over the years.

Contents

Figures

Tables

Boxes

Authors' biographies

Marilyn A. Stone

B.Sc. (Econ.) Hons. (Cardiff UC), Ph.D. (Heriot-Watt), M.Litt. (Heriot-Watt), Diploma Chartered Institute of Marketing (DipCIM), M. Institute of Logistics and Transport, M. Institute of Learning and Teaching (MILT)

Marilyn Stone is a senior lecturer at Heriot-Watt University, Edinburgh, in international marketing and logistics at both undergraduate and postgraduate levels. She is director of the international management degree and associate director of the international business and languages (IBL) degree, managing the exchange student programmes. She speaks fluent Spanish and French. Her research interests relate to the implementation of the Single European Act (1986) and the Single European Market in relation to European third-party logistics service provision. She has been a senior academic partner in six Teaching Company Schemes concentrating on strategic marketing and operations management in third-party logistics provision (for TDG), timber importing and processing, and kitchen furniture manufacture. She is a member of the editorial board of *European Business Review*. Her research papers include Literati club *European Business Review* outstanding paper 1996 (MCB University Press) for 'Strategic development related to Europeanization of UK logistics and distribution services suppliers'. She trained in international marketing with Philips, Delta Metal and Rubery Owen, after which she joined Heriot-Watt University.

J.B. McCall

J.B. (Ian) McCall consults in cross-cultural business management, having particular interests in Japan and West Africa. He gained considerable experience through working in Nigeria over a number of years as a government official in marketing tropical products concentrating on cocoa, groundnuts, palm products and rubber. He was marketing and sales manager with Thomas Broadbent, the sugar engineering business, having global responsibilities for the export of centrifugal machines. Latterly, he developed his academic career as a lecturer in International Marketing at Sheffield Polytechnic and went on to Napier University, Edinburgh were he was closely involved in developing courses in European marketing. He is regularly invited to run seminars on international negotiations in Argentina, Finland, France, Sweden and the UK. He has published two leading texts on international negotiation and has contributed to academic journals and press. He is currently working on a personal history of the economic history of Nigeria which is available on www.ianmccall.co.uk.

Preface

At the beginning of the twenty-first century it is appropriate to reflect on the ever-more critical role that Europe is playing within global marketing. Movement towards a true Single European Market in which products, services and capital can flow freely across national borders whilst people enjoy similar freedom to go on holiday, to work or to live has progressed a long way. The European Union (EU) continues to evolve. While there still remains some inevitable discord between its members, slowly but surely it is becoming more harmonious and more cohesive. It is steadily developing into a liberalized 'common market' in which products and services and associated marketing are more similar than, say, twenty years earlier when the Single Europe Act (1986) was enacted. Courageously, even ambitiously, the European 'club' is now preparing for another step in its enlargement, bringing in the nations of Central and Eastern Europe. While, lately, the unity of the European Union has been tested in the turmoil of Middle Eastern politics, its future seems secure.

Against this background, Europe plays an increasingly critical role within the global market. It is the strategic marketing approaches used by Europeans within international marketing that is the focus of interest in this text. These are considered as they apply both internally across European national borders, and externally, within the global market.

Over the past two decades, working towards becoming a 'European' while still being proud of national roots, has been a personal goal. Overseeing international student exchanges has encouraged this effort, especially those supported through EU programmes. Principal amongst these is SOCRATES, which aims to encourage the spirit of European citizenship, improve linguistic expertise and raise the level of co-operation between institutions. Within SOCRATES, ERASMUS supports higher education student exchanges, seeking to bring about more appreciation of cultural similarities and differencs within Europe and beyond. It is these experiences on which this text draws, alongside a background of international marketing within the manufacturing and logistics sectors.

There are rich cultural features distinguishing national and regional peoples which influence strategic marketing across Europe, e.g. language, different approaches to working hours, interpretation and attitudes toward promotional messages. Although Europeans are becoming more similar, differences ensure that strategic international marketing continues to be challenging, while working internationally at a global level is even more demanding. It is these issues that are addressed within this text.

ONLINE RESOURCES

Designed for lecturers and students as an accompanying online resource, this textbook has its own website which includes a Lecturer and Student Support Section: featuring five full-length case studies with discussion topics and comprehensive answer guide, plus a Lecture Slide for each chapter with learning objectives and sub-topic listings.

The website can be found at: www.routledge.com/textbooks/0415314178.

The text has been developed and written by Dr Marilyn A. Stone, Heriot-Watt University, ably supported by Ian McCall. Although both authors have discussed at length and contributed to the whole text, particular responsibility for the individual chapters has been as follows:

Marilyn A. Stone
    Chapter 2: Framework for international marketing
    Chapter 3: European marketing
    Chapter 4: International Marketing Information Systems: marketing research
    Chapter 7: International promotion
    Chapter 9: International marketing planning and implementation

Ian McCall
    Chapter 1: Introduction to international marketing
    Chapter 5: International product development
    Chapter 6: International pricing
    Chapter 8: International channels of distribution

Once the draft chapters were prepared, the authors read each other's contribution to link the chapters of the text. Examples have been drawn from a range of countries and situations, which it is hoped will help students to relate to the issues being discussed. The overall editing of the text was completed by Marilyn Stone.

Additionally, I am most grateful to Dr Calin Gurau for his contribution of the section on the Central and Eastern Europe in Chapter 3: European marketing. He has drawn on his own experience of being born and brought up in Romania, and comments upon the strategic marketing perspective as seen from the point of view of one who well understands the region.

Others who have supported the preparation of this international marketing text include Professor Chris Eynon, managing director, and Ms Katherine McIsaac, research director, of NFO WorldGroup. Both have been most encouraging. They have both read the draft of Chapter 4: International Marketing Information Systems: marketing research, and made useful comments concerning methodology used within consumer marketing research. They highlighted the critical role of qualitative research alongside the more popularly known quantitative survey techniques. Their comments have been taken on board, although ultimately the responsibility of what has been written lies with the text authors.

Thanks are due to all the others who have encouraged the authors to complete the text. In particular, thanks are due to the IT computer support at Heriot-Watt University given by Keith Aitchison and Guiliano Broccato, and to Duncan Hothersall, production director at CAPDM. Without them all I might never have managed to print out some of the files. Thanks should also go to my students over the years who, with their enthusiasm, have helped to stimulate my interest in developing international and global marketing cases. I should like to thank my other colleagues at Heriot-Watt University who have encouraged me to persevere.

Finally my thanks go to my extended family for bearing with me in the ups and downs of getting thoughts to paper. In particular, thanks to Phil for having confidence that the text would one day be completed, to Juliette and Anthony for their pride in their 'Mum', and to Nuala and Robert for giving their children an international outlook.

Despite all the support and the effort made to prepare a fair review of European strategic marketing as seen by myself and Ian McCall, the ultimate responsibility for what has been written rests with the authors. While it is intended that this should be as accurate as possible, any mistakes or omissions that may have been made are of our making and not of those others who have supported us in the task.

Marilyn A. Stone
29 August 2003

Abbreviations

ACD	automatic cash dispenser (sometimes referred to as 'automatic teller machine' (ATM))
ANCOM	Andean Common Market
ASEAN	Association of South East Asian Nations
ATP	Association of Tennis Professionals
ATR	Audience Television Research
BARB	Broadcasters' Audience Research Board
BCG	Boston Consulting Group
BETRO	British Export Trade Research Organization
BMRA	British Market Research Association
BOTB	British Overseas Trade Board
BSE	Bovine Spongiform Encephalopathy
B-to-B	Business-to-Business
CAD	Computer Aided Design
CAM	Computer Aided Manufacture
CAP	Common Agricultural Policy
CAPI	Computer Assisted Personal Interviewing
CASI	Computer Assisted Self Interviewing
CATI	Computer Assisted Telephone Interviewing
CAWI	Computer Assisted Web Interviewing
CEE	Central and Eastern Europe
CIF	Cost, insurance and freight (named port of shipment)
CIM	Chartered Institute of Marketing
CIP	Carriage and insurance paid to (named place of destination) RoRo and containers
CIS	Commonwealth of Independent States
CJMR	Carrick James Market Research (agency)
COFACE	Compagnie Française d'Assurance pour le Commerce Exterieur (French credit insurance authority)
DDP	Delivered duty paid (named port of destination)
DOB	distributor own brand (own label brand)
ECB	European Central Bank

ECGD	Export Credits Guarantee Department (UK)
ECSC	European Coal and Steel Community
ECTS	European Credit Transfer Scheme
ECU	European Currency Unit (= euro)
EDI	electronic data interchange
EEC	European Economic Community
EFAMRO	European Federation of Associations of Market Research Organisations
EFTPOS	Electronic Funds Transfer at Point of Sale
ELUPEG	European Logistics Users and Providers Group
EMBS	European Master in Business Science (degree)
EMRS	Export Marketing Research Scheme
EMU	European Monetary Union
EPOS	Electronic Point of Sale
ERM	Exchange Rate Mechanism
ESOMAR	European Society for Opinion and Marketing Research
EU	European Union
EURATOM	European Atomic Energy Community
Eurostat	Statistical Office of the European Communities
EX-IM Bank	Export-Import Bank of the United States
EXW	Ex Works, factory, warehouse, etc.
FCA	free carrier (named place) RoRo containers
FDA	Food and Drugs Authority (US)
FDI	foreign direct investment
FMCG	Fast Moving Consumer Goods
FOB	Free-on-Board (named place of shipment)
FOE	Friends of the Earth
FT	*Financial Times*
GATT	General Agreement on Tariffs and Trade
GDP	Gross Domestic Product
GM	General Motors
GM	genetically modified (of food)
GNI	Gross National Income
GNP	Gross National Product
H&M	Hennes & Mauritz (Swedish clothing retailer)
HERMES	Euler Hermes Kreditversicherungs-AG (German credit insurance authority)
ICC	International Chamber of Commerce
ICT	information and communication technology
IMF	International Monetary Fund
IMP Group	International Marketing and Purchasing Group
ISO	International Standards Organization
ISP	Internet Service Provider
IT	information technology
KFC	Kentucky Fried Chicken (fast food outlet)
lip-sync	lip-synchronization

ABBREVIATIONS

M&S	Marks & Spencer
MBO	Management buy-out
MD	managing director
MERCOSUR	Southern Cone Common Market (South America)
MIS	Marketing Information System
MNC	multinational corporation
MRS	Market Research Society
NAFTA	North American Free Trade Agreement
NFC	National Freight Corporation (leading UK logistics service provider)
OECD	Organisation for Economic Cooperation and Development
OFT	Office of Fair Trading
PC	personal computer
PEST	political, economic, social and technological
PIN	personal identification number
PLC	product life cycle
3PLP	third-party logistics service provider
PPP	Purchasing Power Parity
PPS	Purchasing Power Standard (= PPP but expressed in euros)
PR	public relations
R&D	research and development
RoRo	Roll on – Roll off (term used for lorries/trucks and/or short haul ferry services)
SBU	strategic business unit
SEM	Single European Market
SME	small to medium-sized enterprise
SMMT	Society for Motor Manufacturers and Traders
SMP	Single Market Programme
TGI	Target Group Index (consumption and lifestyle survey)
UK	United Kingdom
UN	United Nations
UNECE	United Nations Economic Council for Europe
US	United States
USSR	Union of Soviet Socialist Republics
VAT	value added tax
VW	Volkswagen (German car manufacturer)
WTO	World Trade Organization

Chapter 1

Introduction to international marketing

INTRODUCTION

This chapter will introduce you to the field of international marketing and, in partic-ular, to the environment within which international marketing decisions are taken. It will demonstrate how it pervades nearly every aspect of our lives.

We are enmeshed as citizens, as individuals and as members of society, including that of organizations, in a network of global linkages that makes countries dependent more than ever on other countries and on other organizations. The so-called economic melt-down in South East Asia in 1997–8 made its effect severely felt as far away as Russia, Brazil and Japan, and to a lesser extent the rest of the world. Policy makers have less capability than formerly to deal effectively with the effects of the globalization of business. Markets have the power to dictate the destiny of countries. An example of this was the ejection of the UK and Italy from the Exchange Rate Mechanism (ERM) of the European Union (EU) in 1993 when the markets showed their lack of confidence in their currencies. The currencies fell outside the permitted deviation limits of the mechanism and were automatically excluded. There remains considerable authority on the part of governments to carry out actions in relation to interest and exchange rates. This is especially the case when they are not constrained by supra-national legislation related to taxation, competition policy, direct influence on large projects deemed to be of national importance or co-operation with other governments. There is a host of other levers, often seen in the enactment of laws and any regula-tions made under them, by which legislators can create, if they are wise, a climate in which business can flourish to the benefit of all.

However, markets are themselves subject to the vagaries of changes in the environ-ment. While the function of markets is to match segments of supply and demand by bringing together buyers wanting to exchange money for goods or services with sellers wanting to exchange goods and services for money, any events likely to influence supply or demand will affect the stability of markets. In a free market economy this will have implications for the allocation of resources among both buyers and sellers. The destruction of the twin towers of the World Trade Center in New York on 11 September 2001 is a classic example of an unpredictable occurrence affecting the market. It sent stock prices in stock exchanges throughout the world into a steep fall. They lost 20 per cent during the year 2002 alone. A long-term bear market underscored once more the dependence of such services as personal pensions on a stock market with a steady growth in share price. The collapse of share prices provided the lesson that international marketing takes place against a background of uncertainty which is in no way diminishing in the current climate.

Technology and communication have combined to provide an infrastructure in which information flows are immediate and facilitate the movement of funds around the world. The transfer of processes associated with production technology such as ordering, delivery documentation, invoicing and the payment of goods and services were not possible ten years ago. The development of these technologies, aided by the plummeting cost of computer memory, has given an added fillip to the globalization process. This, in turn, has created new organizational forms in which companies have to cross borders not only to access customers, but also to communicate with other parts of the organization, exposing personnel to new forces which they have to learn to handle. People in other cultures, whether as consumers, colleagues, partners, suppliers or legislators and functionaries, constitute groups which often think and act in different ways from their counterparts in the domestic market and indeed from each other. International marketing is distinguished from its domestic form by a high level of diversity.

LEARNING OBJECTIVES

The objectives of this chapter are to:
- introduce you to the field of international marketing;
- identify current issues in the economic, political/legal, socio-cultural and technological environment;
- underscore the implications of globalization for organizations;
- examine the organizational structures appropriate to the globalized market;
- derive some of the skills needed to communicate successfully across national borders.

When you have completed the chapter you should:
- be familiar with the nature of the global market place;
- recognize the inter-relationships between the various factors in the environment and identify their potential to affect marketing decisions;
- show understanding of organizational structures in the global environment;
- indicate awareness of the problems of communicating across cultures and give evidence of knowledge of some possible solutions;
- distinguish the special importance of the Internet within international marketing.

DEVELOPMENTS IN INTERNATIONAL EXPANSION

International trade goes back a long way. Even before the rise of the Roman Empire, the Phoenicians, from their base in the eastern Mediterranean, are believed to have explored the West African coast with a view to expanding their trading activities. Artefacts found in various sites in Italy, France, Spain and Britain bear witness to the trade that the Romans did with the Greek states and the Egyptians. Later, other traders like the Venetians connected with the trade routes to the East. By the Middle Ages, Europeans had set out to engage in the spice trade, which led to the keenest of competition for that trade between the British and the Dutch in the East Indies. Portuguese and, latterly, the British, Dutch, French, Swedes and others embarked on trading expeditions to the Guinea Coast of West Africa. At the same time, the Portuguese and Spaniards sought to find fresh sources of wealth in the New World which, in turn, led to the infamous slave trade as well as the development of the trade in sugar and tobacco. By the end of the industrial revolution and prior to the Great War of 1914–18, there was a truly international market. It differed from the global market of today in that there was greater emphasis on commodities being bought by the developed countries and manufactured products by the less developed countries. It reflected the comparative advantage possessed by nations although there were already companies involved in direct international investment. Today, there is a market where multinational corporations (MNCs) have transferred expertise to other, less industrialized, countries. These provide sources of cheap labour for manual skills as in Indonesia and Thailand, intellectual skills such as the computer software industry in India, and production expertise as in the example of the Republic of Korea. Bangalore, indeed, the centre of the Indian high-tech business, is becoming a fully fledged research and development centre to rival Silicon Valley in the US. In an economy where competitiveness is global, companies have to take advantage of resources available in organizations in other countries to retain competitive advantage whether in innovation, cost, quality or speed of production and delivery.

Some latter-day concepts in international expansion

Research suggests that firms expand into new markets based on their collective experience in other markets (Clark *et al.*, 1997). This moves us on from earlier theories that a company

3

will only export when a product reaches maturity and suggests that firms choose to inter-nationalize in incremental stages following predictable paths. These were appropriate to their time. Today's organizations operate in complex networks and internationalize to support their membership in their networks (McKiernan, 1992). Companies prosper if the network does. International marketing decision-making in MNCs operate as a network rather than through a headquarters–subsidiaries structure. In pursuit of the ideal network, the Japanese car manufacturer Mazda has encouraged its suppliers to forge global links by entering equity alliances with foreign component makers to enhance their international competitiveness. Similarly, Nissan, linked over the last few years with Renault, has been selling shares in its component groups to foreign and Japanese buyers and merging other parts makers to generate cash flow and streamline parts procurement to meet international standards in costs and technology.

In the ever-burgeoning services sector, the generally accepted view that all services are fragmented is changing. Service-dominant industries apart from separated services like films, books, patents and computer programs, have internationalized by developing economies of scale and scope (Segal-Horn, 1993). While they must stay close to the customer by the interactive nature of the delivery, they are more like product-dominant industries than had been believed. Cross-border mergers and alliances among lawyers, and more ambitious ones between firms of accountants and lawyers, have strengthened their international competi-tive position (Akroyd, 1999).

Globalization is driven by market, cost, government, competition and other factors (Yip, 1992) as well as by the motives of managers. Given the global strategic perspective, the corollary that it should be accompanied by a universal standardization is difficult to sustain as such a stance is product oriented and in defiance of the marketing concept. It is also apparent that different nationalities buy similar products for different reasons and different versions of a product for reasons of values, custom and preference as well as price. There are various models to assist in the decision about the extent of standardization and adapta-tion. In particular, differentiation and integration pressures are identified by Prahalad and Doz (1987) as critical to deciding whether a multi-domestic or global strategy should be pursued. They add a third dimension in 'global strategic co-ordination' which implies that a firm centralizes certain strategic resources while adapting where there is a need to do so. Such thinking has given rise to the saying 'Think global, act local'.

COUNTRY RELATIONSHIPS WITHIN THE INTERNATIONAL ECONOMY

Within the global economy a number of trends can be observed which are not obvious if the markets are individually considered. Countries can no longer be self-contained even if they have the resources to exist as such.

Specialization

Countries specialize sometimes in different products but often in particular varieties of a product rather than the full range, usually because the greater the scale of activity, the lower the costs become and the more price competitive a company is likely to be. Some products are more susceptible to this process than others. Over the last twenty years or so average costs in research-intensive industries such as the microchip industry have tended to fall quickly. The electronics industry, like pharmaceuticals and agro-chemicals, is typified by high rates of product innovation shortening the product life cycle. Producers need to generate a high level of sales relatively quickly to recover their fixed research and development costs.

A second factor increasing the degree of specialization within a country is the size of the market, which is related to the returns to scale mentioned above. The large and wealthy economy of the US is often quoted as an example of the gains from the very 'bigness' of the domestic market. The abolition of tariffs within the EU, and the establishment of a single market, achieved a similar enlargement of the market which has encouraged firms to increase production plant size to reduce unit costs and has eliminated inefficient producers. The success of companies like Nestlé, the chocolate manufacturer, and the pharmaceutical company Sandoz, based in a small country like Switzerland, show that looking to other countries as markets can create market size.

A third factor influencing the way a country specializes lies in the decisions of MNCs about where to locate their production. MNCs can easily switch production from one location to another aided by developments in technology which will be discussed later. Ireland has become a favourite place to locate high-tech production and research as well as financial services because of the factors favourable to it. These include a good education system, the English language, low company taxation levels, a good infrastructure helped by substantial regional grants from the EU and its being a founder member of the single currency, the euro. It has become a net exporter of the products in which it has become an expert producer. Specialization means countries must trade with each other to obtain the benefits that it bestows.

Specialized production in one country can be one part of an international product, other parts of which are produced in different countries and with final assembly in yet another location, raising the question of its place of origin (see Figure 1.1). While the places in which different parts of cars are made in different parts of Europe will change with new models, recent productivity comparisons and government incentives, the global organization of motor car production and the ease of changing patterns of production and assembly are evident. There is a coloured representation of Peter Dicken's network on the Internet. Search on 'Ford Fiesta production' on Alta Vista.

Foreign direct investment (FDI)

FDI is investment undertaken by companies wanting to expand internationally. It may involve buying the necessary land, plant and buildings of an existing domestic company in a host country or setting up a green-field site there. At the other end of the scale it can mean setting up a local sales company with warehousing from which to attack a market from inside for the first time. Large acquisitions are more likely to be made when a country's currency is weak. European and Japanese investment in the US peaked when the dollar dipped to a low level in the early 1990s. Due to the collapse of some East Asian currencies in the crisis

5

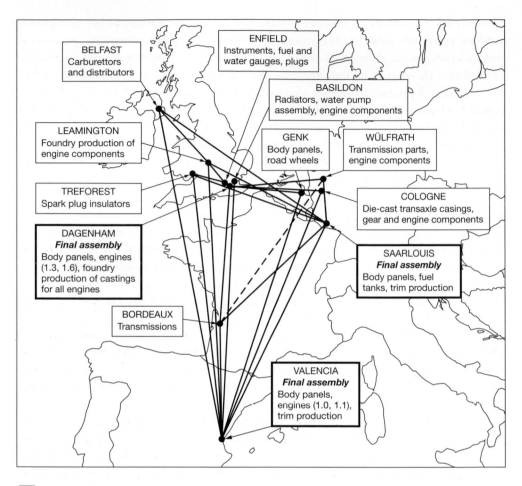

Figure 1.1 The Ford Fiesta production network in Europe (Dicken, 1998; reprinted with permission of Sage Publications)

of 1997–8, their values fell by up to 50 per cent making buying into the market a temptation for companies in countries less affected by the economic downturn.

Making such an FDI does not only involve a transfer of funds changed into the currency of the country receiving the investment. It has to be supported by other resources including transfer of technical and marketing skills and technology. It can be used as a substitute for alternative means of doing business like direct sales or, as is more likely, it can be used to complement trade.

Payments and the foreign exchange market

There is a complex web of international payments that links countries. Payment for goods and services is normally made through the banking system. The exporter's bank balance is credited and the exporter's bank settles with the importer's bank. However, what the exporter gets in his own currency is not a fixed return. Exchange rates vary, determined largely by short-term rates of interest. This means that the exporter may have to 'sell forward', that is to be put in funds by the bank which will cover itself in the discount market and receive payment when it falls due. An appreciation of a currency makes exports more expensive to overseas buyers (and imports cheaper to domestic consumers). A depreciation has the opposite effect; the value of exports will increase while the volume of imports may fall and imports become dearer for domestic consumers. The adoption of the euro by a majority of the EU countries has eliminated that risk within the group of countries embracing the European Monetary Union (EMU).

Purchasing Power Parity

According to many economists, exchange rates equalize in the long term. This is known as the Purchasing Power Parity (PPP) theory. This suggests that in the long term an identical basket of goods should cost exactly the same in all countries. In the meantime, short-term variations in the rates are taking place, sometimes with violent swings, and it is within this shorter term that decisions are taken. The US dollar has in the years between 1993 and 2003 varied widely in relation to other major currencies. Wide variations underscore the difficulties confronting a seller when exchanging the foreign currency on his export earnings for domestic currency as the level of earnings on similar transactions at different times may differ, which is why most companies prefer to enter some form of hedging of transactions.

When making decisions concerning markets to enter or develop, marketers can profit from statistics which attempt to equalize these variations by expressing the economic performance of all countries in terms of the US dollar adjusted to reflect PPP. Within the EU, Eurostat, the Statistical Office of the European Communities, adopts a Purchasing Power Standard (PPS) expressed in euros. These approaches give a better idea of the economic performance of nations and are widely used for marketing decision-making. Table 1.1 gives some examples of the economic statistics used.

While these statistics are useful, they are not precise, being based variously on surveys or on regression estimates or extrapolated from earlier PPPs. What goes into national Gross Domestic Product (GDP) which is a constituent part of Gross National Income (GNI, formerly Gross National Product, GNP) can vary. For example, it can include large expenditure on building and maintaining prisons, and installing security systems as well as the cost of providing socially useful products and services. It can also include taking out theft insurance cover in countries where the crime rate is high and, since the events of 11 September 2001, the cost of premiums for damage caused by terrorism. Even the vast amounts spent on lawyers' fees in a country given to litigation like the US can inflate the GDP and hence the GNI per capita calculation. Nevertheless, the column headed 'GNI per capita PPP US $ 2000' is a better reflection of standards of living between countries than would be the case using the column headed 'GNI per capita US $ 2000'. For this reason alone, it is important for international marketers to understand the notion of PPP. It is used because it provides the best available basis on which to compare economies.

7

Table 1.1 *Comparison of world economic statistics, 1990–2000*

Country	Total GNI millions US $ 2000	GNI per capita US $ 2000	GNI per capita PPP US $ 2000	Life expectancy at birth 2000	FDI as percentage of GDP 2000	GDP per capita av. annual real growth 1990–2000	Average annual inflation 1990–2000
Argentina	276,228	7,460	12,050	74	4.1	3.0	5.2
Austria	204,525	25,220	26,330	78	4.8	1.7	2.1
Belgium	251,583	24,540	27,470	78	7.9	1.8	1.9
Brazil	610,058	3,580	7,300	68	5.5	1.5	207.7
China	1,062,919	840	3,920	70	3.6	9.2	7.1
Denmark	172,238	32,280	27,250	76	21.1	2.1	2.2
Finland	130,106	25,130	24,570	77	7.5	2.4	1.9
France	1,438,293	24,090	24,420	79	3.3	1.3	1.5
Germany	2,063,734	25,120	24,920	77	10.1	1.2	2.1
India	454,800	450	2,340	63	0.5	4.1	7.9
Indonesia	119,871	570	28,330	66	1.2	2.5	15.5
Ireland	85,979	22,660	25,520	76	24.3	6.5	3.5
Italy	1,163,211	20,160	23,470	79	1.2	1.4	3.8
Japan	4,519,067	35,620	27,080	81	6.2	1.1	0.1
Korean Republic	421,069	8,910	17,300	73	2.1	4.7	5.1
Malaysia	78,727	3,380	8,330	73	1.9	4.4	3.9
Mexico	497,025	5,070	8,790	73	2.3	1.4	18.9
Netherlands	397,544	24,970	25,850	78	14.8	2.2	1.9
Nigeria	32,705	260	800	47	2.6	-0.4	28.5
Poland	161,832	4,190	9,000	73	5.9	4.5	23.4
Portugal	111,291	11,120	16,990	76	5.9	2.5	5.3
Singapore	99,404	24,740	24,910	78	6.9	4.7	1.3
Spain	595,255	15,080	19,260	78	6.4	2.3	3.9
Sweden	240,707	27,140	23,970	80	9.7	1.6	2.1
UK	1,459,500	24,430	23,550	77	9.5	2.2	2.9
US	9,601,505	34,100	34,100	77	2.9	2.2	2.1

Source: data selected and adapted from *World development indicators* (World Bank, 2002a). These data are also contained in the *World Bank atlas 2002* (World Bank, 2002b)

Using macro-economic and social 'facts'

Consider the market for a consumer durable such as a hypothetical electro-widget costing about US $900 in Argentina, Brazil, India, Korea and Sweden. If we go to the indicators shown in Table 1.1, we see that GNI, formerly GNP, per capita, on a purchasing power parity basis (in 2000) is $23,970 in Sweden and $17,300 in Korea. Both Sweden and Korea are wealthy countries. Income distribution in Sweden is comparatively even and details are readily available in an open and statistically minded society. The electro-widgets would be well within the buying capacity of most Swedes. In Korea, the income distribution is harder to ascertain. An authoritative source, Daniel Cohen, the eminent French economist, considers that Korea and Taiwan are among the most egalitarian countries in the world – more egalitarian than France (and presumably the US and the UK) and almost on a par with Sweden (Cohen, 1998). The market in Korea would also seem attractive and large due to the wide distribution of income among the population.

In Brazil, with a population of 170 million and GNI per capita (PPP) of US $7,300, the distribution of income is heavily skewed. Much of the wealth is concentrated in the hands of a relatively small proportion of the population. Income distribution figures are not available. A large market is unlikely to exist among ordinary inhabitants for the electro-widget. Where distribution data are not available, good proxies are the mortality statistics according to Amartya Sen (1998), social economist and Nobel prize-winner. There is a strong correlation between life expectancy at birth and the success of government policies, including how well the benefits of these policies are spread among the population. Brazilians have a life expectancy of 68 years. Like its neighbour Argentina, with a population of 37 million and GNI per capita of US $12,050, Brazil has enjoyed rapid growth rates but life expectancy has risen only modestly because wealth remains concentrated. Argentina, with a life expectancy of 74 years, is worth researching further as a potential market since the spread of income is much wider than in Brazil and the proportion of the population constituting a market relatively higher.

India, where in the same year the GNI per capita (PPP) was US $2,340, would appear at first sight to offer little opportunity for the sale of electro-widgets. Here again, the income distribution is heavily skewed, which is concealed by the raw data. An estimate quoted by management guru Tom Peters a decade ago indicated that as many Indians (there are over 1,015 million of them) as Americans had an annual income of over US $40,000. The vast majority live in the cities and are easily accessible, making them possible purchasers of the hypothetical electro-widgets.

POLITICAL ENVIRONMENT

Incentives to global growth

Policy makers find themselves confronting the power of the market. They seek to diminish any adverse impact of global trade on their own manufacturers and on employees by putting restrictions on imports, e.g. by 'voluntary' import restraints that are applied selectively against trading partners. This has been shown in the US by its disregard of the principle of free trade in such industries as automobiles, steel and textiles when they appeared threatened by foreign competition. Such an approach does not take account of the fact that foreign exporters may not have caused the decline in the domestic industry, which is usually driven by the pressure to maintain jobs and profits. A second way aimed at containing competition from foreign imports is through the application of quotas and tariffs or other measures such as requiring companies to make import deposits prior to bringing in the goods from abroad, thereby increasing the cost of importing. They also exercise the right to implement rules on dumping when a commodity is sold in a foreign market below marginal cost, e.g. to dispose of a surplus or to 'buy' market share.

A more subtle method of restricting exports is through non-tariff barriers. These are more difficult to detect or prove. Examples would be a campaign to 'buy British' or using national standards that are not comparable, providing preference to domestic over foreign tenderers or requiring a particular design that favours the domestic tenderer rather than have a performance-related requirement. The negative aspect of international trade is that the spirit of free trade is less likely to be observed if national and organizational interests are threatened.

There is, however, good reason to emphasize the positive aspects to be seen in the global environment. Privatization and deregulation have resulted in the opening up of markets to trade where previously it had not been possible. In the telecommunication sector, for example, national monopolies have been dismantled in places as far apart as Italy and Argentina. The last ten years have witnessed the breaking up of government monopolies and the removal of regulations that hindered trade which has been dramatized by the sale of organizations such as the national telecommunications and other public utilities. Sales of government-owned businesses have created opportunities for expanding companies in Central and Eastern Europe. Pilkington Glass, for instance, has a joint venture with a former nationalized Polish glass company. The introduction of competition in these industries has provided an incentive to world trade growth since the collapse of the Communist system in Eastern Europe. They present an opportunity for marketers intent on finding new markets. On the other hand, Nigeria, to cite just one example, still has more than a thousand companies in the public domain not exposed to competition and not operating as well as they could as a result of inefficiency, corruption and lack of motivation to excel.

Role of the state

The extent to which the state intervenes in trade and business activities varies from country to country. In the US there is an antipathy to government intervention, emotively referred to frequently as 'interference'. On the other hand, India, for decades a protectionist, centralized economy, has of recent years opened up its market to allow a degree of liberalization to encourage inward investment. In Japan and France, governments play a central role in the management of the economy, although, recently, both have been observed to ease their grip on certain sectors. For example, France has agreed to the privatization of France Télécom but has retained a measure of control through the *noyau dur* or hard-core shareholding. Strongly interventionist governments need to be assessed more closely when entering markets with substantial FDI support than when entering those that operate a more *laissez-faire* policy.

10

BOX 1.1 *'LAISSEZ-FAIRE'* IN A COMMUNIST STATE?

China is an example of an economy trying hard and successfully to move to a capitalist type economy despite the centralization of government control and its tradition of a command economy. It already has a GDP in excess of that of Italy and is expected to become the third largest economy in the world by 2007 after the US and Japan (McRae, 2003). With China's entry into the World Trade Organization (WTO) and the opening of its markets to comply with its commitments to the WTO, the move by Hong Kong and Taiwanese manufacturers to invest heavily in mainland China has received an added fillip. Political barriers to investment in once-strategic industries like semi-conductors, oil and banking are crumbling. There are signs that political integration of Hong Kong is being paralleled by an economic one just as Taiwan is also being integrated economically. Scientists and managers of Chinese origin are returning to China from Silicon Valley in droves as the economy points upwards. Thousands of Taiwanese are pursuing degrees in Chinese rather than US universities. The World Bank estimates that Greater China will overtake the EU in five years in terms of purchasing power. These Taiwanese and Hong Kong entrepreneurs have, with the local mainland organizations, been building up networks of influence together with the Koreans, Japanese and other Asians, which will be difficult for foreigners to match. If China learns to protect intellectual property and respect for personal freedoms, the inflow of foreign talent will further increase and mainland inter-national centres of innovation are likely to emerge. The fulcrum of international wealth and power appears to be shifting to the Far East.

In those countries that have adopted a political system in which people feel included, such as those with proportional representation, there is likely to be a wider influence on govern-ment policy. In countries with a high power distance between strata of society, where there is less participation by the population, it is more likely there will be sudden and violent political change.

International organizations

The international marketer has to be aware of the impact on international trade of organiza-tions with worldwide influence on business decisions. The WTO, for example, is opposed to restrictions like non-tariff barriers mentioned above. In particular, it may be asked to adjudi-cate on disputes arising from the increasing number of non-tariff barriers and from regional trade arrangements. One company's actions in gaining a large market share in another coun-try may lead to the serious injury of an industry in, say, a developing country. The WTO may be asked to decide what should be done if there is a case made by the developing country's government for protection. Conversely, countries can protest that protection is excessive and prejudicial to free trade.

Another international organization that can influence marketing decision-making is the Organisation for Economic Co-operation and Development (OECD), a grouping of some thirty wealthy, industrialized nations. It makes decisions in the interest of economic growth and financial stability and is also concerned with promoting trade with third world countries. Member countries have agreed, among other actions with similar objectives, to forbid government buyers in their jurisdictions to impose 'offset' measures in civil contracts on sellers from developing countries. 'Offset' is where part of the value of a contract is fed back into the buyer country's economy, e.g. in terms of part manufacture or designs or technology transfer, all of which create local employment. Knowledge of such conditions can be critical for marketers in developing countries.

BOX 1.2 WORLD TRADE ORGANIZATION AND THE BANANA WARS

In the early 1990s the US filed a complaint with the World Trade Organization (WTO) against the European Union (EU). It charged that an EU scheme giving banana producers in former colonies in the Caribbean special access to European markets breached free trade rules. At the time only 7 per cent of Europe's bananas came from the Caribbean and were distributed by European firms. The EU position sprang from a 1970s agreement, the Lomé Convention, whereby each Caribbean country was given a banana export quota. This, the EU hoped, would enable the economies of such developing countries to grow without their having to depend on overseas aid. It protected Caribbean farmers, typically holding small parcels of land, from competition from the large-scale, mechanized plantations run by US MNCs producing the Chiquita, Dole and Del Monte brands. The Dublin-based Fyffes, and its associate company, Geest, is a large supplier in Western Europe but sources only in Belize where it shares control with the various interests there including the government. It does not have the political clout exercised by the powerful American companies.

The large MNCs could reduce the cost of producing bananas far below that of the small peasant farmers in islands like the Leeward Islands and St Lucia. The scheme envisaged that it would close the dollar gap between the cost of Caribbean and Latin American bananas. Three-quarters of the bananas supplied to the EU come from Latin America and are supplied by these same MNCs through the producing companies they own in Central and South America. Indeed, Chiquita Brands International had about 40 per cent of the European market before the new system was introduced in 1993. By 2001, its share fell to less than 20 per cent, contributing to the group's near bankruptcy position (Alden and Bowe, 2001). The MNCs also control the distribution of these bananas. The US itself does not export any bananas to Europe. Caribbean bananas are shorter and sweeter than those grown in Latin America. Countries in the EU like Sweden and Germany buy solely the 'dollar bananas'.

The Latin American governments involved, including countries like Ecuador, Honduras and Mexico, also made representations to the WTO in support of the US complaint. In 1997, the WTO ruled in favour of the US. The EU was perceived by US interests to be dragging its feet in abiding with the WTO's judgement which eventually led to the US exercising its right under WTO approval to retaliate in 1999 (Jonquières and Dunne, 1999). It slapped import tariffs on a range of European luxury goods, including Parma ham and Scottish cashmere sweaters, to a value of US $308m (£209m) of imports (Norman and Alden, 2001).

Eventually, after some nasty exchanges, the feared confrontation was avoided. The agreement reached was that there would be a transitional regional regime under which the Caribbean producers would have a specific quota up to the end of 2005 after which there would be no more quotas. Thereafter uncertainty remains. There will be no support after 2005 except by tariff preference which has to be negotiated, although there may be an aid package to producers to enable them to diversify. Many Caribbean banana producers have already gone out of business with the fall in banana exports. As US MNCs can market at a cost that threatens the continued existence of Caribbean producers, those still active in production believe that they will have to appeal to the ethical judgement of European consumers to survive in their traditional work. Another suggestion mooted is to have the bananas marketed under a fair-traded label in a similar manner to the Central American coffee producers. In this dispute, the Caribbean producers are not the only losers. The flaws in the WTO dispute-settlement mechanism have been highlighted. Countries will not negotiate seriously if they cannot later be held to their commitments, which may be at odds with other commitments as in this case.

Regional groupings

Regional economic integration has been one of the most significant developments in the international market over the last 50 years and originates in political decisions which have wide economic implications. The most advanced of these is the EU which has developed a single market with the majority of its members using the common currency, the euro, within the Eurozone. Further political integration is expected. There are other economic groupings, like the Association of South East Asian Nations (ASEAN) which has established a free trade area in the South Pacific comprising Indonesia, Singapore, Malaysia, the Philippines and Thailand with Myanmar as a relatively recent addition. MERCOSUR in the cone of South America, comprising Argentina, Brazil, Paraguay and Uruguay with Chile and Peru as associate members, is a customs union with tariffs abolished and a common external tariff on goods entering from outside. The North American Free Trade Agreement (NAFTA) links Canada, the US and Mexico in a free trade area of over 300 million people. Organizations outside NAFTA seeking to be price competitive in the US can gain access to the American market through FDI in Mexico where labour costs are lower than in Canada and the US. By the same token, a Mexican or US supplier can enter the European market through operating within the EU in lower cost producing areas like Portugal and Spain. Increasingly, MNCs are moving their production to Eastern Europe to countries preparing to enter in the next wave of the EU enlargement. Poland, which has a relatively high growth rate, even lower costs and good communications to the EU heartland, is expected to enter into the EU in June 2004.

Business/government relations

In these days of potentially high mobility of capital, labour and production, companies can choose the most favourable country in which to operate. If a company will not give a country what it wants, another one probably will. Swedish companies have moved production and/or headquarters out of Sweden because of its high personal tax. Germany has the highest rate of corporate tax in Europe, encouraging Siemens to employ more people outside Germany than inside it, a reversal of the earlier situation. The relationship between companies and governments is one of mutual power and influence in which the bargaining power of each will depend on the relative power being exercised.

Relations with the home government reflect this mutual influence. Governments are in a position to compel certain actions if the companies are legally registered in it. They can define what constitutes monopoly, control the flow of technology and restrict the movement of people. They are, however, dependent on a successful business sector to raise money in taxation and provide employment, which makes the business sector influential. Managers seek to persuade their parliamentary representatives to propose, or support, actions in the company interest; many lobby the appropriate government ministers and even employ public relations (PR) professionals to do this. As a result, home country governments can be of great assistance to companies. Governments have in the past used the promise of aid and other incentives, or the threat to withhold them, as a means of getting the best possible terms for host governments alongside the best possible return for company investors.

It is an established principle in international law that foreign firms should receive equal treatment with home firms. However, they are often discriminated against, in effect, if not in intention. For example, in the area of taxation, the imposition of high taxes may discourage the repatriation of a foreign company's profits. In the area of law the host government sometimes only allows local nationals to act as sales distributors. This can preclude large minority sections of the population who do not come within the 'local' national definition as well as persons with a majority local shareholding in a locally established company. Some countries insist on a certain domestic content of components in the production of goods in their subsidiaries to protect their national interests.

LEGAL ENVIRONMENT

In a world in which the accelerating pace of change is a predominant feature of the environment, it is only to be expected that changes in attitudes and their interaction with technological, cultural, economic and political factors, will be reflected in the laws which regulate the conduct of business. Consequently, governments are more than ever concerned

BOX 1.3 THE US, GENETIC FOOD, AGRI-CHEMICAL MANUFACTURERS AND THE NEW ZEALAND GOVERNMENT

New Zealand has a Freedom of Information Act under which Cabinet documents of the New Zealand government revealed that the US government threatened early in 1998 to pull out of a potential free trade agreement with that country over its plan for labelling and testing genetically modified food. It was alleged that this was to protect the global ambitions of the agro-chemical firm Monsanto. The Cabinet minutes dated 19 February 1998 noted that the US was concerned in principle about the kind of approach being advocated by the Australia and New Zealand Food Standards Council and the effect this could have on others, including the EU. Apparently, it was linked with a bilateral trade agreement being brokered by representatives of the two governments and, reportedly, could impact adversely on the outcome. Friends of the Earth (FOE), the environmental group, said the New Zealand documents made the US international strategy on genetically modified (GM) food clear for the first time. 'This is the first visible evidence of the lengths the US will go to in getting countries to accept unproven genetically engineered foods', claimed Adrian Bebb, FOE's food and bio-technology campaigner. 'It is nothing short of international bullying' (Woolf, 1998). A British Liberal Democratic spokesman on food safety claimed that it was evident that the US government was acting on behalf of Monsanto to force its GM food worldwide on unsuspecting consumers.

to emphasize the legal basis under which goods are made, distributed and sold within their countries. These laws, and regulations made under them, embrace issues like the degree of competition to be maintained, the extent to which restrictive practices are permitted, whether and how intellectual property is to be protected and how consumers and users are to receive protection in their economic exchanges. They also address the relationship between industry and government in its capacity of a politically motivated entity and defender of the public interest including controlling the degree of foreign ownership and expatriate management tolerated, and the means of settling disputes in connection with marketing agreements. The emphasis on the issues and the ways in which governments give effect to their established aims differ from country to country. For instance, most governments are concerned to ensure that patents, which convey a monopoly for a given period – usually 16 to 20 years – are not used to restrict competition. In the UK there is provision for compulsory licensing if the product is not being worked. In some countries the importing of patented goods constitutes working, but local working of the product is required in most industrialized countries. There is no compulsory licensing in Argentina or Italy, but failure to work is penalized by the total loss of patent rights. In the US there is no requirement for working the patents, which is unique outside Russia and the other countries of the former Soviet Union, with the result that an unprincipled licensee can use a US patent as an obstructive weapon. In the case of copyright, it has a duration of 75 years in the UK, but only 25 years in Japan. It will be noted that in Japan you can buy cheap CDs of the recordings of the Beatles, but you cannot buy them for resale in those countries where the copyright is still in force.

International and supranational law

Where there is a dispute as to which law applies, that branch of law known as private international law or conflict of laws is called on to determine the law applicable and the jurisdiction that will pass judgement. Parties should agree the law of the contract to avoid conflict of laws. The United Nations Economic Council for Europe (UNECE) has devised model forms of contract for contracts between organizations working within different legal systems. The Vienna Convention (see the next section) went a long way to resolving the danger of the conflict of laws by establishing straightforward rules. These provide for a sales contract to be regulated by the domestic laws agreed by the parties. Failing designation by the parties, the domestic law of the country in which the seller has his/her habitual residence applies. There are a couple of exceptions to the latter rule that need not be considered here.

Supranational law has been developed to meet the needs of regional economic and political 'blocs'. In the EU, for example, there has evolved a body of case law which takes precedence over domestic laws wherever the conflict occurs. An important aspect of this is competition law which is based on the principles laid down by the founding fathers in Articles 85 and 86 of the Treaty of Rome. This law, in effect, says that with tariffs abolished, there is no way in which any agreements in restraint of trade will be permitted and that any attempt to abuse a dominant position will be dealt with severely. In 1998 Volkswagen was fined ECU 102m (= €102m) for restricting intra-Community trade by prohibiting its Italian dealers operating through its Italian distributors, Autogerma (100 per cent owned by VW), from selling Volkswagen and Audi cars to foreign buyers, mainly in Germany and Austria (OJEC, 1998). EU law is much tougher than member country laws in that it is not possible to call on patents, registered trade marks, brands and copyright if these are associated with restrictive agreements.

Law and marketing agreements

Knowledge of the law under which an agreement is made is essential for sales people negotiating sales agreements because it may affect eventual outcomes. Knowledge of the commercial law of one's own country is not enough. The required knowledge covers the UN Convention on Contracts for the International Sale of Goods, sometimes referred to as the Vienna Convention, which a purchaser might want to regulate a contract. It would also cover the custom of merchants which has been a successful source of the harmonization of international trade law and is embodied in *Incoterms 2000* (ICC, 2000) which can form part of the contract of sale if so agreed. Acquaintance with the performance of contracts is necessary especially as it refers to delivery, the passing of property, the passing of risk and how arbitration rules and practices change to meet the cultural needs of different countries. The minimum knowledge of process needed is that of 'offer' and 'acceptance' and how any prior exchanges are usually excluded in a large buyer's formal contract documents.

Distributorship, agency agreements and licensing agreements are surrounded in the US by a complexity of laws stemming from the Sherman Act which prohibits contracts in restraint of foreign trade and monopoly. Agreements, the sole effect of which is to restrict competition, are void. Granting exclusivity to a distributor of a territory or brand is increasingly seen as violation of the law irrespective of its competitive effects. In most Arab countries there are commercial codes in which there is provision for disputes to be taken before local courts but it is normal for disputes to be referred to arbitration for quick settlement. This can be at the International Court of Arbitration in Paris or locally. The local court has the discretion to set aside judgements under certain conditions. Under EU law, agents are exempt from a general prohibition on agreements likely to affect trade between states because they are seen as an extension of the sales arm of the company they represent. Distributors are only exempt from such prohibition where they have a market share below a given percentage in a market area or have a joint turnover with a supplier of more than a given value in euros. These are specified and updated in the Official Journal (of the European Communities) from time to time to take account of inflation. Equally, under the concept of parallel imports, an entrepreneur can buy where goods are cheapest. This applies even where there is a (restrictive) distributorship agreement in a territory for the sale of these goods. There is no protection for the parties to the agreement. This lack of protection occurs even when a brand name or a patent has been registered or granted.

Where an agreement is not considered to affect trade between countries, then the law to be relied on is that agreed between the parties, although which law can be critical. It may be advantageous to agree to the law of the other party, as the following example showed:

> In the United Kingdom the law of agency is weak. Agency agreements can be terminated easily and normally only by giving the notice usually contained in the agreement itself. In France, Germany, the Netherlands and some other countries, the law presumes the agent the weaker of the parties and provides for compensation if an agent's services are dispensed with. It is therefore to the interest of a British agent to have an agreement with a French supplier under French law; for the French supplier English or Scots law provides an advantage should that supplier wish to terminate the agreement. If a French supplier discovers that an English agent is unaware of this, then he can trade off to his advantage an apparent concession to agree to English law in return for one of substance. In Belgium there is a law specific to distributorship that provides for compensation under specific rules for the goodwill which the distributor is assumed to have built up for the supplier.
> (McCall, 1996)

A directive from the European Commission has given agents within the EU the rights of employees, making it possible for compensation to be paid where an agent has incurred losses as a result of the termination of an agreement. Where both parties are not in the EU, it is wise to be aware of the other party's law. For example, a whisky distributor may make an agreement with its Venezuelan distributor under Scots law only to find in the case of a dispute that Venezuelan law applies where the contract is performed in Venezuela.

SOCIAL ENVIRONMENT

Perhaps the greatest long-term problem in the social environment is the contraction of populations in the industrialized countries of the world due to falling birth rates, while the opposite takes place in the developing world. If economic performance is measured on the basis of GNP per capita, i.e. the GNP of a country divided by the number of people in it, then the higher the birth rate the harder the economy has to work, even to maintain the current situation. A major concern arising from the contraction of population in Europe is that the smaller population paying taxes will have to support a larger population of older people. The UK has a social security system originally planned when there were seven working people for every pensioner; the proportion is now nearer two to one. The picture may be even worse in France and Germany where there are high social costs which support the advanced welfare system in Germany and the high proportion of pensionable civil servants (*fonctionnaires*) in France that are unsustainable in the new conditions. The 'pensions time bomb', as it has been called, may well lead to a complete restructuring of social security systems. Insurance companies across Europe are merging in the hope of creating a competitive presence when this happens. Marketing in the developing countries may be aimed at increasing the use of contraception in those countries trying to increase living standards for their peoples, and to reduce the expectations of people in the belief that frustrated hopes lead to social unrest.

International customer

The international customer does not exist except as a consumer of a few global brands like Coca-Cola and L'Oréal. The international market has to be segmented, or to have an identifiable niche, to be meaningful for the vast majority of companies. Again, the division between developed and developing countries is a useful distinction to make. People in developing countries often do not have the spare cash to buy what international companies are offering. In these circumstances, it may be necessary to embrace alternative technologies to satisfy that market. This can involve designing for a particular market, e.g. by building a cheap, simple load-carrying vehicle suitable for local needs or a washing machine that replicates in cold water and hand-operated mode the action of the automatic washing machine at an affordable price. The alternative is to target only that percentage of the population with the money to pay for an automatic machine. The distribution of income among a population can be a significant factor in this decision, but such data are not available in most countries. It has already been demonstrated that in India, despite a GNI per capita of only US $2,340 (PPP), income distribution is heavily skewed and conceals a large and accessible wealthy sector. A country's population as a bare statistic is only a starting point for understanding markets. The Irish population is the youngest in the EU but it is no longer growing at the rate it did ten years ago. The youth market is in excess of what its population might indicate. Ireland is the country with the highest average annual growth rate in Europe in private consumption per capita, indicating a latent demand at the luxury end of the market.

Need to look beyond the 'facts' for decision-making in developed countries

Consider a US illustrator specializing in illustrated book covers contemplating entering the EU market. The temptation is to give countries with a small population a low priority which could lead to missed opportunities. Denmark, for example, has some five million inhabitants. Informed research can establish that in the US the number of new titles published each year is 0.2 per thousand of the population. The Danish figure is 2.0 per thousand – equivalent to 50 million people in US terms. Denmark exhibits cultural traits which reflect embedded reading habits with a quarter of the two million Danish households belonging to one or more book clubs.

The preferences of consumers in individual countries are determined by their values. The factors bearing on a purchasing decision include the language spoken, which will reflect the culture and evoke certain responses. This could be the beliefs of people such as religion, their attitudes towards time, wealth acquisition and risk-taking as well as the way in which relationships are organized. The level and importance of education, material culture development, technology and the notion of aesthetics all contribute to consumer preferences.

TECHNOLOGICAL ENVIRONMENT

Nowhere is there greater change than in the environment of information and communication technologies (ICTs) which are the result of the convergence of the integrated circuits of microelectronics through digital representation of information and telecommunications. The ICTs include computer types like mainframes, desktops, laptops and workstations, as well as local and wide area networks, Intranets and the Internet, mobile telephones and the various software applications.

Internet

The Internet is the current public face of computer networking and is expanding at an incredible rate. It provides the carrier for the operation of other services including international e-mail, browsing of documents on the world wide web (www) and other functions. The world wide web can give easy access to databases providing information long before the printed word becomes available, e.g. the data on countries drawn from *World Development Indicators* shown in Table 1.1 were found by visiting the World Bank website at http://www.worldbank.org/data.

On-line transactions are increasing with increased usage of the Internet. While it can be a good medium for advertising, it can go beyond that in a way useful to users if it establishes and reinforces a dependence. It is now possible through the Cirrus facility to use a bankcard to withdraw cash in most countries. One of the authors recently obtained cash from an automatic cash dispenser (ACD) in Buenos Aires, Argentina, thanks to the Royal Bank of Scotland's alliance with Spain's Banco Santander, now BSCH since its merger with the Banco Central Hispano. Goods can be ordered on-line. Retailers are moving into the era when goods can be displayed electronically, selection made and delivery carried out without the buyer leaving home. The electronic intermediary is already providing examples

19

with firms like Amazon Books On-line which sells books 24 hours a day to customers in over 100 countries. It competes by providing a database of two and a half million titles, which is five times that of the largest bookshop. Orders are passed on immediately to the publisher who forwards the book required direct to the customer. Whether it can replace the knowledge and advice of the innovative small bookseller is open to question, but without doubt the Internet is changing fundamentally the dynamics of competition. Investors can buy and sell shares on the Internet from New York, US, to Taipei, Taiwan, and Christmas shoppers can buy toys at eToys. It is also an increasing source of information for marketing decisions through the various search engines like AltaVista and Google.

Electronic data interchange

Electronic data interchange (EDI) facilitates exchange of data with customers and automates the traditional order, progress, shipping advice note, invoice and payment systems. The *Incoterms 2000* mentioned earlier were revised in that year to facilitate this electronic processing. EDI also enables international carriers to keep track of every item being handled within their organization and with other carriers with whom they are in alliance. International EDI can incorporate a set of trading standards, e.g. Tradanet network which supports electronic transactions between wholesalers and retailers spanning 100 countries and 23 time zones.

Other uses of electronic data

One early electronic data system is the French videotex system, Minitel, which is a system that allows people at computer terminals to retrieve information from a central database, usually over a telephone connection. Minitel is a public service providing in excess of 24,000 services that reach into more than 6 million homes and offices in France and is used by many private companies for their own use. Terminals are free to users and payment is through the telephone bill. This allows the smallest companies to gain economies of scope in marketing (users can explore any service at low cost) and distribution (companies do not have the expense of collecting small sums of money from thousands of users each month). Consumers can use Minitel for tapping into databases, for home banking, for getting tele-phone numbers or train times, for tracing the movements of vehicle fleets and parcels and for hundreds of other applications.

The French garment manufacturer Vestra, which uses it to link its US subsidiary to its manufacturing company in Strasbourg, illustrates Minitel's versatility. Tailors take essential measurements of the US customer and enter them in a terminal. Every night the data are sent by satellite to France by way of a central computer in New York. In the morning a computer-controlled laser cutter selects the appropriate cloth and cuts the garment. Tailors add the finishing touches and the item is flown back within four days.

Other uses of electronic technology are demonstrated by the use of bar codes combined with customer account numbers to implement loyalty schemes in large retail outlets. These data can be collated for each customer and the retailer can observe the pattern of the customer's purchases and use that together with those of other customers to determine

BOX 1.4 SOME LATTER-DAY APPLICATIONS OF TECHNOLOGY

A minute piece of silicon or other semi-conducting material on which microcircuits can be printed gives us the benefits of credit cards with secure memory and personal identification number (PIN) access only, giving greater security for cardholders. Microchips can also be used on a windscreen disc to record the numbers of journeys a car can make on toll roads and can immediately pinpoint motorists who have not paid for the privilege. Keychain memory pods can be used to plug in to personal computers anywhere to eliminate the need to carry personal computer (PC) laptops around to access files and data for day-to-day business. Many more applications are being developed.

marketing strategy. It is used to customize the requirements of individual customers without losing the economies of mass production (Pine, 1993), and to customize packaging to the needs of individual retailers, e.g. to produce 'own-brand' labels for home and foreign customers as well as the company brand name without adding to variable costs. Robots can be programmed to manufacture to a given quality to meet identified market needs.

ORGANIZATIONAL ENVIRONMENT

As the economic and commercial environment becomes progressively more global, so organizations have to adjust to the changing scene. The structures that served a market based on export no longer provide a solid basis for organization when FDI and dispersed foreign production are prevalent and competition comes from quarters previously regarded principally as markets.

Changes in organizational structures

What distinguishes the globalized market place is a complex form of internationalization implying a degree of functional integration between dispersed economic activities. Fewer and fewer industries are orientated to local, regional or even national markets. Consequently, organizations have had to be structured to meet the changing circumstances. There is a move away from the international organization, which relied on export-based strategies, and the transfer of the parent company's knowledge and products, necessitating a dialogue between customers, intermediaries and suppliers and the people directly involved in the worldwide diffusion of knowledge. There is a move towards multinational organizations geared to the markets in which they operate, sensitive and able to communicate meaningfully with them. Problems with head office specialists and country managers in this type of organization are cross-cultural in nature. If the subsidiary manager is an expatriate, the problems between the headquarters and the subsidiary may be few, but the problems between the subsidiary, the host government and other locals can be considerable. Having local managers reverses the communication problem.

The last two decades of the twentieth century saw the emergence of global organizations which seek to achieve cost advantages through centralized global scale operations. Global/regional strategies involve specialization and integration of cross-border production and distribution. Subsidiaries are rationalized manufacturers supplying intermediate products and/or final assembly as part of a vertically integrated network across countries. There is a greater need for good communication between units because of the increasing number of interactions. The most recent and fastest growing organizational type is the transnational organization which recognizes that the world is more than a portfolio of market places as in international and multinational organizations. It is more than a collection of specialized production, distribution and assembly units, as in the global organization; it is also made up of resources and capabilities. It is the ability to exploit these and link them on a worldwide basis that is the source of the transnational's competitive advantage. It displays national responsiveness and flexibility, and exhibits the characteristics of global innovation and learning (Bartlett and Ghoshal, 1991).

Formal and informal co-operation

Intimately linked to the arrival of an integrated global market and a further increase in the number of cross-border interactions is the flood of foreign acquisitions, mergers and strategic alliances. Organizations are re-defining their core competencies to compete more effectively and seeking to supplement these with the competencies of others across the world by indulging in one or other of these activities. Microsoft – since Windows 95 – is concentrating on its competitive advantage in software creation and strategic marketing agreements with PC suppliers and has abandoned the manufacture and distribution of its output. Instead, it manages its relationships with manufacturers and distributors, so releasing funds for innovation formerly tied up in fixed manufacturing and distribution costs. The growth of outsourcing is re-shaping relationships across the information technology (IT) industry. IBM set up a division to sell its skills in IT to companies like Dupont (US) and General Accident (UK). It is likely that the majority of IBM's profits in the next decade will come from these activities. The perspective is one that views the development of relationships with other organizations as a necessary condition for the effective harnessing of resources across them.

Politics and negotiation

If network members want to obtain the best outcomes for themselves, as far as their continuing membership of the network allows, their behaviour is political. Politics with a small 'p' is about the use of influence and power to persuade others to do something they might not otherwise have done. Within organizations, managers are losing many of the mechanisms once considered essential to the job. The need to reduce overheads to compete on a global scale has left fewer people to do the managing, and the enhanced role of alliances has removed many functions of managerial control. Increasingly, managers are responsible for tasks carried out through others over whom they have no hierarchical control. In the exercise of the political skills to succeed, negotiation is a key activity. Since negotiation outcomes are interaction and information dependent, achieving the desired outcome and eliciting the information require an understanding of the other party's culture. Cross-cultural negotiation is not only a process whereby suppliers, customers and distributors in other countries are influenced to behave in a particular way; it is also a process which goes on within organizations. Interpersonal communication is critical to achieve understanding between all concerned.

CROSS-CULTURAL COMMUNICATION AND MEANING

A communication approach to culture is relevant to global marketing. It is a thrust that views communication as a number of parallel activities each of which makes a contribution to overall meaning. Language on its own is a poor conveyor of meaning. It is assisted by non-verbal communication associated with the cultures in question. When the non-verbal behaviour contradicts the oral one, the non-verbal signal is the one to rely on (Morris, 1977). The oral and non-verbal factors are mediated by the situation in which an interaction occurs, e.g. the 'soft sell' and the 'hard sell' is utilized for different market conditions.

Social context and structure

The final, and perhaps the most significant, mediator of meaning is social context and structure. People brought up in a national culture unconsciously absorb the commitments and strictures that the social structure imposes on them. Unconsciously, they make assumptions and draw inferences from the way their language classifies and labels. These hidden assumptions are the most important aspects of non-verbal communication in that they cannot be observed.

It would be expected that the words 'Yes' and 'No' would have the same meaning in every language. Nothing could be further from the truth. The scenario in Box 1.5 illustrates this in relation to the Arabs and the Japanese, and underlines the need to find out as much as possible about an unfamiliar culture, especially the hidden assumptions people make. It shows how their language reflects the way the Japanese avoid confrontation by the use of affirmatives as negatives. Japanese vertical relationships and the behaviours that sustain them are a positive disadvantage when solving problems. The logical, or dialectic, style is guided at all times by the interpersonal relations between the speakers. The premises underlying thesis–antithesis are parity and confrontation on an equal footing which will develop into, or permit the possibility of, synthesis. The lack of discipline for relationships between equals and reluctance to be adversarial in a culture that values harmony discourages the Japanese from practising these three basic steps of reasoning, handicapping them in advancing any issue brought under discussion.

Ethical dimensions of cross-cultural interaction

As soon as national borders are crossed there is exposure to dilemmas that do not appear in the domestic scene, or which manifest themselves in different ways. What should be done when an agent in Mexico includes in a price agreed with a buyer a 'confidential

23

BOX 1.5 A CROSS-CULTURAL SCENARIO

This imaginary encounter attempts to create a scenario which will make the characteristics of the Japanese and Arabs easy to remember.

Japanese do not like confrontation which threatens loss of face. For this reason they tend to say 'Yes' when they mean 'Maybe' or 'No'. The Japanese word 'Hai' means 'Yes' but 'Yes, I understand' not 'Yes, I agree'. There are many oblique ways of saying 'No' in Japanese, as for example, drawing in a deep breath and saying 'It is very difficult' or 'I'll see what I can do'. In spatial terms, they like to maintain a similar distance between each other as North Europeans. However, in terms of gaze, they tend to avoid direct eye contact which symbolizes confrontation in a culture which needs harmony to maintain vertical relationships. They have long silences between turns of talking which can be disconcerting to the uninitiated.

Arabs have a language which is expressive and beautiful and which is classical in origin being founded largely in the Holy Koran. It is not particularly suited to nuances of meaning in a commercial setting. Arab language requires exaggeration to convey everyday meanings and cannot be translated into English without losing some of its meaning. Within their own countries, Arabs need to make strong assertions or over-exaggerate to communicate meaning to other Arabs. In this way, when an Arab says 'No' another Arab may not accept it as a direct negative if not supported by flowery, expressive words of embellishment like 'No, a thousand times no'. They also like close physical contact. There is a classic photograph of Presidents Nasser and Kennedy in which Nasser is half-facing Kennedy and has a hand on his (Kennedy's) thigh. Associated with this proximity is a tendency to direct eye contact. The Arabs are an example of a people who believe that the eyes are the windows of the soul which reflects their warmth and spontaneity. Such characteristics leave little time for silence.

The situation could arise where a Japanese who says 'Yes' when he means 'No' is talking to an Arab who says 'No' when he means 'Yes'. The Japanese likes to maintain a good physical distance between himself and another while the Arab prefers a close contact. The Japanese avoids gaze and the Arab likes to hold it. The Japanese likes to leave long silences between turns of talking and the Arab loves to fill them. The likelihood of miscommunication is high.

(McCall and Cousins, 1990)

commission' of 10 per cent? Or when a hotel company specializing in long haul destinations is confronted with environmental groups opposing a projected golf course supported by government policy in Thailand. The environmentalists claimed it would deplete the water stocks available for irrigation and force small farmers to carry water long distances for irrigation. These are just two examples of everyday occurrences facing the international marketer in a world where values regularly clash. They show the richness of diversity in the international environment that reaches into all aspects of the marketer's work.

CONCLUSION

The elements of the international marketing environment are inter-linked and do not exist in isolation. The global economy could not exist to any degree without the technology that makes it possible; pressure from the market provides incentives for further technological innovation. Many markets previously closed by regulation and public control have been prised open as a result of political action. It is political will that produces blueprints for growth such as the creation of free trade areas. Equally, political balances counter excesses in the commercial sphere. Growth in international trade has led to experimentation with organizational structures to meet the new needs, multiplying the number of cross-cultural interactions on which its success depends, and emphasizing the need for effective communication at different levels of the organization. The result has been the increasing dependence for marketing decision-making on the ability of organization members to use the communication technology available and to improve their ability to cross the cultural divide. The global market makes unprecedented demands on the international marketer.

REVIEW QUESTIONS

1.1 Examine the uses and limitations of the data in Table 1.1 as a basis for comparing the countries as markets.

1.2 Given that the relationship between government and business is one of mutual power and influence, identify the forces that give the relative bargaining power to:

a   countries; and
b   companies.

1.3 Are we moving to a world of transnational companies?

1.4 Think of a cross-cultural experience that you have had, on holiday for example, and isolate the behaviours that have made the greatest impression on you.

1.5 New examples of the use of the Internet or communication technology are emerging all the time. Show how you have been keeping abreast of developments by giving a couple of examples.

1.6 Examine the ethics of the actions of the principal participants involved in the WTO decision in the 'banana wars' in Box 1.2.

REFERENCES

Akroyd, R.I. (1999) Personal communication, Aston University Business School.

Alden, E. and Bowe, C. (2001) 'Banana group sues EU over trade curbs', *Financial Times,* 26 January, p. 10.

Bartlett, C.A. and Ghoshal, S. (1991) *Managing across borders*, Boston, Mass.: Harvard Business School Press.

Clark, T., Pugh, D.S. and Mallory, G. (1997) 'The process of internationalization in the operating firm', *International Business Review*, Vol. 6, No. 6.

Cohen, D. (1998) *The wealth of the world and the poverty of nations*, Cambridge, Mass.: MIT Press.

Dicken, P. (1998) *Global shift: the internationalization of economic activity,* London: Sage Publications.

ICC (2000) *Incoterms 2000*, Paris: International Chambers of Commerce.

Jonquières, G. de and Dunne, N. (1999) 'A partnership in peril', *Financial Times*, 8 March, p. 19.

McCall, J.B. (1996) 'Negotiating sales, export transactions and agency agreements' in Ghauri, P.N. and Usunier, J.-C. *International business negotiations*, Oxford: Pergamon.

McCall, J.B. and Cousins, J. (1990) *Communication problem solving: the language of effective management*, Chichester: John Wiley.

McKiernan, P. (1992) *Strategies of growth: maturity, recovery and internationalization*, London: Routledge.

McRae, H (2003) 'Here is the news for the next five years', *Independent,* 8 January.

Morris, D. (1977) *Manwatching: a field guide to human behaviour*, London: Jonathan Cape.

Norman, P. and Alden, E. (2001) 'US threatens EU with new sanctions', *Financial Times,* 8 March, p. 37.

OJEC (1998) 'The community vs Volkswagen AG and others', *Official Journal of the European Community*, 13 July.

Pine, B.J. (1993) *Mass customization: the new frontier in business competition*, Boston, Mass.: Harvard Business School Press.

Prahalad C.K. and Doz, Y. (1987) *The multinational mission*, New York: The Free Press.

Segal-Horn, S. (1993) 'The internationalization of service firms', *Advances in Strategic Management*, Vol. 9.

Sen, A. (1998) Report in the *Observer*, 18 January.

Woolf, M. (1998) 'Revealed: how US bullies nations over genetic food', *Independent on Sunday*, 22 November.

World Bank (2002a) *World development indicators*, Washington: World Bank.

World Bank (2002b) *World Bank atlas 2002*, Washington: World Bank.

Yip, G.S. (1992) *Total global strategy*, Eaglewood Cliffs, NJ: Prentice Hall.

Chapter 2

Framework for international marketing

INTRODUCTION

This chapter reviews the literature related to international expansion and interprets it within the context of international marketing. It examines the marketing management strategies that can be used for international expansion. The routes used to achieve international expansion are identified and assessed. Finally, some international expansion strategies and models are discussed in relation to international marketing.

LEARNING OBJECTIVES

The objectives of this chapter are to:
- introduce you to the concept of international growth as related to manufacturing and service industries;
- identify the influences on the internationalization process of these industries;
- examine the strategic options for international expansion;
- consider the market entry methods whereby international expansion can be implemented.

When you have completed the chapter you should:
- understand the theoretical framework to international marketing;
- know the major influences on international marketing development;
- appreciate how international marketing has evolved;
- be aware of the contribution of strategic analysis to international marketing theory;
- appreciate the link between international marketing theory and international marketing planning.

INTERNATIONAL EXPANSION OF MANUFACTURERS

Early literature on international expansion concentrated on the manufacturing industry, in particular, as it related to multinational corporation (MNC) expansion involving consumer products and industrial equipment, e.g. Levitt (1983), Ohmae (1985), Porter (1986); Douglas and Craig (1989). These authors examined the expansion of MNCs from their domestic base into international and multinational markets alongside changes in approach to global corporate culture. After the late 1980s, this research widened to cover MNCs within the service provision sector by commercial and investment banks, airlines, hotels and express freight providers, e.g. Segal-Horn (1992, 1993).

During the 1960s and 1970s, economic theory was used to interpret the international expansion of business. Rostow (1960) considered international expansion to be an extension of the stages of economic growth where each host country influenced the marketing activities of international firms. Vernon (1966) and Vernon and Wells (1986) examined international expansion as an extension of the domestic product life cycle (PLC) related to international investment and international trade. Dunning (1988) also drew on economic theory to explain the transnational activities of enterprises. He, like Vernon, studied the international production of MNCs, examining foreign direct investment in terms of advantages to the MNC of international ownership, incentives and location.

Another approach to international expansion research has been to concentrate on analysing the international experience through case study. Johanson and Wiedersheim-Paul (1975), Bilkey and Tesar (1977), Cavusgil and Nevin (1980), Czinkota (1982) and Ford and Leonidou (1991) used this approach in developing their models, which concentrated on exporting from a home base. For example, the Cavusgil and Nevin (1980) model shows the firm selling in the home market (domestic marketing) before progressing to the preliminary evaluation of the feasibility of exporting (experimental involvement) and the systematic exploration of expanding international marketing activity (active involvement) with long-term commitment in international markets. Olson and Wiedersheim-Paul (1978) emphasized the pre-export behaviour of firms within their model of export propensity.

Generally, these models identified three states of international expansion through which firms can proceed. Paliwoda and Thomas (1998) highlighted these states as being:

1   stimuli for international experimentation;
2   active international involvement;
3   committed international involvement.

State 1 occurs when a firm operating in the domestic market experiences external and/or internal stimuli which encourage it to begin exporting. External stimuli can take the form of unsolicited orders from buyers, of having distributors abroad, and/or of using domestic export agents. Firms that start exporting through external enquiries exemplify a passive approach to international marketing. This involvement is fortuitous, marginal and intermittent with short-term profits. As the firm becomes more involved, it moves to State 2, becoming active internationally. It undertakes systematic exploration of marketing opportunities that often impose considerable physical, financial and managerial demands on the firm's resources. At this stage the firm can still retract from its international interests, but it may choose to proceed to State 3, as a committed participant in international marketing.

Until the early 1980s, international expansion was viewed as a stage of incremental growth. Earlier studies had considered international development in terms of exporting from the domestic base, e.g. Root (1966) explained international expansion using a model showing the export planning process. It proceeded through three stages which were:

1   identifying and measuring market opportunities;
2   developing the export marketing strategy;
3   implementing the strategy.

Later, Root (1987) broadened his concept of international marketing beyond simple exporting (selling domestic goods to a buyer in another country) to show marketing practices with the marketing mix encompassing an international dimension, involving a measure of overseas investments and co-operation with an overseas business firm. He emphasized the importance of the marketing research contribution to successful international expansion. Models were developed that used marketing research to prioritize management decision-making associated with international expansion. In these, after studying the enduring international characteristics of a market such as target market geography, topography and demography, market segmentation was used to identify critical characteristics of the market such as consumer buying patterns and consumption (Wind and Douglas, 1972). Other researchers also emphasized the need to concentrate on key markets by using market segmentation to avoid spreading resources too thinly (BETRO (British Export Trade Research Organization) 1975 and 1979; Paliwoda and Thomas, 1998).

Douglas and Craig (1983) developed a model using marketing research to prioritize international marketing options. Goodnow (1985) extended it to cover the setting of marketing objectives such as return-on-investment or market share targets which could be used alongside marketing research to select international market strategies and methods of entry. Harrell and Kiefer (1981) also used marketing research to determine a country matrix to ascertain the most favourable countries for international operations. Estimations of the attractiveness and competitive strength of each country enabled favoured multinational strategic market portfolios to be decided. Harrell and Kiefer applied their model to evaluate the favoured global markets for Ford tractors.

Phases of international market expansion

Douglas and Craig (1989) were among the first researchers to consider international expansion beyond the stage of initial entry to a new market. Their model (shown in Figure 2.1) shows the phases of international expansion for manufacturers and indicates the strategic decisions required. The phases progress through initial entry, local market expansion and global rationalization:

> *Phase 1: initial entry* During Phase 1, management selects the countries and the entry methods for the expansion. Entry methods could range from establishing

wholly owned subsidiaries using green-field sites to the use of mergers and acqui-sitions, joint ventures, strategic alliances and information partnerships. Progress in Phase 1 influences the timing and sequencing of a move to Phase 2.

Phase 2: local market expansion In Phase 2, the firm extends its activities within each selected country. The marketing strategy and marketing mix are adapted to meet each country's demands. As expansion widens, there may be co-operation across countries in developing international brands, promotion and distribution strate-gies.

Phase 3: global rationalization Over time, Phase 3 global expansion leads to the inte-gration of operations and increased marketing between countries. Rationalization and co-ordination of the marketing mix and supply chain are encouraged to achieve a balance between the firm's product portfolio and growth.

The triggers for these three phases of global marketing evolution vary and are specific to each firm. They can be both external and internal. External triggers are environmental factors including industry trends and competitive pressures; internal triggers cover sales, profits and management initiatives. Certain internal triggers can be directly related to external factors, e.g. increased competition from foreign firms may lead to declining sales. Firms will respond in their individual ways to these triggers to generate their strategic thrust.

Douglas and Craig (1989) suggested that for Phase 1, initial market entry, triggers could include:

- saturation of domestic market;
- movement overseas of domestic customers;

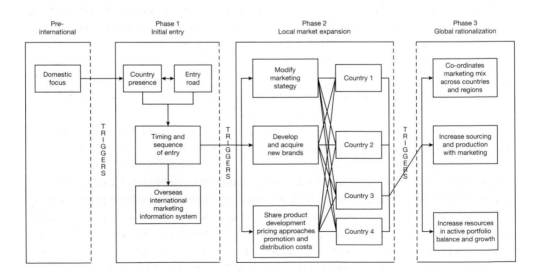

Figure 2.1 Global marketing evolution (adapted from Douglas and Craig, 1989, Figure 25.2, p. 371)

- diversification of risk;
- sourcing opportunities in overseas markets;
- entry of foreign competition in home market;
- desire to keep abreast of technological changes;
- government incentives to export;
- advances in communications technology and marketing infrastructure.

Triggers at Phase 2, local market expansion, might be:

- local market growth;
- meeting local competition;
- local management initiative and motivation;
- desire to utilize local assets more effectively;
- natural market boundaries.

In Phase 3, global rationalization, the triggers could be:

- cost inefficiencies and duplication of efforts between countries;
- learning through the transfer of ideas and experience;
- emergence of global customers;
- emergence of global competition;
- development of global marketing infrastructure.

The Douglas and Craig model assumes that there is a range of influences on the firm's international expansion. In this way, the international expansion of a domestic customer is likely to demand support from its suppliers so that they, too, are obliged to become international, whether or not they had intended to follow a strategy of international expansion. The customer/service provider relationship has obliged many suppliers to enter the international arena because of the influence and, sometimes, the dominance, of a customer. In this way, international expansion has often occurred as part of a piggyback relationship, the domestic supplier piggybacking on the international expansion of a domestic customer. For example, the UK-based Marks & Spencer retailer obliged its suppliers to expand internationally to match its own expansion strategy; similarly, car component manufacturers have had to follow the major car producers to their assembly locations.

Szymaski *et al.* (1993) also emphasized the role of the globalization triggers or 'drivers', strategy levers and business performance that influence the firm's control over its international strategy. Samiee (1994) extended the Douglas and Craig model to provide a conceptual framework for assessing the influence of the country of origin on customer evaluation of products in a global market. This assesses how international growth proceeds along a geographical continuum from regional to national coverage, from country to country towards global coverage. However, traditionally few firms reach full globalization; they usually remain with more limited international cross-border coverage. Those exceptional firms that do expand globally have become the MNCs of today with brands such as Coca-Cola, IBM, McDonald's and Microsoft that have become household names throughout the world.

Other approaches to international marketing model development have included the need to adapt the marketing mix to reflect the features of the export market as well as the characteristics of the company, product and industry of the expanding firm (Cavusgil *et al.*, 1993). Cavusgil *et al.* concentrated on the product and promotion components of the marketing mix, comparing those used in the home and host countries. Similarly, Jeannet (1981) developed the work of Bartels (1968) using the marketing mix as a function of the existing environment. Chan and Hwang (1992) evolved a model to identify the influences on global strategy and entry method choices of MNCs, emphasizing the role of global concentration, synergies and strategic motivations on environmental and transaction-specific variables. In this way, models have become more complex, attempting to take into account a range of issues that affect the influences on international marketing.

Role of purchasers in international market expansion

While research into international expansion has concentrated on manufacturing experiences, it has also encompassed the role of the supporting supply chain, in particular, industrial purchasing. In the 1980s, the International Marketing and Purchasing (IMP) Group compared international customer service among industrial purchasers within France, Germany, Italy, Sweden and the UK. Turnbull and Valla (1986) provided a country-by-country perspective of international industrial marketing strategies and the relationships between national suppliers and their customers. They developed the multistrat model which showed the strategic marketing decisions that firms make related to technology, choice of market segments, product or service offering and choice of customers. The model recommended that firms look for one or more of these dimensions from which to establish competitive advantage.

Other approaches to international expansion analysis

Other international marketing models have used case studies to describe international expansion. One such study of IKEA showed that its competencies were linked to following its customer demands (Terpstra and Sarathy, 1997). Takeuchi and Porter (1986) used the case of the Canon AE-1 camera to show that market segments and positioning strategies had been matched to demand within three country markets using three distinct marketing approaches to achieve the desired global strategy. Nichols (1994) also used case studies to develop company models to evaluate international decision-making.

Summary of international expansion methods for manufacturers

Researchers have used various approaches to assess the development of international marketing. Early studies extended economic theory to marketing theory to interpret international expansion. These studies largely concentrated on the situation for manufacturing industry, considering phases of incremental expansion from domestic to export marketing. Models of international expansion began by concentrating on export activities and the role of marketing research. Typically, a firm was shown to expand incrementally from country to country and then co-ordination evolved between operational and marketing activities on an increasingly global level.

INTERNATIONAL EXPANSION OF SERVICE INDUSTRIES

Research related to international expansion within the service provision sector has shown that, although there are similarities between the international behaviour of manufacturers and service providers, they are not identical. While research related to manufacturers can be used as a baseline for examining the international expansion of the service sector, it is usually adapted to match the specific considerations of the service industry.

Channon (1978) studied the international expansion of the UK service industry, including the transport industries but excluding the nationalized air and land-based (road, rail and bus) transport which had their international expansion constrained. Nevertheless, he considered that, in 1978, the state owned National Freight Corporation, the fore-runner of the UK-based NFC plc, had 'a relatively aggressive European expansion strategy', similar to that of UK manufacturers. Channon found that deliberate overseas expansion strategies were most common among those firms with a medium level of international activity and, in particular, among those engaged in building and construction as well as in the provision of hotels, leisure, banking and financial services. These firms diversified domestically, but had concurrently, or shortly after, also expanded their principal activities to overseas markets. This strategy was pursued vigorously, with investments being concentrated in the developed regions of Western Europe, North America and the higher economic growth countries.

Segal-Horn (1992, 1993) followed Chandler (1977, 1986 and 1990) and used his model to analyse different types of service firms in terms of the economic and cultural barriers affecting their international expansion. Chandler studied manufacturers, especially those within the oil and pharmaceutical industries characterized as having high technology and low labour intensity. His model showed that these firms sought scale economies for cost advantages and scope economies of capacity utilization through international expansion. Scale economies were achieved through increased volume of production/sales, while scope economies occurred when the cost of producing two products jointly was less than the cost of producing each product separately. During the 1980s, many service industries became more like manufacturing industry in approach and they began to internationalize (Segal-Horn, 1992). Larger service firms pursued scale and scope economies to reduce risk and take full advantage of international expansion. Simultaneously, changes in technological, market and regulatory conditions created more favourable conditions for this expansion. Nevertheless, there were still many service firms which operated within local or regional boundaries and remained inappropriate candidates for global marketing strategies.

Dicken (1986) found that large manufacturers were changing their international production from separate bases for each product within each country (multinational operations) to single-source production (transnational operations) using specialist core production competencies in each country. These inter-linked country production units were developed to provide economies of scale with associated cost reduction for logistics provision. International marketing organization was expected to reflect these changes in manufacturing organization, with more cross-country coverage, but it did not necessarily mirror the production organization. Marketing organization evolved to match the needs of marketing management and sales force structure which was itself closely linked to customer demographics. Appreciation of the influence of national and regional cultures precluded marketing organization following the rational approach to location of production plants. While customers showed less concern as to where their purchases were produced, they expected to be served by persons appreciative of their local cultural expectations.

SUMMARY OF INFLUENCES ON INTERNATIONALIZATION

Firms have been encouraged to internationalize through the influence of:

■ globalization of markets;
■ cheaper communications;
■ removal of barriers to trade and foreign investment;
■ targeting of economies of scale in business;
■ innovation in logistics;
■ environmental considerations.

These factors have become increasingly interdependent. For example, the globalization of economies has been linked to the increasing standardization of products and services (or economies of scale within business) which, in turn, has been related to more efficient communication through the advancement of information technology (IT) and management information systems. The move towards the removal of barriers to trade, such as those within the Single European Market, has led to more international expansion (see Chapter 3 for further discussion).

STRATEGIC OPTIONS FOR INTERNATIONAL EXPANSION

International expansion has also been considered in terms of strategic development with strategic approaches for the domestic market being extended to have international, and global, coverage.

Product portfolio strategy

Various methods have been used to determine favoured strategies for development using product/market matrices. Ansoff (1965) considered that the strategic options available to firms depend on the relationship between their existing or new product portfolio in their established or new markets (see Figure 2.2). Within the existing framework, firms in their established markets can use penetration or product development strategies related to those currently being undertaken. The firm with existing products in existing markets has the options of withdrawal, consolidation or market penetration. If considering a new market, the firm can follow market development and diversification strategies involving related or unrelated diversification (Johnson and Scholes, 2002).

	Existing product	New product
Existing market	Penetration strategies • withdrawal • consolidation • market penetration	Product development strategies
New market	Market development strategies	Diversification strategies

Figure 2.2 Strategic related options for growth (adapted from Ansoff, 1986, p. 99)

Entry into new markets with an existing product portfolio requires measures to ensure market development such as increased expenditure on promotion or investment in channels of distribution. New products for markets in which the firm is already established might require product development strategies, while new products in new markets might require a combination of related and unrelated diversification strategies. Related diversification can be effected through vertical (backward or forward) and/or horizontal integration within the supply chain. Unrelated diversification could occur where firms decide to diversify into markets and products outside their present range of activities. However, unrelated diversification is a high-risk strategy dependent for its success on a firm's resources in terms of finance and skills. Strategies with lower risk are those which extend the core business, namely those involving related developments in Ansoff's terms. Related diversification is more likely to be appropriate than unrelated diversification, but the choice will depend on the market conditions at the time.

With Ansoff's approach, firms are likely to favour expansion strategies using related developments rather than to follow higher risk diversification strategies. Firms prefer to apply their established expertise within new markets, rather than diversify into new activities within new markets. However, as the market becomes more competitive, with profit margins under pressure, some market leaders may diversify their interests along the value chain, despite the higher associated risk. Referring to Figure 2.2, firms prefer to use strategies that develop their existing products and services, that is, penetration and/or market development strategies. Within existing markets, market penetration is usually favoured in place of withdrawal from the market or consolidation of operations, as it will pose least risk, e.g. the firm may look for more customers within an existing market. Nevertheless, as price competition increases together with the associated reduced profit margins, the market penetration option may become less attractive. Then the firm may be obliged to consider new product development or other diversification strategies.

Since the 1990s, firms have favoured moving towards strategies that concentrate on core products and services, making diversification strategies less popular. Many holding companies have reviewed their group strategies to focus on targeted industrial markets and countries. Unrelated diversification is not now generally favoured, although many firms have implemented it in the past. The favoured strategy, at present, is to encourage developments related to those services already offered.

Boston Consulting Group (BCG) growth-share strategic analysis

During the late 1960s, BCG introduced its growth model for strategic planning which classifies a firm's portfolio of products in terms of their market growth rates and their market shares (BCG, 1971). The BCG model is normally used to show individual firms' favoured product portfolios. The product groups are categorized as 'stars', 'cash cows', 'question marks' and 'dogs' (see Figure 2.3).

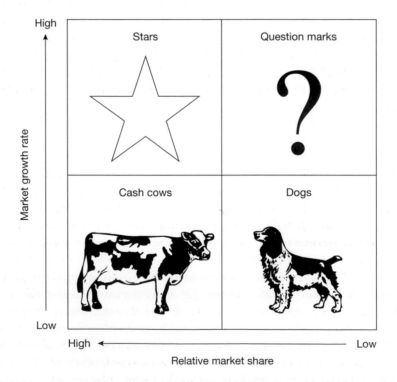

Figure 2.3 Boston Consulting Group (BCG) growth-share matrix (based on BCG, 1971)

Star products have high market growth rates with relatively high market shares and higher than average industrial performance. They are likely to be new products at the beginning of their PLC (see below for explanation), which require considerable financial support. They have good future prospects, but their immediate return on capital is often low.

Cash cow products have relatively high market shares with associated low market growth rates. These products are usually well established in the market, often at the mature stage of their PLCs. They require limited financial support and should reap higher than normal returns.

Question mark products have relatively low market growth rates with low market shares. They incur high risk and, like 'stars', demand considerable financial support. They may be products at the beginning of their PLCs with uncertain potential for growth. Financial rewards are likely to be low and can be negative.

Dog products have both relatively low market growth rates and low market shares. Such products are reaching the end of their PLCs. Financial rewards are limited with such products and they often incur losses.

Summary of BCG growth-share strategic model application

The BCG model identifies the favoured product/service portfolios which provide steady profit earners, the 'cash cow' products/services. Industry leaders are likely to use the income from 'cash cows' to develop new products and services or 'stars' which should provide higher profits and 'cash cows' for the future. They will try to phase out the problematic, less profitable 'question marks' and 'dogs' by disposal or sub-contracting the production, or service. Increasingly, industry leaders are focusing on the provision of the more profitable products and services and do not themselves undertake the provision of the full range of products and services, rather they sub-contract, or 'outsource', the less profitable operations. Within the context of international marketing, leaders try to concentrate on serving the more attractive markets, encouraging others to take up opportunities in the less attractive markets.

Product life cycle

The product life cycle (PLC) is a product's pattern of consumption which proceeds along given phases that can be measured, in particular, by monitoring sales. When applied to international trade theory, the PLC refers to international trade and production patterns. Country production passes through trade cycles. In this way, countries and their manufacturers initially may act as exporters; then, over time, they may lose export markets, so that once exporting countries can become importers of the product (Wells, 1968). Rugman *et al.* (1986) using the US example developed a trade cycle model to show importing and exporting trade between the US, Canada, Europe, Japan and the rest of the world. This model highlights the fluctuations that occur over time as these countries' trade changes between importing and exporting status. While the market growth rate and relative market share influence strategic direction and choice of market sector, as shown by the BCG model above, the PLC also has an effect on international trade and direct investment (Vernon, 1966). Furthermore, trade in physical goods influences the pattern of international expansion of service provision.

37

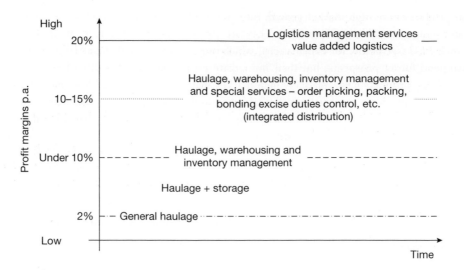

Figure 2.4 Logistics services development and profit over time (Stone, 1998)

Walmsley (1989) used the trade cycle model to emphasize the positive relationships between international PLC and international commitment. His model shows international involvement progressing from an initial passive stage, when the firm targets its efforts on the home market and accepts exports as they occur, to a more positive international marketing stage with aggressive marketing of a similar scale and approach to that used in the home market. The fully international firm uses constant probing of international markets together with marketing research to prolong the international and domestic PLC for its products.

Services have life cycles which operate in similar ways to PLCs except that they apply to services. For example, the logistics industry services range along a continuum – through general haulage, storage, inventory management, integrated distribution and logistics management – associated with increasing profitability, as shown in Figure 2.4 (Stone, 1998). These services have become more specialized and ever more dependent on IT. Hauliers increasingly offer services at differing levels of sophistication, ranging from open lorries through to specialized temperature-controlled vehicles and beyond. Each service will be at its own particular stage of the PLC, within either introduction, growth, maturity or decline. Throughout the PLC, profit margins vary with the more sophisticated services usually gaining the higher margins, although even these can be low. In effect, in terms of the evolution of logistics services, the different sectors have different stages of development and progress rates.

Industry profitability strategic assessment

Another approach to determining the strategic direction of an industry, or firm, has been developed by Porter (1980, 1985, 1986, 1987, 1990 and 1991). Porter showed the five factors (or forces) that influence the market dynamics of supply and demand and the profitability of the average firm in an industry to be (see list on facing page):

38

1   competition among existing firms;
2   threat of new entrants;
3   threat of substitute products (and technologies);
4   strength of buyers;
5   strength of suppliers.

These forces individually follow their own life cycles and will operate in different ways in different international markets.

A company's ability to obtain profits above an average level depends on its building a sustainable competitive advantage. Porter (1985, 1986) highlighted the fact that to achieve this advantage, the firm can select from four broad strategic options which he termed:

- cost leadership;
- cost focus;
- differentiation;
- differentiation focus.

Cost leadership relates to achieving lower costs than competitors by using more efficient production methods. Cost leadership is closely related to cost focus which concentrates on cost rather than other managerial issues. Differentiation considers the ways in which the product (or service) can be distinguished from competing products; differentiation focus concentrates on this strategy. Innovation may be one way of differentiating products. In practice all four options can play a part in a firm's strategy although firms usually concentrate on one approach. Many firms endeavour to move from cost-based strategies (cost leadership and cost focus) towards differentiation, moving from commodity businesses to niche players (Doyle, 1994).

MARKET ENTRY METHOD OPTIONS

Manufacturers have used various entry methods to achieve international expansion, but not all are applicable to the service sector. Manufacturers can produce their goods in their home country and export them to other countries using their own resources, i.e. their own export marketing expertise and transport fleet. Alternatively, the producer may use the services of specialist freight forwarders, sales agents and distributors. If exporting is not appropriate, the manufacturer can produce the goods in the country of sale, using a range of entry methods. These could include developing a green-field site for production in the country in question, licensing the manufacturer's 'know-how' to another producer, entering a joint venture agreement with an established local producer, or acquiring a producer of similar goods operating within the country being targeted. Paliwoda (1993) considered the international market entry methods for manufacturers to be as follows:

Freight forwarder	acts on behalf of producer to provide documentation and delivery service to foreign destination.
Export house	acts as an administrative link between producer and overseas customer. It represents a buyer abroad and can provide documentation service for the buyer.

Agent	sells a product to the end customer without taking title of the goods. An agent usually handles more than one company and/or product line and is paid by commission.
Distributor	extends the agency agreement to take title of the goods being traded. A distributor usually is given exclusivity of sales territory.
Piggybacking	uses the distribution channels of another company in a similar way to agents and seeks to ensure distribution outlets and products are complementary. In the same way as an agent, payment is usually by commission. These agreements may be linked to strategic alliances.
Consortium exporting	links smaller companies to combine their skills and resources in bidding for projects as a group of independents.
Licensing	confers a right to utilize a company-specific manufacturing process on the licensor, usually including a know-how agreement incorporating production training. It encourages the export of the licensor's components often embodying advanced technology.
Franchising	introduces the small independent entrepreneur to a proven business concept. It transfers the right to use the company's name, logo and all that may be identifiable with the company.
Management contract	transfers company-specific know-how and management control systems. Frequently such contracts are used in the service sector, e.g. logistics service providers.
Joint venture	joins together partners to manage a business. Traditionally, this involves joint equity investment and contracts may be of fixed or undefined duration.
Strategic alliance	is a flexible version of a joint venture with an agreement between partners which is continually evolving and has limited investment commitment. It brings firms together to focus on shared objectives aiming to enhance their joint competitive positions, i.e. firms share costs, skills and access to global markets with each partner contributing that at which it is best. Strategic alliances are sometimes termed strategic partnerships.

Manufacturers have a variety of entry methods for their international expansion and select the appropriate method according to the product being traded, the market, the customer and the resources available. However, services are intangible and cannot be readily exported by any intermediary other than the provider themselves. Consequently, not all of the international expansion entry methods used by manufacturers are appropriate for the service sector, e.g. third-party logistics service providers (3PLPs) use some, but not all, of the international market entry methods used by manufacturers. Thus, while freight forwarding, export houses, agents and distributors are not appropriate expansion entry methods for 3PLPs, entry methods such as setting up in green-field sites, joint ventures with local firms and acquiring established firms in the countries targeted can be used. 3PLPs may link their expansion with that of their established customer base by piggybacking on the customer's expansion. Strategic alliances and information partnership agreements are used much less frequently and involve relatively low investment commitment to extend the service coverage until it is appropriate to use more formalized expansion methods, such as joint ventures or acquisitions.

Other service providers will use appropriate entry methods to suit their particular service and the resources of the firm concerned. They may, but need not necessarily be, similar to those used within the logistics service provision industry. For example, a hotel group providing services directed at the tourist market might expand by building new hotels on green-field sites; it could also enter joint venture agreements with locally established hotel operators and/or it could acquire established hotel businesses within the targeted countries. It might also use other arrangements such as strategic alliances/partnerships to support this expansion, as for example linking informally with a package tour operator or airline to offer holiday packages to tourists. Further discussion of international market entry methods is given in Chapter 8: International channels of distribution, pp. 203–10).

The choice of method for international expansion will depend on circumstances – including the expansion stage (or 'phase' in the terms of Douglas and Craig, 1989) – such as the firm's resources and the nature of the product. A common route is to acquire another firm in the country targeted for expansion. Yet, such expansion routes can pose problems, as indicated by Porter (1987) who cautioned against acquisition for its own sake and advised that firms should undertake three tests to reduce the risk of acquisitions, namely to consider the attractiveness, cost of entry and better-off tests.

CONCLUSION

While many manufacturing firms have expanded internationally, traditionally, service firms have not expanded outside their own domestic markets. However, since the mid-1980s, factors such as customer demand and the desire for economies of scope and scale have encouraged service firms to internationalize (Chandler 1977, 1986, 1990; Channon, 1978). Other factors that have encouraged firms to internationalize have been the globalization of markets, cheaper communications, removal of barriers to trade and increased foreign investment (Cooper, 1993, 1994; Segal-Horn, 1993). During the 1990s, the rapid development in IT, especially the advent of e-commerce through the Internet, has helped and promoted international expansion.

Product portfolio matrixes can help to assess routes to international strategic development within a firm or an industry. These evaluate strategic options for firms in terms of managing their existing or new product portfolios in established or new markets which, in turn, may lead to related or unrelated diversification opportunities (Ansoff, 1968; Johnson and Scholes, 2002). Another approach to determining strategic options is to compare market

41

growth rate and relative market share of the portfolio of products or services being provided (BCG, 1971). The objective is to have a combination of products, or services, that will give a high level of 'cash cows' and 'stars' rather than 'question marks' or 'dogs'. For any individual product, or service, the categorization may change at different stages of the PLC, so, 'cash cows' may over time become 'dogs' or 'question marks'. Such categorizations only apply as generalizations, but they do provide a framework for showing the favoured products and service offerings which, in turn, are influenced by their positions on the PLC continuum. The PLC concept considers the evolution of products or services, taking the stages to be those of the emerging, high growth, mature and declining market phases.

Just as products or services have life cycles, customers also have their own life cycles that affect market development. Douglas and Craig (1989) identified the stages of international expansion that were undertaken by manufacturers. At the initial entry phase, they relate to the selection of the country(ies) in which to operate and the method of entry. This may be followed by local market expansion and global rationalization phases *en route* to achieving global market coverage.

The literature highlights difficulties in establishing the cause and nature of the strategies used by firms. Mintzberg and Waters (1982) and Mintzberg (1994) considered that strategies may be 'enacted', partly as an outcome of unintended actions. They concluded that:

> there is . . . no reason to believe that strategies should, can, or actively do change on a regular schedule, let alone an annual one. Indeed, all evidence is to the contrary: real strategic change is *ad hoc* and irregular, with strategies often remaining stable over long periods of time and then suddenly changing all at once.
>
> (Mintzberg and Waters, 1982)

In this sense, strategic international expansion is often the consequence of various interrelated factors rather than due to the implementation of one particular action. For example, the move towards cross-border expansion in Europe was influenced by the Single European Act (1986), but the development of the Single European Market would not alone oblige firms to pursue a strategy of pan-European coverage. Customer demand, competitor activity and resource constraints would all influence following a strategy of increased European activity. These influences should be considered in the general assessment of international expansion.

The five forces model introduced by Porter (1980) can provide a framework for examining the influences on the strategic direction being used by an industry as well as by the players in the industry. A firm's performance can be compared with the industry average to assess its ability to achieve sustainable competitive advantage, i.e. strategies followed that give cost leadership, cost focus, differentiation or differentiation focus. Differentiation can be implemented through price, image, support, quality and design. Segmentation also plays a part, as do niche and customization strategies (Mintzberg and Quinn, 1991). The approaches of Ansoff (1979), Ansoff and McDonnell (1990) and the BCG (1971) provide depth to Porter's framework.

International marketing theory provides a framework for international marketing implementation and practice, showing how international marketing has evolved and how it is likely to develop. These issues will be discussed further in this text. Those related to the

Marketing Information System (MIS) are discussed in Chapter 4 and those defining the marketing mix are discussed in Chapters 5, 6, 7 and 8. International market planning and its implementation are considered in the concluding Chapter 9.

REVIEW QUESTIONS

2.1 Discuss the framework that international marketing theory can provide for the practitioners of international marketing.

2.2 Consider the ways in which information technology has changed the traditional progress of international expansion to enable the potential for instantaneous global coverage provision.

REFERENCES

Ansoff, H.I. (1965) *Corporate strategy*, New York: McGraw-Hill.

Ansoff, H.I. (1979) *Strategic management*, London: Macmillan.

Ansoff, H.I. (1987) *Corporate strategy*, revised edn, Harmondsworth: Penguin.

Ansoff, H.I. and McDonnell, E. (1990) *Implanting strategic management*, 2nd edn, Englewood Cliffs, NJ: Prentice Hall.

Bartels, R. (1968) 'Are domestic and international marketing dissimilar?', *Journal of Marketing*, July, pp. 56–61.

BCG (1971) *Growth and financial strategies*, Boston, Mass.: Boston Consulting Group (BCG).

BETRO (1975/1979) *Concentration on key markets*, British Export Trade Research Organisation (BETRO) report, London: British Overseas Trade Board (BOTB).

Bilkey, W.J. and Tesar, G. (1977) 'The export behaviour of smaller sized Wisconsin manufacturing firms', *Journal of International Business Studies*, Spring, pp. 93–8.

Cavusgil, S.T. and Nevin, J.R. (1980) 'Conceptualizations of the initial involvement in international marketing' in Lamb, C.W. and Dunne, P.M. (eds) *Theoretical developments in marketing*, Chicago, Ill.: American Marketing Association, April.

Cavusgil, S.T., Zou, S. and Naidu, G.M. (1993) 'Product and promotion adaptation in export venture: an empirical investigation', *Journal of International Business Studies,* Vol. 24, No. 3, p. 485.

Chan, K.W. and Hwang, P. (1992) 'Global strategy and multinationals' entry mode choice', *Journal of International Business Studies*, Vol. 23, No. 1, pp. 29–53.

Chandler, A.D. (1977) *The visible hand: the managerial revolution in American business*, Cambridge, Mass.: Harvard University Press.

Chandler, A.D. (1986) 'The evolution of modern global competition' in Porter, M. (ed.) *Competition in global industries*, Boston, Mass.: Harvard Business School Press, Ch. 13, pp. 405–48.

Chandler, A.D. (1990) 'The enduring logic of industrial success', *Harvard Business Review*, March–April, No. 2, pp. 130–40.

Channon, D.F. (1978) *The service industries: strategy, structure and financial performance*, London and Basingstoke: Macmillan.

Cooper, J.C. (1993) 'Logistics strategies for global businesses', *International Journal of Physical Distribution and Logistics Management*, Vol. 23, No. 4, pp. 12–23.

Cooper, J.C. (ed.) (1994) *Logistics and distribution planning: strategies for management*, 2nd edn, London: Kogan Page.

Czinkota, M.R. (1982) 'Internationalization process involves both learning sequence and export stages' discussed in Ford, D. and Leonidou, L. 'Research developments in international marketing: a European perspective' in Paliwoda, J. (1991) *New perspectives on international marketing*, London: Routledge.

Dicken, P. (1986) *Global shift: industrial change in a turbulent world*, London: Harper and Row.

Douglas, S.P. and Craig, C.S. (1983) *International marketing research*, Englewood Cliffs, NJ: Prentice Hall, pp. 16–19 and pp. 306–25.

Douglas, S.P. and Craig, C.S. (1989) 'Evolution of global marketing strategy: scale, scope and synergy', *Columbia Journal of World Business*, Vol. 24, No. 3, Fall, pp. 47–59.

Doyle, P. (1994) *Marketing management and strategy*, Hemel Hempstead: Prentice Hall.

Dunning, J.H. (1988) 'The eclectic paradigm of international production: a restatement and some possible extensions', *Journal of International Business Studies*, Vol. 19, No. 1.

Ford, D. and Leonidou, L. (1991) 'Research developments in international marketing: a European perspective' in Paliwoda, J. *New perspectives on international marketing*, London: Routledge.

Goodnow, J. (1985) 'Developments in international mode of entry analysis', *International Marketing Review*, Vol. 2, No. 3, Autumn.

Harrell, G.D. and Kiefer, R.O. (1981) 'Multinational strategic market portfolios', *MSU Business Topics*, Winter, p. 13.

Jeannet, J.-P. (1981) 'International marketing analysis: a comparative-analytic approach', working paper quoted in Jeannet, J.-P. and Hennessey, H.D. (1995) *Global marketing strategies*, 3rd edn, Boston, Mass.: Houghton Mifflin, p. 195.

Johanson, J. and Wiedersheim-Paul, P. (1975) 'The internationalisation of the firm: four Swedish cases', *Journal of Management Studies*, Vol. 12, No. 3, pp. 305–22.

Johnson, G. and Scholes, K. (2002) *Exploring corporate strategy: text and cases*, 6th edn, Harlow: Financial Times/Prentice Hall.

Levitt, T. (1983) 'The globalization of markets', *Harvard Business Review*, May–June, pp. 92–102.

Mintzberg, H. (1994) *The rise and fall of strategic planning*, New York: Free Press.

Mintzberg, H. and Quinn, J.B. (1991) *The strategy process: concepts, contexts, cases*, 2nd edn, Englewood Cliffs, NJ: Prentice Hall.

Mintzberg, H. and Waters, J.A. (1982) 'Tracking strategy in an entrepreneurial firm', *Academy of Management Journal*, Vol. 25, pp. 465–99.

Nichols, N. (1994) 'Scientific management of Merck', *Harvard Business Review*, January–February, pp. 95–6.

Ohmae, K. (1985) *Triad power – the coming shape of global competition*, New York: Free Press, pp. 122–4.

Olson, H.C. and Wiedersheim-Paul, F. (1978) 'Factors affecting the pre-export behaviour of non-exporting firms' in Ghertman, M. and Leontiades, J. (eds) *European Research in International Business,* New York: North-Holland, p. 285.

Paliwoda, S.J. (1993) *International marketing*, 2nd edn, Oxford: Butterworth-Heinemann.

Paliwoda, S.J. and Thomas, M.J. (1998) *International marketing*, 3rd edn, Oxford: Butterworth-Heinemann.

Porter, M.E. (1980) *Competitive strategy: techniques for analysing industrial and competitors*, New York: Free Press.

Porter, M.E. (1985) *Competitive advantage: creating and sustaining superior performance*, New York: Free Press.

Porter, M.E. (1986) *Competition in global industries*, Boston, Mass.: Harvard Business School Press.

Porter, M.E. (1987) 'From competitive advantage to corporate strategy', *Harvard Business Review,* Vol. 65, No. 3, May–June, pp. 43–59.

Porter, M.E. (1990) *The competitive advantage of nations*, London: Macmillan.

Porter, M.E. (1991) *On competition and strategy*, Boston, Mass.: Harvard Business School.

Root, F.R. (1966) *Strategic planning for export marketing*, Scranton, Penn.: International Textbook Company, p. 5.

Root, F.R. (1987) *Entry strategies for international marketing*, Lexington, Mass.: Lexington Books, p. 5.

Rostow, W.W. (1960) *The stages of economic growth*, New York: Cambridge University Press.

Rugman, A.H., Lecraw, D.J. and Booth, L.D. (1986) *International business: firms and the environment*, New York: McGraw-Hill.

Samiee, S. (1994) 'Customer evaluation of products in a global market', *Journal of International Business Studies*, Vol. 25, No. 3, p. 587.

Segal-Horn, S. (1992) 'The logic of international growth for service firms', working paper SWP 42/92, Cranfield University School of Management, Cranfield, Bedford.

Segal-Horn, S. (1993) 'The internationalisation of service firms', *Advances in Strategic Management*, Vol. 9, pp. 31–55.

Stone, M.A. (1998) 'The expansion of UK-based logistics service providers', unpublished Ph.D. thesis, Heriot-Watt University, Edinburgh.

Szymaski, D., Bharadwaj S.G. and Vradarajan, P.R. (1993) 'Standardization versus adaptation of international marketing strategy', *Journal of Marketing*, Vol. 57, October, p. 4.

Takeuchi, H. and Porter, M. (1986) 'Three roles of international marketing in global strategy' in Porter, M. (ed.) *Competition in global industries*, Boston, Mass.: Harvard Business School Press.

Terpstra, V. and Sarathy, R. (1997) *International marketing*, 7th edn, Fort Worth: Dryden Press, Fig. 8.3, p. 373.

Turnbull, P.W. and Valla, J.P. (1986) *Strategies for international industrial marketing*, London: Croom-Helm.

Vernon, R. (1966) 'International investment and international trade in the product life cycle', *Quarterly Journal of Economics,* May, pp. 190–207.

Vernon, R. and Wells, L.T. (1986) *Manager in the international economy,* 5th edn, Englewood Cliffs, NJ: Prentice-Hall.

Walmsley, J. (1989) *The development of international markets,* London: Graham & Trotman.

Wells, L.T. (1968) 'A product life cycle for international trade?', *Journal of Marketing,* July, pp. 1–6.

Wind, J. and Douglas, S. (1972) 'International market segmentation', *European Journal of Marketing,* Vol. 6, No. 1.

RECOMMENDED FURTHER READING

Albaum, G., Strandskov, J. and Duerr, E. (2002) *International marketing and export management,* 4th edn, Harlow: Pearson.

Bennett, R. (1996) *International business,* London: Pitman.

Bradley, F. (2002) *International marketing strategy,* 4th edn, Harlow: Pearson.

Bridgewater, S. and Egan, C. (2002) *International marketing relationships,* Basingstoke: Palgrave.

Chee, H. and Harris, R. (1998) *Global marketing strategy,* London: Financial Times/Pitman.

Czinkota, M.R. and Ronkainen, I.A. (2004) *International marketing,* 7th edn, Mason, OH: Thomson South-Western.

Daniels, J.D., Radebaugh, L.H. and Sullivan, D.P. (2004) *International business,* 10th edn, Upper Saddle River, NJ: Pearson/Prentice Hall.

Dicken, P. (2003) *Global shift: reshaping the global economic map in the 21st century,* 4th edn, London: Sage.

Doole, I. and Lowe, R. (2001) *International marketing strategy: analysis, development and implementation,* 3rd edn, London: Thomson.

Dwyer, F.R. and Tanner, J.F. (2001) *Business marketing: connecting strategy, relationships and learning,* 2nd edn, New York: McGraw-Hill.

Griffin, R.W. and Pustay, M.W. (2002) *International business: a managerial perspective,* 3rd edn, Upper Saddle River, NJ: Prentice Hall.

Hollensen, S. (2001) *Global marketing: a market-responsive approach,* 2nd edn, Harlow: Prentice Hall.

Jaffe, E.D. and Nebenzahl, I.D. (2001) *National image and competitive advantage: the theory and practice of country-of-origin effect,* Copenhagen: Copenhagen School Press, Handelshojskolens Forlag.

Jeannet, J.-P. and Hennessey, H.D. (2001) *Global marketing strategies,* 5th edn, Boston, Mass.: Houghton Mifflin.

McAuley, A. (2001) *International marketing: consuming globally, thinking locally,* Chichester: John Wiley.

Mühlbacher, H., Dahringer, L. and Leihs, H. (1999) *International marketing: a global perspective*, London: Thomson.

Rugman, A.M. and Hodgetts, R.M. (2000) *International business: a strategic approach,* 2nd edn, Harlow: Pearson.

Schlegelmilch, B.B. and Keegan, W.J. (2001) *Global marketing management: a European perspective*, Harlow: Financial Times/Prentice Hall.

Wright, S. (1997) *The Financial Times marketing casebook,* London: Pitman.

Chapter 3

European marketing

INTRODUCTION

This chapter will introduce you to the European Union (EU) and the operations of the Single European Market (SEM) within international marketing. It will consider the influence of the European environment in which marketing decisions are made and will comment on the move towards a common culture across Europe. It will demonstrate that while the political goal is for a united Europe of member states, in practice, there is a long way to go to achieve the 'ideal'.

LEARNING OBJECTIVES

The objectives of this chapter are to:
- introduce the changing role of Europe in global markets;
- identify current issues in the EU economic, political/legal, socio-cultural and technological environment;
- examine the effect of EU influence on national legislation and control within member states;
- evaluate the implications of an enlarged EU on international marketing;
- assess the implications of the SEM on marketing practice.

When you have completed the chapter you should be able to:
- give evidence of knowledge of the interaction of marketing in the EU and global marketing;
- relate marketing decision-making to the SEM;
- review current inter-relationships between EU institutions and member states as well as between member states themselves;
- envisage the marketing challenges associated with the proposed enlargement of the EU;
- assess the extent to which a harmonious SEM has been achieved to enable organizations in member countries to compete successfully in the global market.

ROLE OF EUROPE IN THE GLOBAL MARKET

The move towards an EU made up of member countries or states reflects the development of the United States of America (USA) in the aftermath of the Wars of Independence. However, in the case of the United States (commonly shortened to 'US') this has taken place over more than two centuries, whereas the EU only began to take shape from 1951, and formally in 1957 (see p. 50). The European Economic Community (EEC), which since 1992 evolved to become the EU, aims at an internal European market among its member countries through the freedom of movement of goods, people, capital and services. The goal is to have a cohesive region that serves its 'European' citizens in a similar way to citizens in the US. At the same time as trade barriers within the EU are being reduced to encourage internal trade and co-operation, it is intended that the EU should be a powerful trading 'bloc' within the global market.

A typical example of the relatively rapid move in the changing flow of trade is the UK's move from a traditional pattern of trading partners based on its links within the British Commonwealth and the US towards trading with EU members, as shown in Tables 3.1 and 3.2. In 1970, prior to the UK's entry into the EEC in 1973, around one fifth of exports and imports by value were traded with EEC members, almost the same as the share of trade with the British Commonwealth countries. North America had between 15 and 20 per cent share while Latin America had a low 4 per cent. After the UK's accession to the EEC, trade with its members was encouraged at the expense of the British Commonwealth. In particular, preferential agreements to import Australian and New Zealand dairy and meat produce (especially butter and lamb) as well as fruit, such as apples, were reversed in favour of similar produce from France and the Benelux countries. In this way by 1980, over 40 per cent of UK exports and imports were with EEC members, with only 11 to 13 per cent with the British Commonwealth. By 1988, with the enlargement of the EEC to include Greece in 1981 as well as Portugal and Spain in 1986 (see p. 50), this trend was even more in evidence with over half of UK exports and imports going to the EEC. Subsequent expansion of the EU to 15 member countries in 1995 with the addition of Austria, Finland and Sweden has increased the UK's trade within the EU to around 65 per cent of its imports and exports.

At the same time, trade with the world's developed economies has become ever more concentrated as shown by the share of UK trade involved with the Organisation for Economic Co-operation and Development (OECD) representing 36 or so developed economies from Europe, North America, Australasia and the Far East. While in 1970, it took about 45 per cent of UK trade, by 1988 it accounted for almost 80 per cent of UK trade. Globally this shows that international trade increasingly involves the established developed economies to the disadvantage of developing and underdeveloped economics, especially those in Africa, Latin America and Central Asia.

OPERATION OF EUROPEAN UNION POLITICAL INSTITUTIONS

The EU operates through a European Parliament with members elected within its member states. A President rotating between member states for a six-month term of office oversees

Table 3.1 *Share of UK exports by value (%)*

Trading area	1970	1980	1988
EEC	21.8	43.4	51.3
North America	15.3	11.3	15.5
British Commonwealth	21.0	13.0	11.0
Latin America	3.5	2.2	1.4
OECD	45.4	72.2	78.9

Table 3.2 *Share of UK imports by value (%)*

Trading area	1970	1980	1988
EEC	21.1	41.3	52.4
North America	20.5	15.0	12.1
British Commonwealth	23.8	11.2	7.9
Latin America	3.6	2.1	1.4
OECD	41.3	76.2	84.8

it. Legislation is determined through the Parliament located at Brussels (Belgium) and Strasbourg (France) and moderated by the European Council of Ministers in a similar way to the UK House of Commons and House of Lords. The European Commission, based in Brussels, administers the working of the EU. Further details of the EU operation process can be obtained by reference to Artis and Nixson (2001) and Swann (1995).

EUROPEAN UNION INFLUENCE ON NATIONAL LEGISLATION AND CONTROLS

Single European Market (SEM)

The Single European Act (1986) sought to implement aims of the founding treaties of the European Community, namely:

■ European Coal and Steel Community (ECSC) (1951);
■ Treaty of Rome (1957), which brought in the European Atomic Energy Community (EURATOM), and the other Treaty of Rome (1957) which started the European Economic Community (EEC).

On 25 March 1957 the EEC was formed between Belgium, France, Germany, Italy, Luxembourg and the Netherlands, bringing countries together to work towards economic and social collaboration. On 1 January 1973 it was enlarged, adding Denmark, Ireland and the UK, and, in 1981, Greece was added, followed by Portugal and Spain in 1986. In 1995

Austria, Finland and Sweden were brought in to make the EU of 15 member countries with a total population of 375.3 million. Currently, 12 more countries are preparing for membership, which would give an enlarged EU of about 482.5 million population. The candidates are predominantly from Central and Eastern Europe (CEE), namely, Poland, the Czech Republic, Slovenia, Slovakia and Hungary, Latvia and Lithuania, Bulgaria, Romania and Turkey, as well as Malta and Cyprus (see pp. 53–62).

The Single European Act (1986) provided new decision-making powers for the Council of Ministers and European Parliament to implement the aims of the EEC treaty to speed up the process of completing the SEM. The SEM, sometimes termed the Single Market Programme (SMP), placed economic and social policy within the ambit of the European Community, focusing on monetary co-operation as well as social, regional, science, technology and environmental policies. However, as the key objective of the single market was 'free movement of goods, people, capital and services within the EU' new challenges were created that needed to be addressed.

SEM supporting treaties

While the Single European Act (1986) moved towards providing a cohesive 'common' market across its member states with increased harmonization of practice to encourage trade, there was frustration that decisions were being taken within the European Commission administrative bodies that were at some distance from people. Consequently, the Maastricht Treaty (1991) was agreed, which aimed at 'devolving power to the lowest appropriate national and regional level' and to increase effective implementation of the SEM. The intention was to reduce the administrative bureaucracy centred on Brussels and to have decisions made at national and regional levels that would bring about a more cohesive Europe.

The Maastricht Treaty (1991) formally set up the EU, comprising the European Community with the Council of Ministers, the European Parliament (sitting in Brussels and Strasbourg), the European Commission and the Court of Justice. A common foreign and security policy and a home affairs and justice policy were agreed on an inter-governmental basis. The concept of *subsidiarity* was put forward whereby decision-making was to be, as far as possible, devolved from Brussels to member states and the regions. Brussels should take only strictly necessary decisions. A Committee of Regions was set up. The Treaty also put in place the framework for the European Monetary Union (EMU), creating the single currency (euro) controlled by the European Central Bank (ECB) which was introduced in January 2002 within the Eurozone (see Chapter 6: International pricing). European citizenship was introduced. The Treaty of Nice (2000) reinforced the concept of 'subsidiarity'.

The Barcelona Summit (2002) considered the problems facing the EU, in particular, the challenges of global competition, EU enlargement and the high overall EU 8 per cent unemployment level. Unfortunately, there was limited progress in addressing these critical issues due to the distractions of the impending elections in France and Germany.

The subsequent Copenhagen Summit held in December 2002 concentrated on working towards the EU enlargement, especially making arrangements for the financing of the new union of 25 countries, admitting a united Cyprus and considering Turkey's application to join the EU (Dempsey and Reed, 2002). Other diversions raised for discussion included Estonia's right to hunt bears and the Czechs' attempts to reach agreement with the Germans

51

over the use of haulage trucks throughout the EU. The ten candidates were offered €40.5bn for 2004–6 although Poland, Hungary, the Czech Republic and Slovakia had been looking for a further €2bn. The major bone of contention was between Poland and Germany regarding more money for farmers (Wagstyl, 2002a). It is anticipated that the enlargement of the EU will proceed in June 2004 with the EU expanding from 15 to 25 members, but Poland, Estonia, Latvia, Slovenia and Malta are concerned as to the timing of the implementation of the expansion. Members and candidate countries have to pass through a ratification process involving parliamentary approval for current members and national referenda for new ones which may prove challenging (Dempsey and Reed, 2002).

Moreover, enlarging the EU from 15 members to 25 will pose enormous administrative challenges, not the least of which is the cost of interpreting and translating. For example, 'when the applicant members attended a special enlargement debate in the European Parliament [in November 2002], an army of interpreters was needed to cope with more than 500 possible linguistic permutations' (Parker, 2002d). The annual bill for translation in the Council of Ministers alone is €50m (US $50.4m) and that does not include interpreters and translators in the European Parliament and the European Commission. Some countries are prepared to simplify the system and have proposed a 'request and pay' system for meetings in the Council of Ministers, where member states pay for interpreters if they want to use their own language. However, other countries, France in particular, are expected to resist any plan that formally entrenches the position of English as the EU's main language.

At the same time it is important that the administration of the EU is seen to be equitable to all members, allowing them all to have a voice in decision-making. In an attempt to address this issue, the ECB agreed on a 'three speed' model for voting rights in its rate-setting governing council once the Eurozone includes new members from the CEE countries (Major and Krosta, 2002). The proposed reform will cap the number of voting members at 21 but include a complex rotational voting system to ensure states are not unrepresented for long periods. But the model also ensures that the five largest countries in terms of GDP and population will have a decisive say in the decision-making process.

However, the Brussels Summit (2003) held at the height of tensions created by the build-up to the war in Iraq exposed the frailty of Europe's attempts to forge a common foreign policy and opened divisions between 'old' and 'new' Europe (Parker, 2003). Decisions regarding the future of Europe were postponed, causing more concern for the enlargement. The crisis damaged relations between the EU and future members after they angered France by backing the US line. It is unlikely to delay the accession of the ten countries due in 2004, but it could complicate the planned accession of Romania and Bulgaria in 2007 due to their strong US support.

European Union constitution

A survey of opinion undertaken between 18 March and 30 April 2003 covering 16,000 persons across Europe indicated a general move towards overriding national and regional governance. It showed that Italy, Greece, the Netherlands, Sweden and Belgium were most in favour; Finland, Denmark, the UK and Ireland were less supportive, while Spain and Austria came in the middle range of opinion (see Table 3.3). Overall 63 per cent of those surveyed were in favour of a European constitution (Yárnoz, 2003).

Table 3.3 *Survey of opinion regarding proposed European Union constitution*

EU member state	% in favour	% against
Italy	77	5
Greece	75	14
Netherlands	71	16
Sweden	69	13
Belgium	68	11
Luxembourg	65	10
Spain	64	9
Austria	63	8
Germany	62	12
Portugal	61	8
France	61	7
Ireland	54	9
UK	52	9
Denmark	43	37
Finland	44	39
EU average	**63**	**10**

Source: Yárnoz (2003)

These ideas were taken on board at the Thessaloniki Summit in Greece (2003), which outlined the EU's first constitutional treaty with potential implications going far beyond those of Maastricht and the Single European Act. The treaty provides for a much more federal Europe, where issues such as foreign affairs and law and order are decided on a European rather than a domestic basis and where elections to the European Parliament would be as important as any national vote. It could even force countries to choose between signing up and leaving the EU (Parker and Dombey, 2003). New policies in fields such as justice and home affairs, including immigration, would be at EU level. The new treaty aims to bolster democratic accountability and transparency by giving a role to national parliaments to veto legislation. This draft constitution will have to proceed through an intergovernmental conference of member states, scheduled to end in the first half of 2004, *en route* to its implementation.

European expansion: Central and Eastern Europe (CEE)

The end of the 1980s and the beginning of the 1990s witnessed dramatic changes in the social, political and economic structure of Europe. The CEE countries replaced their Communist regimes and started their transition process towards a market economy and political democracy. These developments in Eastern Europe and the former Soviet Union have provided

Western businesses with new opportunities and challenges within this potentially large market. While most Western firms have been adjusting their strategies to accommodate increased integration of the EU within a SEM of 376 million people, they have largely neglected the substantial opportunities available in Eastern and Central Europe. The ten agreed enlargement candidates have a total population of 74 million with a further 54 million people in the Balkan states, making the population potential for the EU around 569 million (Wolf, 2002a). Most of the CEE countries are in desperate need of investment to support technological development associated with consumer and industrial goods and services.

However, there are challenges related to these emergent markets, which have experienced enormous changes over the last decade. Currently in most CEE countries, there are democratically elected governments that are committed to establishing market economies based on free competition and pluralist ownership. Most of these countries have transfer of technology agreements and improved trading links with Western economies as their top priorities. Yet, these reforms have been hindered by high levels of inflation, unemployment and economic instability related to the restructuring of the national economic systems compounded, predictably, by the different paces and the successes of reforms across these countries.

Most of the CEE countries have removed their trade barriers and launched ambitious privatization programmes that explicitly welcome foreign investment. Nevertheless, Western companies remain cautious. These countries' ability to attract foreign investment depends on their market conditions, including:

- speed and the smoothness of the transition to the privatization process;
- upgrading of the residential and commercial infrastructure for foreign firms and investors;
- improvement in communications, especially telecommunications and physical infrastructure;
- economic and political stability related to banking and currency;
- reform of the legal system, particularly property and privatization rights;
- incentives given to foreign firms and investors, such as tax holidays, favourable conditions for expatriates and remittance of profits as well as improved efficiency related to official approvals and permissions.

Geographical boundaries

Geographically, Central and Eastern Europe lies to the east of Germany, Austria and Italy and extends eastwards to the Ural Mountains and the Caspian Sea. The broad political and cultural regions are as follows:

- Baltic States: Estonia, Latvia, Lithuania;
- Central Europe: Czech Republic, Hungary, Poland and Slovakia;
- Eastern Europe: Bulgaria and Romania;
- Former Yugoslavia states: Croatia and Macedonia;
- Bosnia and Herzegovina, Montenegro, Slovenia and Serbia;
- Commonwealth of Independent States (CIS) comprising Belarus, Ukraine and the Republic of Moldavia;

54

- Russia;
- Albania, which remains largely isolated and does not readily fit into any of the regions.

Hungary, Poland and the Czech Republic are the economic leaders in terms of market reforms. Slovenia, Slovakia and the Baltic States, i.e. Estonia, Latvia and Lithuania, are also well advanced in the transition process. Their geographical position as neighbouring developed industrialized countries, together with their more liberal national economies, have helped them to attract foreign inward investment. Romania and Bulgaria are lagging behind the leading countries with slower rates of improvement in their infrastructure and administrative systems, associated with more acute economic crises and instability. The war and the social unrest within the former Yugoslavia and Albania reduced their ability to attract foreign investment. Successful economic reforms are needed to improve their social and political life.

Economic transition towards a market economy

The CEE countries have reached different phases of economic development, related to their experience of:

- Communist system influence;
- economic and political reform;
- traditional links with Western European countries.

COMMUNIST SYSTEM INFLUENCE

Initial conditions played a role in determining the degree and speed of reform policies in the transition from Communist influence to Western privatization. In this regard, Poland, Hungary and Slovenia have had considerable advantage, as they were exposed to market approaches prior to transition. Bulgaria and Romania, in contrast, suffered from having tighter Communist control of their economies and bureaucracy. The Baltic States did not introduce market reforms until 1991 when they became independent.

ECONOMIC AND POLITICAL REFORM

The initial political conditions of the CEE countries had an impact on the political elite regime changes (or lack of them) at the beginning of the transition. The countries that experienced the greatest political elite change also undertook bolder and more rapid economic and institutional reforms. In this respect, Hungary, Poland and the Czech Republic led the group of countries in Central Europe, while the Slovak Republic, Romania and Bulgaria lagged behind. The different performance of the Baltic countries, with Estonia leading in the reforms, emphasizes the importance of political regime change. However, macroeconomic stabilization and structural reforms sometimes offset the initial conditions. For example, Estonia, despite negative initial conditions, once it started reforming, quickly caught up with some of the more advanced candidate countries.

The CEE countries differed in the speed and scope of implementing economic reforms and, consequently, experienced different levels of economic performance. The transition experience of the CEE countries shows that growth recovered only after the economies were stabilized and inflation was controlled and substantially reduced. Those countries that did not manage to stabilize their economies early on, such as Bulgaria and Romania, have continued to fall behind in structural reforms.

Strong positive associations have been found between enterprise privatization and restructuring, and between privatization and higher productivity growth in the transition economies. The release of valuable assets, in particular, infrastructure, equipment and human capital, associated with privatization can help the change. The transition experience has highlighted the importance of institutional factors in sustaining growth, especially reforms of the legal and judicial system, restructuring of the education system, reform of central and local administration and the control of corruption.

TRADITIONAL LINKS WITH WESTERN EUROPEAN COUNTRIES

Traditional links between some CEE countries and Western European countries have provided a critical catalyst for growth and successful transition through sustained foreign direct investment (FDI), transfer of knowledge and regional programmes for structural development. For example, Hungary, Poland, the Czech and Slovak Republics, Slovenia and the Baltic States have benefited from their traditional relations with Austria, Germany, Italy and the Scandinavian countries (Wagstyl, 2002b).

Phases of economic and political evolution

The economic and political evolution of the CEE countries can be divided into four main phases:

- start of democratic transformation (1990–1);
- reform programmes (1993–4);
- economic stabilization and continuation of economic reform (1995–8);
- signs of success (1999–2003).

PHASE 1: START OF DEMOCRATIC TRANSFORMATION (1990–1)

After the Communist regimes were overthrown, the political and social institutions of these countries needed restructuring. The organization of free democratic elections and the intro-duction of new constitutions achieved the restructuring, although for some only amendments were made to the existing ones.

The elected political institutions (parliaments and their governments) took the initial steps to transform the economy from a centralized system to a free market system, with appro-priate supporting institutions. New economic and financial legislation had to be introduced to encourage private economic initiative and entrepreneurship. Fiscal policy was required which provided incentives for foreign investors to attract the much needed capital for eco-nomic and market restructuring and development. The results of this liberalization and restructuring were not always positive. Initially, all CEE countries experienced decline in their GDPs due to their losing their traditional markets and associated economic structures. In many cases, the rapid liberalization of trade was not matched by the liberalization of prices, which created favourable conditions for a substantial black market based on price differentials among different regions of the same country, or between neighbouring countries.

PHASE 2: REFORM PROGRAMMES (1993–4)

In this period, CEE country governments introduced more complex reform programmes. Some states, such as Poland and Hungary, decided to use 'shock therapy' on the centralized economy to accelerate the transition process, while others, in particular, Romania and Bulgaria, have adopted a more gradual approach to transition. These reform programmes included privatization of state-owned enterprises, encouraging private initiative and the promotion of small and medium-sized enterprises as well as price and trade liberalization.

These reforms had mixed effects on the economy and standards of living. The increased freedom of trade provided opportunities for many entrepreneurial people. However, the collapse of the centralized economic system led to rises in unemployment and inflation. The difference in social and economic opportunities between citizens created social and economic polarization of the society, resulting in a few rich people with many poor people in place of a more egalitarian society.

PHASE 3: ECONOMIC STABILIZATION AND CONTINUATION OF ECONOMIC REFORM (1995–8)

During this period, a number of CEE countries succeeded in stabilizing their economies at the 1989 level of GDP, in particular, Poland, Slovenia and the Czech Republic. However, other countries experienced a slower rate of economic growth together with a fall in economic reforms. New legislation was introduced to restructure the political and economic infrastructure in these countries. The regulations started to emulate EU requirements and standards, to ease these countries in their future integration within the Western European system. The continuation of economic reforms created challenges and social tension, associated with high levels of inflation and unemployment.

PHASE 4: SIGNS OF SUCCESS (1999–2003)

As a result of cumulative reforms, many CEE countries started to display signs of economic success, although substantial differences remain between the most successful transition economies such as Poland, Hungary, the Czech Republic and Slovenia, and the least successful ones like Romania and Bulgaria. The rates of inflation have been brought under control and, although still at high levels, unemployment growth has been substantially reduced. Economic, legal and political restructuring continues, with stronger emphasis on EU standards. In social terms, a prosperous middle class has started to evolve, formed from local entrepreneurs and independent professionals. Improvements in the infrastructure have improved standards of living for citizens and have attracted more foreign investors. Privatization objectives have been achieved in many countries.

It should be noted that the descriptive model discussed above is predominantly characteristic of the Baltic States and the CEE countries. It does not fit the experience of the Commonwealth of Independent States (CIS), which has had a less favourable pace of development, with many structural reforms still waiting to be implemented, or enforced. The conflict in former Yugoslavia slowed down the process of economic and political transition in some of the countries from this region, especially Serbia, Macedonia and Montenegro.

EU integration

EU membership represented an essential objective for the CEE countries. Ten of these countries have applied to become EU members: Bulgaria, the Czech Republic, Estonia, Hungary, Latvia, Lithuania, Poland, Romania, the Slovak Republic and Slovenia. In order to join the EU, they need to fulfil the economic and political conditions known as the 'Copenhagen criteria', according to which a prospective member must:

- be a stable democracy, respecting human rights, the rule of law and the protection of minorities;
- have a functioning market economy;
- adopt the common rules, standards and policies that make up the body of EU law.

As a recognition of their success in the process of political and economic reforms, on 9 October 2002, the European Commission recommended completing negotiations with the Czech Republic, Estonia, Hungary, Latvia, Lithuania, Poland, the Slovak Republic and Slovenia (see Copenhagen Summit (2002) discussed on pp. 51–2). They will be joining the EU in May 2004. Two other Eastern European states, Romania and Bulgaria, are scheduled to become EU members in 2007, if they fulfil the required entry criteria.

Population mobility

Apart from the high costs associated with the enlargement of the EU, there is major concern regarding a perceived likelihood of massive east–west migration (Parker, 2002c). However, although the EU membership confers the right of free movement, that right will not apply immediately to the ten countries expected to join from 2004 onwards. Free movement will not be available for up to seven years after accession, with Germany and Austria especially determined to impose lengthy transition. Research and previous experience, as when Spain and Portugal joined the European Community, suggests the fears of uncontrolled migration to the west may be unfounded. The European Commission's research predicts the long-run migration potential from the candidate countries is about 1 per cent of the current EU population, but that is likely only after many decades of steadily declining flows. In the early years, between 70,000 and 150,000 from the former Soviet bloc are estimated to be likely to move west every year. Many of these would be workers on temporary, particularly agri-cultural, contracts. Little eastward migration from the current EU member states is expected as the research shows that most Europeans prefer to stay at home (Parker, 2002c).

Challenges and opportunities for international business in Central and Eastern Europe

The decision to become active in Central and Eastern Europe depends mostly on a firm's strategic motives and objectives for internationalization. Usually, firms initiate and develop international operations to achieve corporate growth, sustainable competitive advantages, or to improve their strategic positioning in relation with competitors. These motives are valid for the international expansion in CEE countries. Frequent additional motives for entering these markets are:

- a high cultural and historical affinity with some of the countries in the region;
- the opportunity to access cheap raw materials as well as low-cost, well trained local work force;
- the high growth potential of some of these markets;
- economic, trade and fiscal incentives.

The decision to develop business, or trade, in the CEE region is also driven by the current strengths and weaknesses of various countries. Some of the strengths are large populations, low wages, geographic proximity to Western Europe, privatization opportunities, low market entry costs and long-term growth potential. However, weaknesses to be overcome include low per capita income, limited management skills, low productivity, overdrawn expectations, poor infrastructure, an unstable business environment and large bureaucracies as well as short-term decline and associated crises.

Strengths and weaknesses differ from country to country and from industry to industry. Central and Eastern Europe is not an economically homogeneous bloc, and disparities in the pace and depth of transformation continue to widen the differences between countries. Rather than standardized strategies, differentiation is required to meet the needs of heterogeneous markets and customers in these countries.

Another strategic consideration concerns the competitive orientation of a company entering this market. The high level of demand in the region, combined with a weak purchasing power of many potential customers, suggests the adoption of a cost leadership strategy would be advantageous. Firms can prolong the product life cycle (PLC) of their existing products by implementing market penetration and market development strategies. Strategies of product development and diversification can often be delayed, although many major MNCs have taken advantage of favourable opportunities to invest in the most successful CEE countries, substantially increasing competition over the last five years. Some of the local firms have been quick to implement effective business procedures, emerging as important competitors, not only in their domestic markets but also in other CEE countries.

Considering the future potential of this region, many MNCs decided to invest early in CEE countries, even if the prospects of profit were low in the first three to five years of their activity. When using a long-term perspective, Western firms have found it beneficial to pursue a strategy of gradually altering the marketing environment of these countries, to move them closer to a functioning market economy. Such an approach, however, requires appreciation of current societal and economic problems. Furthermore, significant investment is necessary in terms of employee training programmes which focus on facilitating change management associated with behavioural and knowledge adjustment. Well designed public relations (PR) and marketing communication campaigns are required to educate and support local suppliers, customers and policy makers regarding the spirit of a free market economy.

Market entry strategies

Analysing the competitive environment of the targeted countries, as well as its own resources and strategic objectives, a company can identify the most appropriate target market and market-entry mode for international expansion. In addition to the general selection criteria such as market potential, market growth, market volume and market access, an assessment of the transformation process and of specific commercial risks is useful when evaluating CEE markets. Among other factors, the progress of economic reforms, the extent to which state monopolies have been abolished and the direction of the governmental budget deficit need to be carefully considered.

With regards to market entry modes, previously the region was accessible by direct exporting or, exceptionally, in some countries (e.g. Poland, Hungary, Romania) through joint ventures agreements (see Chapter 2: Framework for international marketing and Chapter 8: International channels of distribution). With the changes post-Communism, exporting, direct investment, licensing, franchising, contract manufacturing and management methods of market entry contracts can all be pursued. Many Western companies still favour the traditional approach of exporting, attempting to reduce the costs and risks of entry. However, after successfully exporting to these countries, currently, many companies are expanding their local presence by creating sales subsidiaries, joint venture agreements or manufacturing units. Some firms are pursuing an active opportunistic approach to these markets, attempting to transfer across borders the profits obtained through exploiting market deficiencies.

Marketing mix strategies in CEE countries

The marketing mix policies implemented in CEE countries have to take into consideration the differences between the Western markets and the local economies, in terms of demand, buying behaviour, infrastructure, business practices and technological standards. At the same time they must also consider the strategic objectives and resources of the company concerned.

Product policy

The product policy for CEE markets is strongly influenced by the technological gap between Western industrialized nations and the former socialist countries. As a result, product policy decisions for CEE markets need to focus on the selection of the most appropriate products from the existing company portfolio and the adaptation requirements to the target market environment.

In positioning established products in these markets, branding is an important tool. In the first years of economic transition, generally Western brands were considered of higher quality and preferable to domestic products. More recently, however, CEE consumers have discovered that Western products are not necessarily better than their domestic counterparts. A resurgence of domestic pride and entrepreneurship has led to increased demand for domestic products, such as soft drinks, bread or soap.

Pricing policy

With regard to pricing policy, the situation in the CEE countries is complex and needs to be thoroughly assessed by foreign companies. The reduction in GDP and the high levels of inflation and unemployment have reduced significantly the purchasing power of large categories of population. Frequently, demand is based on price levels, often neglecting quality, for example, a lucrative market for second-hand clothing has developed in many CEE countries. The high level of inflation and undeveloped financial markets create pressures for increasing the price to include a risk margin for potential economic and associated crisis situations.

Pricing decisions must be based on specific market conditions, the target groups envisaged and the company objectives. For the consumer segments with low purchasing power a low-price offer combined with standardized products would appear to be the most effective. However, a growing number of CEE customers are ready, and able, to pay higher prices, especially for high-quality technical products which offer substantial benefits. Any pricing policy needs to include a flexible approach based on a permanent evaluation of the changing conditions in the target markets.

Distribution policy

The liberalization of the CEE economies has given a high impetus to trade, both internally and externally. In terms of foreign trade policy, most CEE countries have attempted to replace their traditional markets with the Soviet Union and other socialist countries by the developed markets from Western Europe and North America. Internally, the infrastructure of these countries has limited the penetration of foreign products. Although reasonably developed, the retailing and transport infrastructure suffered from poor quality standards and low maintenance. However, the situation has changed over the last five years, as all CEE governments have invested in improving the infrastructure.

The privatization of the commercial network has proceeded at a quicker pace than the privatization of manufacturing units. Currently, the distribution networks in the CEE countries are relatively well developed, at wholesaler, retailer and logistical level. Some Western retail chains have identified the growing opportunities in the CEE countries, expanding their networks to the more developed countries of the region, e.g. UK's Tesco has expanded into Poland and Hungary, and Germany's Metro, Rewe and Tengelmann, as well as France's Carrefour, Geant, Auchan and Leclerc expanded into Poland in the late 1990s. In 2002, after the success of its first store in Bucharest, Romania, Carrefour planned to extend its operations by opening a further 23 new supermarkets across the country. As the financial infrastructure, transportation network and the communication services improve in CEE countries, more opportunities for multi-channel distribution will occur.

Marketing communication

In the socialist system, marketing communication such as advertising had a strong flavour of propaganda and was largely controlled by the state. Latterly, an explosive development of media channels and communication services has made possible the use, in almost all CEE countries, of contemporary communication instruments such as advertising, personal selling, PR and sales promotion.

Currently, the most critical communication instrument used is advertising. Although the global reputation of their brands provides an advantage for MNCs, often the advertising campaign needs to be substantially adapted to the local tastes and requirements. The use of local communication agencies can be beneficial, as they provide valuable knowledge of the local market profile and culture.

61

PR communication is important to create a positive image about the company and its activities. The popularization of sponsorship, donations for local charities or educational programmes, can increase substantially the local reputation of foreign firms and socially responsible organizations.

Summary

The existing economic, social, legal and cultural differences between CEE countries makes a standardized approach unprofitable within this economic region. Rather, marketing strategies have to be tailored to the specific requirements of each country. However, few countries in this region have 'commonality', in terms of culture and economic development, which can be exploited for economies of scale.

The transition economies from Central and Eastern Europe offer opportunities for business expansion and development, as well particular challenges. Strategic approaches used by foreign companies need to take into consideration the specific elements of a country's history, economic, political and legal system, social behaviour and traditions to be able to develop effective implementation of the most appropriate marketing mix. The trend for most CEE countries is to develop their market economies and implement Western standards through legislation, technology and manufacturing. Although the development is slower in some countries, and economic and associated crises remain possible, the CEE region represents considerable potential opportunity for the foreign companies capable of adopting a long-term strategic approach to the market.

INFLUENCE OF THE SINGLE EUROPEAN MARKET ON THE REGULATION OF MARKETING PRACTICE

In the late 1980s, considerable restructuring occurred, especially in the European US $700bn per annum food market, to deal with increased competition, changing tastes and products, faster innovation and the advance of European integration through the SEM with many European firms acquiring across national borders. Typically, the large transnational firms bought into continental European business through mergers and acquisitions (see Table 3.4) while others used joint venture arrangements, often *en route* to full acquisition. But, as many of these were new ventures into new markets, many resulted in heavy financial losses. For example, in logistics, Christian Salvesen, one of the top six UK logistics service providers, lost in excess of £2m per annum in its German ventures (Stone, 2001). Indeed, within the food industry, where in 1992 the 20 largest food manufacturers accounted for only about 12 per cent of the European market of 100,000 companies and retailers were ever more dominant, many producers found cost saving synergies difficult to achieve. In response, they turned to other less risky expansion routes such as strategic alliances. Nestlé, once averse to joint ventures, joined with US General Mills to develop the cereals market, with Coca-Cola in canned coffee and with BSN to buy Cokoladovny, a Czech biscuit and confectionery company (Jonquières and Dawkins, 1992).

In the early 1990s, UK business became increasingly cautious regarding expansion to continental Europe due to:

Table 3.4 *Top ten European cross-border mergers and acquisitions*

Bidder	Target	Year	US $bn
Nestlé (Switzerland)	Rowntree (UK)	1988	4.92
Philip Morris (US)	Jacobs Suchard (Switzerland)	1990	3.80
BSN (France)	Smiths Crisps, Walker Crisps, Jacobs (all UK), Saiwa (Italy), Belin (France)	1989	2.50
Nestlé (Switzerland)	Buitoni	1988	1.40
Pepsico (US)	Smiths Crisps, Walkers Crisps (UK)	1989	1.35
Sudzucker (Germany)	Raffinerie Tirlemont (Belgium)	1989	0.99
BSN (France)	HP Foods/Lea & Perrins (UK)	1988	0.34
Ferruzzi (Italy)	Lesieur (cooking oils division) (France)	1988	0.26
Freia (Norway)	Marabou (Sweden)	1990	0.23
Kuwait Investment Office	Ebro (Spain)	1988	0.22

Source: KPMG quoted in Jonquières and Dawkins (1992)

- losses associated with joint ventures and acquisitions;
- shortage of capital;
- associated need to reduce risk;
- effect of recession.

This caused a change of approach and attitude towards involvement in continental European activities. UK firms became increasingly risk averse and many modified their initial enthusiasm towards acquisition to a more cautious approach involving participation in networking and collaboration in European ventures. For example, in the late 1980s the Royal Bank of Scotland and the Spanish Banco Santander (which later brought in the National Westminster Bank in 2000) shared in a strategic alliance to exchange technology expertise. At the same time, Marks & Spencer (M&S), the clothing, food and houseware retailer, joined forces with the third-party logistics service provider, NFC/Exel Logistics, to develop its cross-border continental European operations in Belgium, France and Spain, which were extended to Germany in 1997. However, after losses in excess of £100m in Europe, M&S withdrew from continental Europe to the UK in 2001.

UK involvement in acquisitions within the EU

In 1993, UK firms spent over £5bn per annum on acquiring continental European. The number of acquisitions per annum fell from the previous year, but the size of the individual deals rose. In contrast, in 1993, UK business disposed of interests worth only £5.7m within the EU. For example, in 1993 the UK retailing group, Kingfisher, took over Darty, the French electricals retailer, for £560m, creating one of the largest non-food retailing groups in Europe. Kingfisher, which included the Comet, B&Q, Woolworth and Superdrug chains, was realizing its ambition according to Sir Geoffrey Mulcahy, Kingfisher's chairman, to have 'the muscle to compete in a European basis as well as enhancing growth opportunities in [UK] domestic markets' (Buckley and Rawsthorn, 1993). Darty's chairman, M. Philippe Francès considered the deal was the start of a 'strategic European alliance' which would enable his company to fulfil its potential. From the late 1990s these investments in continental Europe became more and more two-way as continental European firms became associated with mergers and acquisitions in the UK. Indeed, cross-border investment across all of Europe has become much more evident.

Financial services sector

Considerable consolidation within the financial sector has taken place across Europe. For example, in 1997 Zurich Group (Switzerland) acquired BAT (UK), making the new entity worth US $35.7bn. At the same time, Nordbanker (Sweden) and Menta (Finland) merged to establish the largest bank in the Nordic region worth US $10.6bn. Within the insurance segment, in 1998, the French Axa group acquired UK Equity & Law and others.

Automotive industry

Traditionally, in the 1960s and 1970s, the automotive industry was nationally dominated and frequently supported by government subsidy. For example, in the 1980s, France had Peugeot and Citroën; Germany had Volkswagen (VW), Mercedes and BMW; Sweden had Volvo; Italy had Fiat; Spain had Pegaso and Seat (under licence from Fiat) and the UK had Rover and Jaguar. The major US automotive MNCs, especially Ford and General Motors (GM) operated alongside the national groups. However, as the EU competition regulation became more stringent, countering national government protection of strategic industries, and as the movement of capital investment became more open, cross-border merger and acquisition took place in the automotive industry in the 1990s. In particular, in 1997, the German BMW acquired UK Rover, as its strategic alliance with Japanese Honda was coming to an end: later BMW sold some Rover subsidiaries, Jaguar and Range Rover, to Ford.

From the turn of the century, with the increasing challenges associated with mergers and acquisition, there was a shift from acquisitions towards more limited strategic alliance or collaboration projects within the global car industry, as shown in Table 3.5.

Express freight

Similarly, within the European express freight industry there was considerable consolidation in the 1990s as national post offices extended their operations across borders. This was especially evident in 1996, when the Dutch postal group, KPN, which became TPG (derived from TNT Poste Group), acquired Australian-based TNT, to become TNT Post and it, in turn, was acquired by the German based Deutsche Post in 1998. In this way, a formidable European express freight group was formed, bringing together leading national and regional networks. However, considerable challenge was posed in assimilating the differing cultures of the acquisitions which extended across the Benelux countries, Switzerland and France, as well as the UK-managed Australian TNT.

Table 3.5 *Strategic alliance and collaboration projects within the automotive industry, 1995–2000*

Strategic alliance partners	Research project
GM/Honda	Engines
Ford/PSA	Diesel
Ford/Oracle	Internet
GM/Commerce One	Internet
Daimler Chrsyler/Ford	Fuel cells
GM/Toyota	Fuel cells
Renault/Fiat	Buses

Source: Burt (2000)

Scientific publishing

Within the research publications sector, the UK/Dutch group, Reed Elsevier, acquired the Dutch firm, Walters Kluwer, to increase its value to US $20.3bn to support its leading position in this specialist market.

Industrial gas

In 2000, the British group, BOC (previously British Oxygen Company), which primarily produced specialist industrial gases, was jointly acquired by its competitors the French group, Air Liquide, and the US Air Products for US $11.8bn (£7.38bn) (Hargreaves, 2000). The traditional British company had metamorphosed to a European/US model, although the European Commission imposed conditions obliging substantial disposals in the UK and France to meet competition regulation.

Brewing industry

Extensive consolidation has also taken place within the European brewing industry. National and regional firms have been brought together to give five or six dominant European firms, some of which compete within the global market. Once again the liberalization of the movement of capital across EU borders encouraged, and enabled, the growth of the major brewing groups, notably the Dutch Heineken and the UK-based Scottish & Newcastle and Guinness (part of Diageo) groups. For example, in 1992, UK Guinness acquired the largest privately owned Spanish brewery, Cruzcampo, paying a high price in the 'scramble' to expand into continental Europe. But Guinness faced challenges in assimilating the acquisition within its portfolio due to its distinct management culture and the need for substantial investment to upgrade its manufacturing processes. Then, in 1997, UK Guinness and GrandMet merged to form a US $39bn group with the French LVMH having a 10 per cent stake (Wagstyl, 1997) and, in 2000, Guinness sold Cruzcampo to the largest European brewer, Heineken. It bought the Spanish subsidiary for its regional brands such as 'El Aguila', which is marketed through another division, Amstel, as 'Aguila' alongside Heineken's own premium brand, with few consumers being aware of the direct links between them.

65

In this way, at the beginning of the twenty-first century, there is increased appreciation of the complexity of the EU integration goal: firms have moved along the learning curve. Market leaders within European business have moved outside their national borders. Many faced challenges in the 1980s and 1990s as they moved from a 'newcomer' position towards becoming 'established' in the wider markets. For businesses with the resources acquisition and merger activities have increased in size and sophistication as the SEM has become more established, but so, too, has the influence of the European Commission which oversees competition regulation and the need to prevent monopoly. For small to medium-sized enterprises (SMEs) expansion across Europe may still pose major challenges. Nevertheless, there is concern, certainly at a national government level, that foreign ownership of utility industries is becoming more evident. For example, in Britain, almost 25 million people receive water or have their sewage treated by German, French, Spanish and Malaysian companies, while more than 55 per cent of households get power from foreign-owned companies (Taylor, 2002).

Cultural convergence and communication

Increasingly, in the 1990s, UK firms became more aware of the need to link language skills with closer awareness and integration of European cultures. Instead of encouraging 'Berlitz' type language learning, night-class language skills for all persons involved in international marketing, incorporation of 'foreign' languages became more focused within business. Whilst British truck drivers continued to be given basic French tuition before being sent to France (as in the case of TDG) and the managing directors (MDs) of timber merchants in Scotland were sent on weekly language tuition lunches, increasingly the language expertise of local nationals was used. For example, in the early 1990s, UK logistics service providers, notably TDG, employed management trainee graduates from France, the Netherlands, Belgium and Spain, in particular, to widen the expertise of the UK workforce. At the same time, UK nationals were employed in TDG's continental European operations alongside local nationals. Previously, restrictions on employing non-nationals would have prevented this exchange of experience of different cultures and associated languages.

Other moves towards EU harmonization

Other moves that have led to more harmonization include:

- environmental regulation;
- labour 'freedom of movement';
- Social Charter covering conditions of employment;
- financial controls.

Environmental regulation

LOGISTICS, TRANSPORTATION AND DISTRIBUTION
As part of the preparation for the Single European Act (1986), to liberalize the market for haulage, national restrictions concerning *cabotage,* the movement of goods by non-national

hauliers, licences and quotas were abolished, making it possible for trucks to move goods across Europe. Alongside this liberalization of transport provision EU legislation to standardize vehicle specifications, trailer length/weight, vehicle emissions and so on has been put in place. Currently, a critical issue is the introduction of the Working Hours Directive controlling drivers' conditions in terms of the number of hours worked, rest breaks, etc.

However, the environmental argument has been used to protect local interests, including national hauliers, and has been taken to be anti-competition. For example, pressure was put on France to allow Italian heavy trucks (over 19 tonnes) to pass through the Mont Blanc tunnel which re-opened in March 2002 after its closure due to a commercial vehicle fire in 1999. Italy also has problems with Alpine freight using Switzerland's Gotthard tunnel. There have been similar arguments related to safety with the Channel Tunnel and illegal immigrant entry continues to pose political and security difficulties between the UK and France.

EU regulation has also affected the private car driver. The compulsory use of safety belts at all times when driving for both drivers and passengers across Europe using national legislation caused considerable debate. While in the UK the resistance to its introduction was limited, in Spain much greater resistance was encountered since general practice there had been that seat belts were only used outside the city boundaries, not within the cities.

POLLUTION CONTROL

The EU has introduced numerous Water Directives – aimed at improving the quality of rivers and waterways, as well as the seas around Europe – which have been implemented across Europe since 1985 (Smith, 2000b). As part of this programme, it has set standards for achieving 'Blue Flag' beach awards which relate to cleanliness of the waters, provision of lifeguard and showers services, the prohibition of dogs on the beach, etc. Attaining the coveted 'Blue Flag' beach award has considerable benefits for encouraging tourism, especially as consumers demand better services. Conversely, if the award is rescinded when waters and beaches fail to reach the required standards, e.g. after the Prestige oil tanker spill off the north-west coast of Spain in November 2002 that adversely affected 70 beaches in the Asturias, there are repercussions on local tourism and its associated fishing industry. The EU applies fishing quotas for fish landings to manage stock in its surrounding waters. It also contributes finance towards de-commissioning fishing fleets where it is considered over-fishing is taking place. Another example of efforts to improve European water are the rules introduced in 2002 on the 'cessation or phasing out of emissions, discharges or losses' of substances such as mercury, cadmium and some pesticides from water sources over next 13 years. In the UK alone implementation of the EU requirement has been estimated to be at least £9bn.

The EU also monitors air pollution in its various guises, e.g. vehicle emission levels and aircraft noise, especially night-time flying around densely populated airports. Indeed production of the French Mobylette, the two-wheeler, two-stroke 49.9cc motorized bicycle termed 'moped', ceased in 2003 due to its not meeting EU legislation on vehicle emission standards (Bell, 2002).

AGRICULTURE

Apart from the control imposed through the Common Agricultural Policy (CAP), which is a specialist topic beyond the bounds of this text, the EU enforces stringent regulations to protect consumer health and safety, and is more powerful in implementing these than regional and national controls which, due to local interest influence, can preclude correct preventive action, e.g. BSE (Bovine Spongiform Encephalopathy), commonly known as 'mad cow disease', in beef, the recurring listeria scares in unpasteurized soft cheeses and salmonella in eggs. The 2001–2 'foot and mouth' controls restricting the movement of cattle and sheep throughout the UK, parts of France, the Netherlands and even Spain, had especially severe effects on UK beef and mutton exports to Europe, as well as adverse consequences for UK tourism directed at rural areas.

Much disquiet has been expressed by the agricultural community and their supporters that EU regulation is unduly bureaucratic, even dictatorial, in its administration of some of these health controls. Consequently, an independent European Food Authority was set up in 2003 which will bring together more than 80 initiatives to control food production, manufacture and distribution, e.g. contamination of food by the cancer-causing chemical dioxin and the use of sewage slurry in animal feed (Smith, 2000a). However the European Food Authority is less powerful than the US Food and Drugs Authority (FDA), having no regulatory powers.

Labour 'freedom of movement'

As part of the EU promotion of labour mobility across national borders there has been increasing acceptance of equivalent educational and professional qualifications between European countries. For example, university degrees in one country can be considered equivalent to a similar degree gained in another EU country. The qualified medical doctor in the UK might be considered able to practise in France, Spain or any other EU country, assuming examinations in local language proficiency are obtained. Previously, it would have been obligatory to study for the qualification in the country in which the individual was practising.

The EU SOCRATES/ERASMUS student exchange programme which has been operating since the early 1980s has further encouraged understanding of the different national tertiary educational approaches. Between 2000 and 2006, €950m (US $901m) has been awarded for the programme, €750m of which is for student grants. Currently, 100,000 students per annum take advantage of the opportunity to study for one year in another EU country, most frequently the UK, France, Spain and Germany. Between 1997 and 2000, there were 5,000 institutional contracts of which 50 per cent were with France, Germany and the UK. A survey of 110,000 participants found that most students (20 per cent) were studying business and they came from 29 different countries.

Equivalent weightings for the studies completed are based on an agreed EU European Credit Transfer Scheme (ECTS) which enables students to be credited for studies in the host country on return to their home country of study. The move towards educational 'equivalence' is shown in the advent of joint degrees awarded between universities for study in different countries, e.g. students studying at Robert Schuman (Strasbourg) in France and Heriot-Watt University (Edinburgh) in Scotland can graduate with degrees from both universities. This experience and qualification aids the graduate job mobility between the two countries. The post-graduate European Master in Business Science (EMBS) degree programme also accommodates students studying in two EU countries.

In a similar move, national professional qualification diplomas are accepted across Europe, e.g. the UK Chartered Institute of Marketing (CIM) diploma should be recognized in France, the Netherlands or any other EU country.

Social Charter covering conditions of employment

Some, but not all EU members have signed up to introduce the EU Social Charter which governs conditions of employment and provision for social welfare. In particular, France has taken on board its provisions whereby its government institutions moved in 2002 to a 35-hour week for its employees. As yet, the UK has not been prepared to accept the associated social costs which industry and commerce consider would be difficult to accommodate to maintain competition within the global market. However, different approaches to implementation of the Social Charter have left employees in one country more vulnerable and less protected than in another. When firms, especially MNCs, downsize their manufacturing workforce, as in the late 1990s and into the twenty-first century, they are likely to do so in a country not following the Social Charter where redundancy payments are lower than alternatives countries where higher costs will be incurred. Consequently, within the automotive industry GM and Ford have reduced their plants and employees in the UK and even in Brazil, while Spanish plants are to be cut back much later due to the redundancy payments of up to five year's wages having to be paid. The UK workforce is paying a price for the more flexible, and competitive, approach to employment.

Financial control

Financial control within the EU is managed through the EMU, the ECB and the Exchange Rate Mechanism (ERM) using the European Currency Unit, the euro within the Eurozone (see Chapter 6: International pricing, p. 160). The euro was introduced within 12 countries making up the Eurozone, namely, Austria, Belgium, Finland, France, Germany, Greece, Ireland, Italy, Luxembourg, the Netherlands, Portugal and Spain (Coffey, 2001). There has been much debate about other EU members joining when they have achieved the required economic conditions and have support from their citizens for the change. Sweden has met its own economic tests and held a referendum in September 2003 but rejected membership. The UK is working towards entry in 2005, although it is more likely that there will be further delay (Parker, 2002a). Denmark's referendum in 2000 emphatically rejected entry, although it may join in due course.

It should be noted that even those EU members officially operating outside the Eurozone are obliged to use the euro for many negotiations with other members. Financial payments within the EU administration are in euros covering transactions between government bodies and EU institutions, e.g. payments for development grants, ERASMUS student exchange grant support, etc. Furthermore, increasingly firms operating across Europe demand consistency in pricing by obliging the use of the euro, e.g. Toyota, the Japanese carmaker, has obliged UK component suppliers to bid in euros (not GB pounds) alongside other European suppliers since 2000 (Griffiths *et al.*, 2000). Similarly, BMW, the German automotive group, predicted an increase in the number of Eurozone suppliers serving its subsidiary, Rover, despite British government moves to protect its components industry (Burt and Brown,

2000). Unilever, the Anglo-Dutch food and household products group, also announced it was 'encouraging' its UK suppliers to invoice in euros (Crooks, 2000).

The major benefit of using the euro is that prices across the Eurozone are more transparent, which encourages price competition between products and services in the relevant European countries. It also eases mobility of people, at least within the Eurozone, especially the movement of tourists who no longer have the inconvenience and costs of converting currency for different countries. The disadvantage has been the high cost to strong currencies, at least in the short term, especially the German Deutschmark which was higher rated than the euro on the international currency market. This is one argument as to why the UK is resistant to losing the GB pound. Conversely, low valued currencies such as the Italian lire benefit from using the higher internationally valued and more stable euro. Certainly, Germany faced severe criticism, as did France and Italy to a lesser degree, from the European Commission when they were ordered to curb their budget deficits within the Eurozone. It remains to be seen whether appropriate corrections to the economies will be made (Parker *et al.*, 2003). These problems have been compounded as German exports have been hit by the rise in the euro currency, as shown by the adverse effects on profits in 2003 for Volkswagen (VW), Europe's largest car producer. Hans Dieter Pötsch, VW's finance-director elect, commented that the rising euro, which was up 24 per cent against the dollar between January and May 2003, cost VW €400m (£281m) (Mackintosh and Harnischfeger, 2003).

Another move towards a more harmonious economic market across EU member states has been the attempt to standardize on taxation, but this has proved difficult to implement. As can be seen from Table 3.6, within Europe Germany, France and Italy have the highest corporate tax (between 57 per cent and 41 per cent) while Finland, Sweden, the UK and Ireland have the lowest (between 28 per cent and 32 per cent), well below the US (40 per cent) and Japan (52 per cent) (Atkins and Harnischfeger, 1999). France and Germany have tried to launch moves to harmonize EU tax policies, challenging the UK government's insistence that taxation must remain subject to national veto, but disagreement continues (Parker, 2002b).

In the EU, even the common value added tax (VAT) has different rates and applications of its use differ between EU members, making for large discrepancies. Under EU rules, goods should be taxed at between 15 per cent and 25 per cent. However, in the UK, rates vary from 0 per cent on children's shoes and clothes to 17.5 per cent for general goods and services, while in Sweden the 24 per cent rate is used. Currently, the European Commission is working towards simplifying the VAT rules. In particular, it is proposing revoking the exemptions in the UK and Ireland on children's shoes and clothes and imposing the full rate of VAT, but the UK government is resisting such a move.

Another major influence on European pricing is the implementation of excise duty, which varies considerably from country to country with substantial differences in car and fuel pricing, alcohol and cigarettes, in particular. Differences also occur in the implementation of luxury tax on goods such as leisure boats. The European Commission's survey found that British beer has an average of €0.99 (60p) in excise duty and €0.17 in VAT on a litre of beer, against €0.12 and €0.02 in Germany, Spain and Luxembourg, while in France taxes on beer are at €0.16 a litre. However, Finland has even higher rates of €1.43 in excise duty and €0.31 in VAT on a litre of beer. Draft proposals are being debated within the

Table 3.6 *International comparison of corporate tax rates, 1999*

Country	Corporate tax rate (%)
Germany	43.6–56.7
Japan	51.6
France	41.7
Italy	41.3
Belgium	40.2
US	40.0
Greece	35.0–40.0
Portugal	39.6
Luxembourg	37.5
Netherlands	35.0
Spain	35.5
Austria	34.0
Denmark	34.0
Ireland	32.0
UK	31.0
Sweden	28.0
Finland	28.0

Source: adapted from KPMG corporate tax rate survey quoted in Atkins and Harnischfeger (1999)

Commission for the UK's high beer taxes to fall into line with those of its EU partners by 2038 with low tax countries such as Germany and Spain rising (Mann, 2002).

The European Commission is working to ensure prices are kept at competitive levels throughout Europe. For example, in 2001, the German car producer, VW, was fined £18.6m for unfair competition in preventing its German car dealers from selling the company's Passat model at a discount for two years after its introduction in 1996. VW prices before tax were higher in Germany than in all other EU member countries, except the UK. In 2002, the European Commission initiated an investigation into the €418m (£255m) subsidy by the German federal government and the regional government of Saxony to BMW towards a new €1.2bn car plant in Leipzig. Under EU law, state aid for car plants cannot exceed the amount of money the company would have saved by moving the project elsewhere. In BMW's case the German authorities told the Commission that the company could have saved more than €500m by building the plant in Kolin, in the Czech Republic, where costs, especially employee wages, are lower. The Commission has taken action against state aid to German carmakers in the past. In 1996 it forced Saxony to reduce the subsidy to a VW plant by €240m after concluding it did not meet EU competition rules (Guerrera and Harnischfeger, 2002). The authority of the European Commission on these matters far exceeds that of national governments.

European product standards and patents

There has been a move from applying national safety standards for products and services, such as the British Standard, towards applying European Standards to prevent the protection of national production. Regarding protection of intellectual property, companies and inventors can apply for:

1   a patent in a specific EU country;
2   an existing European patent, which is a package of national patents covering the EU;
3   a Community patent, a single patent applicable EU-wide being introduced around 2005–6 (Tait, 2003). The latter is expected to be cheaper than the average European patent, although more expensive than similar intellectual property protection in the US. However, there are problems associated with the Community patent concerning:

- language and the extent to which such a patent needs to be translated so that it can be read throughout the EU. The patent claim, i.e. the legal scope of the patent, needs to be translated into all EU languages. The remainder must be in French, German or English. The new patents court will be in Luxembourg, but may not come into operation until 2010;
- location of a central patents court in which a Community patent could be lodged;
- cost to the supervision of national patents;
- administration of the system. The European Patent Office already handles European patent applications and is expected to take on the Community patent work as well, but it already has a backlog of work.

Further discussion of the role of product development in international marketing is given in Chapter 5: International product development.

European promotion harmonization

Increasingly, industry controls related to promotion are governed by European rather than national legislation, e.g. those with respect to tobacco sponsorship of sport, especially Formula 1 racing. In March 2002, there was a Belgian proposal that all car advertisements should contain a warning that the motorist is responsible for safe driving, which would curtail 'go-faster' advertising such as the Hyundai strapline that its car 'disappears faster than a dotcom'.

European channels of distribution ('place')

The reduction, even removal, of border controls in the form of passports, import/export documentation, etc. has greatly eased mobility within the EU, especially across continental Europe. Transport haulage provision has been largely liberalized (Stone, 2001). However, sometimes it has been replaced by protection of national hauliers in the guise of environmental protection. For example, no Sunday commercial vehicles are permitted on the roads in France, Germany and Austria to protect the private car user. An additional 'vignette' tax is raised on commercial vehicles weighing more than 12 tonnes crossing Germany to Eastern Europe and similar charges are made in Austria and Switzerland. France is proposing imposing a tax or fee on all trucks travelling on toll-free motorways or dual carriageways to help fund its new high-speed railway lines and motorways (Lichfield, 2003).

Another example of the European Commission increasing competition is through the deregulation of distribution of cars in Europe. For the past twenty years, there have been car sale restrictions imposed through the 'block exemption' which allowed car manufacturers to escape normal competition law by selling new vehicles through franchised outlets with exclusive selling territories. In 2001, the Commission introduced changes to develop an open market for car retailing, replacing the traditional business model with very low margins on car sales offset by lucrative servicing and repair contracts (Burt, 2001). In future, car manufacturers will be able to impose quality criteria for dealers wishing to sell their cars, be they existing car showrooms, new entrants such as Carrefour and Tesco, or websites on the Internet, but they will not be allowed to grant them exclusive trading areas. Price competition is expected to increase.

Future developments within the SEM

Unfortunately, despite all the moves towards the creation of the SEM there is a long way to go to achieve the goals of free trade and movement. Europe has seen progress towards the ideals give way to red tape and protectionism. For example, 'despite the much proclaimed freedom of movement across the EU's 15 member states, an Austrian baker still needs eight licences to open a shop in Italy, a few kilometres down a borderless motorway' (Guerrera, 2003). The EU's ambition to become the world's most competitive economy by the end of the decade cannot work without a properly functioning single market, and the European Commission reported that this ambition is threatened by a sluggish economy and lack of political will. Progress towards the goals has been made. Between 1986 and 1992, the European Commission proposed, and national governments and the European parliament approved, 280 laws aimed at creating a single market. Since 1993 Brussels has produced an average of more than one legislative proposal a day, most aimed at replacing and harmonizing national legislation.

According to a European Commission study, the SEM added €877bn (equivalent to US $926bn or £577bn) to EU income over the past ten years and increased annual GDP by 1.8 per cent, creating some 2.5 million jobs in the process. It did this by allowing products to circulate freely, giving consumers more choice and businesses a wider market (Guerrera, 2003). But while goods can move freely across borders, legal barriers and national regulations hinder providers of services, which account for 70 per cent of the EU economy. The European Commission estimates that bringing EU services in line with the US would create 36 million jobs. To that end, legislation is being sought to remove the major barriers. However, member states do not fully trust one another, often raising barriers to foreign service providers. Similar attitudes hamper EU efforts to remove barriers to the movement of capital. Progress on the Financial Services Action Plan launched in 1999 to create a single European financial market by 2005 has involved 34 of the 42 laws designed to create an EU-wide financial market being agreed, covering laws against insider dealing and help for companies raising funds across the EU. But further development has suffered through disagreement between member states, the European Commission and the European Parliament. Such delays are expensive. According to the European Commission, a single financial market would add an extra 1.1 per cent to the EU's GDP, or €130bn (US $153bn, £94bn) over the next decade (Guerrera, 2003; Guerrera and Norman, 2003).

While progress is being made towards achieving the key objectives of the SEM of free movement of goods, people, capital and services (see p. 51), challenges remain. While travellers roam freely across the EU, legal and financial barriers restrict workers. At present, EU citizens typically face problems in getting their professional and academic qualifications recognized, although some progress has been made in this respect (see p. 68). Companies that wish to move workers across the EU have to pay extra costs as a result of the lack of rules for a Europe-wide pension. Even in the area where the single market has worked best, i.e. free movement of goods, problems persist. Despite the absence of internal borders, prices of everyday goods differ more than they should in a single market. Table 3.7 shows price differences in a range of MNC branded goods across Europe, e.g. a bottle of Evian water in Finland costs four times what it does in France where it is produced, while Germans pay half as much for Heinz tomato ketchup as Italians. National regulations, red tape and uneven competition across the EU prompt companies to price their goods differently.

Trading disputes between the EU and the US

In 2001, Pascal Lamy, EU Trade Commissioner, considered the world's two largest trading powers, the EU and the US, were 'elephants of world trade [that] have objectively extremely similar interests' (Norman and Alden, 2001). In the past, usually the US and EU have been able to resist domestic demands for protection by emphasizing their shared interests in larger trade negotiations such as the Uruguay Round and the sectoral agreements that followed on telecommunications, financial services and information technology. However, increasingly these underlying interests have become subject to the pressures of domestic politics as with the US facing demands for trade action in diverse sectors such as beef, steel, timber and even banana producers. The World Trade Organization (WTO) dispute involving the banana trade reflects the EU's wish to protect its spheres of 'colonial' influence in Africa, the Caribbean and the Pacific against the US pull to support its Latin America interests in

Table 3.7 *Differences in prices of general supermarket goods across the European Union*

Multinational brand	Highest prices (in euro cents)	Lowest prices (in euro cents)	Ratio: cheapest/ most expensive
Evian mineral water	Finland 189	France 44	4.3
Barilla spaghetti	Sweden 138	Italy 59	2.3
Heinz ketchup	Italy 138	Germany 66	2.1
Kellogg's cornflakes	Greece 152	UK 71	2.1
Mars bar	Denmark 143	Belgium 73	2.0
Fanta	Sweden 146	Netherlands 77	1.9
Colgate toothpaste	UK 126	Portugal/Spain 76	1.7
Elvital shampoo	Ireland 126	Spain 76	1.7

Sources: European Commission survey (November 2000) quoted in Guerrera (2003)

Central America (see Box 1.2, pp. 12–13). There is EU resistance to US hormone treated beef and to genetically modified (GM) foods, especially those produced by the MNC Monsanto. The US objects to delays in EU approval of GM crops and foods as well as draft EU labelling and traceability rules. The US also disagreed with government aid for the European Airbus A380 'superjumbo' project and there are continuing differences over the EU environmental ban on aircraft 'hush-kit' mufflers to cut airport noise which discriminate against the US (and UK) aviation industries. In March 2002, the US imposed steel tariffs of between 15 and 26 per cent on 15 categories of steel on all imports above set quotas for three years, which triggered EU consideration of retaliatory tariffs on 316 US products. The impasse is likely to be a long and complex legal battle in the WTO. Both the US and the EU have agreed to abide by the WTO rules regarding the dispute, but they disagree over how the rules should be interpreted (Mann and Alden, 2002).

Another cause for concern has been the EU's court ruling that key aspects of bilateral 'open skies' agreements were unlawful (Dombey and Done, 2002). It could lead to dispute between the EU and the US over existing treaties and, even legal action over valuable airline routes. The current agreements remove restrictions on the number of airlines flying to and from the US, as well as airline capacity, frequencies and pricing. But they continue to exclude foreign carriers from the US domestic aviation market and they protect US airlines from foreign take-overs.

These trade disputes aimed at protecting domestic interests have been compounded by political differences between countries leading to consumer boycotts of particular national products. This was especially evident in the adverse reaction in the US to French wine and cheese in the aftermath of France's vocal opposition to the US-led invasion of Iraq in March 2003. Such circumstances are extremely difficult to predict and their distortions on trade countermands normal international marketing planning.

EUROPEAN MANAGEMENT ORGANIZATION STRUCTURES

While necessarily the management of cross-border European organizations is more complex than that of national or regional organizations, a pattern is emerging for the more international group. Where the firm has started in a particular country, usually its headquarters will be located in that country, e.g. the Spanish fashion clothes producer Zara is based in Coruña in north-west Spain (see Box 3.2) and similarly, Benetton, based in northern Italy. But feedback for the Marketing Information System (MIS) is obtained from their networks of international retail outlets. As firms become larger, and certainly for the MNCs, European operations are usually managed from a base in northern Europe, e.g. traditionally based in the south-east of the UK, often in London or the Oxford area, or in the Benelux countries, most frequently in the Netherlands. In this way, firms such as Unilever, Heineken, Shell and Sony manage their international, and European, operations from the Netherlands. As they widen operations across Europe, countries are usually grouped together due to their geographical and cultural proximity, e.g. Spain and Portugal; Germany, Switzerland and Austria; the Scandinavian countries, Denmark, Norway and Sweden together with the Baltic country, Finland; while the UK and France usually remain separate. Logistics and distribution, marketing and sales operations are organized to match national geography and population density with market demand.

ROLE OF EUROPEAN, NATIONAL AND REGIONAL CULTURE IN MARKETING

Traditionally, there has been a large cultural divide between northern and southern Europe. Northern Europe covers Scandinavia (encompassing Finland, Sweden, Norway and Denmark), Germany, the Benelux countries (comprising the Netherlands, Belgium and Luxembourg) and the UK. Southern Europe largely covers the Mediterranean countries – France, Italy, Spain and Greece, together with Portugal.

While all these countries have their own dominant national language, e.g. Spanish in Spain, Swedish in Sweden, tolerance and the use of regional languages and dialects has been encouraged, especially over the last twenty years. In this way, Spain has the official Castillian Spanish but also has Basque in the north-east, Catalan in the north and Valencian further south along the Mediterranean coastal area. Similarly, while English is the common language in the UK, Welsh is spoken and used in parts of Wales and Gaelic in the north-west of Scotland. Indeed, these regional languages are taught in schools and, frequently, government officials are expected to have at least secondary education qualifications in the use of these languages. Marketers operating within these regions are expected to communicate in both the national language and the regional language. In this way, an advertising message in Spain may be given in Spanish as well as Catalan, Valencian or Basque; similarly, in Belgium both French and Dutch/Flemish dialect are used.

Nevertheless, increasingly, and certainly for professional purposes, different nationalities are brought together through the use of the English language. However, the English spoken is not necessarily the same as that spoken in the UK; rather it evolves to suit the persons speaking it, often with specific words that take on different meanings from those used by UK English speakers. For example, the European Logistics Users and Providers Group (ELUPEG) meets to improve European logistics. It has more than 180 members representing MNCs, primarily from the electronics and automotive industries, including Sony, Samsung, Philips, Ford, GM and Mattel as well as logistics service providers such as Exel, Deutsche Post, Christian Salvesen, Hays and Tibbett & Britten. Meetings bring together many nationalities speaking many languages. It is English which is used as the communication language although, occasionally, groups of like-nationalities may break away into their own common language. The use of English is a practical approach to communication, but is not necessarily politically correct, as is apparent by the need for the European Parliament and associated EU administration to be conducted in more than ten different languages, necessitating an expensive interpreting and translating service.

BOX 3.1 WORKING HOURS

Associated with different climate patterns, southern Europe has customarily had different times for working than those in northern Europe. In this way, in Spain, many businesses start at 8.00 a.m., stop for a long lunch of up to three hours in the summer months, in keeping with the close social links between work and leisure. In contrast, generally, a short lunch break is taken in the north in the Netherlands – often taking no longer than half an hour – and interestingly, 'free' milk is provided by the state at work canteens. Spaniards often return to work about 5.00 p.m. until 8.00 or 9.00 p.m. in the evening. Typically, shops open around 9.00 a.m. or even 10.00 a.m., closing at 1.30 p.m. for a long afternoon break to accommodate the long lunch and heat in summer to re-open about 4.30 to 5.00 p.m., closing again at about 8.00 p.m. in the evening. Most shops are not open on Sunday, the exception being bakers, newsagents and tourist shops. The banks and post office (Correos) open at 8.30 a.m. and close at 2.00 p.m. Monday to Friday: the post office opens on Saturdays but not the banks; there is no Sunday opening.

Practices are changing with the influence of international retailers with major food and household retailers in Spain. For example, the Spanish group Mercadona, the French owned Carrefour (previously Pryca), the Alcampo, part of the French Auchan group, and the German discount store Lidl, all open Monday to Saturday between 10.00 a.m. and 10.00 p.m., with no lunch-time closing. Generally, these types of retailers are closed on Sundays, although there has been a recent move to Sunday opening in the summer.

In France, like Spain, the practice has been to have a longer lunch; however, working practices are changing. The 'sandwich' lunch in Paris is becoming much more common, especially as workers learn to appreciate the benefits of an earlier finish to ease home travelling as distances from work to home have increased.

Normally, in the UK, the common working day, Monday to Friday, runs from 9.00 a.m. to 5.00 p.m. or 5.30 p.m. making up a 40–42 hour week. A one hour lunch break is commonly 12.30 to 1.30 p.m. Shops usually open 9.00 or 10.00 a.m. until 5.30 or 6.00 p.m. with no lunch closure, and some have late night shopping on Thursday evenings until 7.30 p.m. However, the major food retailers have been moving towards ever longer, even 24 hour opening, especially in the last decade. Sunday opening has been commonplace in Scotland since 1984 (when it was introduced at Cameron Toll in Edinburgh), although not so prevalent in England and Wales. Department stores and retail chains began opening on Sundays in the two-month lead-up to Christmas and, finding it popular with consumers, have moved to general Sunday opening between 11.00 a.m. and 5.00 p.m. in Scotland.

Differences in national regulation and consumer behaviour between northern and southern Europe are especially evident in the opening hours of licensed bars (or pubs in the UK). Differences occur within the UK, where in England and Wales, pubs typically open at 5.00 p.m. and close at 11.00 p.m., while in Scotland, they open for much longer, moving towards almost 24 hour opening, reflecting the more liberal approach in Continental Europe, especially in Spain, France and Greece. On the other hand, restrictions on the sale of alcohol are much more stringent in Scandinavian countries, which encourage consumers to drink at home rather than go out to pubs.

Other examples of differences in retail hours of opening in the rest of Europe are the practice in Germany of shops closing at 1.00 p.m. on Saturdays, and limited Sunday opening in general on the Continent, although in France some food retailers open in the morning. Surprisingly, in France many petrol stations close on Sunday afternoons.

In summary, where MNCs, e.g. Shell, IBM and Ford, are encouraging a more common approach to hours of working, working practices override national traditional approaches with the need for standardization across the organization, yet there continues to be wide diversion in practice, especially between northern and southern Europe.

BOX 3.2 EUROPEAN YOUTH

Increasingly youth culture is becoming more similar across Europe. Generally, young people are getting married at a later age – many are living with partners, buying homes and working as young married couples did in previous decades. Popular music, while still nationally orientated, has become much more English language based. For example, Céline Dion produces French songs for the French Canadian and French market together with additional English language versions for the more international market.

Clothing fashion, too, is more international with national brands crossing borders to become European and even global brands. National retailers expanding across Europe and beyond in their internationalization have enhanced this process, predominantly through franchising. For example, in 2002, Swedish fashion retailer Hennes & Mauritz (H&M) had more than 770 stores in 14 countries across Scandinavia, the rest of Europe and the US. The Spanish Inditex group opened its first Zara store in Spain in 1975. By 2002, it had expanded its Zara outlets, so that, together with its other divisions – Masimo Dutti targeting the exclusive market, Bershka for teenagers, Pull and Bear for sportswear and Oysho, a lingerie specialist – Inditex had almost 1,300 stores in 39 countries (George and Levitt, 2002). Mango, another Spanish clothes fashion retailer, opened in Barcelona in 1984 and by 1992 had 100 shops in Spain since when it has expanded its operations across Europe. In 1998, it opened its first store in the UK. Similarly, the French Caroll, the Hong-Kong based Esprit and the UK Monsoon fashion retailers are extending their European coverage. These clothes retailers are following the internationalization process of US retailers predominantly targeting the youth market, e.g. Gap and Timberland, alongside US global brands Adidas, Levi's and Nike that have led the way among fashion conscious consumers, especially younger consumers.

Nevertheless, national and regional brands continue to play their part. While a Spaniard could happily breakfast on Bimbo bread and Bonka coffee and pay bills with a Bonka Visa card, it is hard to see these brand names proving successful in Britain or elsewhere. (See Chapter 5: International product development, pp. 133–6 for further discussion of international branding.)

Technology has played its part in forging a common bond between youth in Europe and youth in other parts of the world. Most young people from the age of ten, if not younger, possess mobile phones which are used as sophisticated fashion toys as much as items for communication. Indeed, increasingly young people no longer have land phones, making for difficulties in undertaking marketing research targeted to this market segment, as there are no publicly available directories of mobile phone owners. Sending text messages, using the Internet at home and Internet cafés while away has removed national barriers, providing almost instantaneous communication and expectations within the fashion awareness culture. This poses considerable marketing challenges for all firms servicing this market whether the large MNC or the SME.

CONCLUSION

The EU has been successful in bringing its members together and has prevented internal conflict in the form of a major war for over fifty years since its inception in 1957 through the Treaty of Rome. Increasingly, EU legal controls aimed at liberalization and harmonization of trade and industry override national legislation across its member states. However, some protection of national industries continues.

The EU faces challenges associated with its proposed enlargement that could be costly. As political tensions rise within and around the established EU, with the entry of the CEE countries, Cyprus and Malta, the EU must take more responsibility for what happens on and beyond its borders. There has been an emergence of a European ideology that holds sway among many European citizens identified with defence of freedom, underlining its alignment with the Free World and distancing itself from Europe's fascist past. Intellectuals stress the origins of the distinctively European values in a symbiosis of Christendom and Roman Law. However, the 'Christian club' is wider and, in reality, encompasses Asian and African religions. European values will have to extend in depth to have more appreciation of Europe's rapidly growing Muslim community and, even more so, as Turkey's application to join the EU becomes a reality (Mazower, 2002, Wolf, 2002b). The rich diversity of peoples within the EU will pose both opportunities and challenges for international marketing. The EU should take care not to be over inward looking, protecting its member states at the expense of the WTO ideals.

Marketing practices are becoming more similar across Europe in terms of the marketing mix, pricing, product (and service) development, promotion and channels of distribution strategies, with increasingly common consumer behaviour, especially among European youth. Yet there remain national, and regional, northern and southern European distinguishing features that have to be considered with cross-border marketing. While, frequently, the English language is used as a means of communication among EU peoples, sensitivity is required to assimilate the other languages and regional dialects within Europe, despite the high financial costs involved.

International marketing will benefit from the SEM as it becomes more cohesive and competitive within the global market. While it faces many challenges in bringing together 25 countries and 500 million people within the enlarged EU over the next decade, successful implementation will help to provide world peace and prosperity in the future. The alternative is not a viable long-term proposition.

REVIEW QUESTIONS

3.1 Discuss the challenges faced in implementing the enlargement of the European Union from 15 to 25 members in June 2004.

3.2 How are market entry strategies for Central and Eastern Europe (CEE) likely to differ from those used in the traditional 15 member European Union?

3.3 Critically assess the influence of the Single European Market (or Single Market Programme) on the regulation of marketing practice.

3.4 Review typical organization structures that MNCs use to manage European marketing operations.

3.5 Using examples, evaluate the channels of distribution commonly used by international firms targeting European mass markets.

REFERENCES

Artis, M. and Nixson, F. (eds) (2001) *The economics of the European Union,* Oxford: Oxford University Press.

Atkins, R. and Harnischfeger, U. (1999) 'Lafontaine fights a rearguard action to define tax ambitions', *Financial Times*, 3 March, p. 2.

Bell, S. (2002) 'France's Mobylette moped the latest victim of EU legislation', *Scotsman*, 9 December, p. 12.

Buckley, N. and Rawsthorn, A. (1993) 'Kingfisher £560m takeover of Darty boosts share 30p' and 'Takeover creates Europe-wide retailer', *Financial Times,* 19 February, pp. 1 and 17.

Burt, T. (2000) 'Slow road to merger', *Financial Times*, 7 January, p. 14.

Burt, T. (2001) 'Blocked out', *Financial Times*, 7 September, p. 18.

Burt, T. and Brown, K. (2000) 'Rover expects more euro-zone suppliers', *Financial Times*, 16 February, p. 2.

Coffey, P. (2001) *The euro: an essential guide,* London and New York: Continuum.

Crooks, E. (2000) 'Unilever urges invoicing in euros', *Financial Times*, 21 August, p. 17.

Dempsey, J. and Reed, J. (2002) 'Prodi backs more generous deal for entrants', *Financial Times*, 11 December, p. 10.

Dombey, D. and Done, K. (2002) 'EU throws doubt on "open skies" deals', *Financial Times*, 6 November, p. 1.

George, N. and Levitt, J. (2002) 'Retail leaders aim to show they're more than just a passing fashion', *Financial Times*, 19 September, p. 21.

Griffiths, J., Bennett, R. and Crooks, E. (2000) 'Toyota demands contracts in euros', *Financial Times,* 11 August, p. 1.

Guerrera, F. (2003) 'Europe sees progress give way to red tape and protectionism', *Financial Times*, 14 January, p. 11.

Guerrera, F. and Harnischfeger, U. (2002) 'Brussels to probe subsidy for BMW', *Financial Times,* 4 April, p. 13.

Guerrera, F. and Norman, P. (2003) 'Brussels warns of deadline for single financial market', *Financial Times*, 2 June, p. 7.

Hargreaves, D. (2000) 'Brussels may be strict on BOC takeover', *Financial Times*, 13 January, p. 1.

Jonquières, G. and Dawkins, W. (1992) 'An appetite for acquisitions', *Financial Times*, 27 January, p. 14.

Lichfield, J. (2003) 'France to pay for high-speed rail links by taxing lorry trips', *Independent*, 21 May, p. 12.

Mackintosh, J. and Harnischfeger, U. (2003) 'Volkswagen profits hammered as rising euro takes toll on exporters', *Financial Times*, 8 May, p. 23.

Major, T. and Krosta, A. (2002) 'ECB agrees three-speed voting model', *Financial Times*, 11 December, p. 10.

Mann, M. (2002) 'Sobering truth of European beer tax survey', *Financial Times*, 17 May, p. 4.

Mann, M. and Alden, E. (2002) 'EU hits at US "unilaterilism" on steel', *Financial Times*, 14 March, p. 10.

Mazower, M. (2002) 'Beyond the Christian club of Europe', *Financial Times*, 12 December, p. 21.

Norman, P. and Alden, E. (2001) 'US threatens EU with new sanctions', *Financial Times*, 8 March, p. 37.

Parker, G. (2002a) 'Brussels seeks EU stability pact reforms', *Financial Times*, 25 November, p. 1.

Parker, G. (2002b) 'France and Germany call for EU tax accord', *Financial Times*, 2 December, p. 1.

Parker, G. (2002c) 'Fears of big move west may be unfounded', *Financial Times*, 10 December, p. 10.

Parker, G. (2002d) 'Intake of new members threatens EU gridlock', *Financial Times*, 12 December, p. 6.

Parker, G. (2003) 'EU summit seeks to mend rifts opened by Iraq crisis', *Financial Times*, 19 March, p. 11.

Parker, G. and Dombey, D. (2003) 'The European Union: "not perfect but more than we could have hoped for": Europe's draft constitution', *Financial Times*, 20 June, p. 19.

Parker, G., Simonian, H., Mallet, V. and Barber, T. (2003) 'EU orders Berlin to curb budget deficit', *Financial Times*, 9 January, p. 6.

Smith, M. (2000a) 'Brussels sets out food safety proposals' and 'EU has three years to fulfil its bold agenda for food', *Financial Times*, 13 January, p. 8.

Smith, M. (2000b) 'Brussels warns on dirty beaches', *Financial Times*, 12 December, p. 2.

Stone, M.A. (2001) 'European expansion of UK third-party logistics service providers', *International Journal of Logistics: Research and Applications*, Vol. 4, No. 1, pp. 97–115.

Swann, D. (ed.) (1995) *The economics of the common market*, 8th edn, London: Penguin.

Tait, N. (2003) 'Third way opens up for patents', *Financial Times*, 10 March, p. 14.

Taylor, A. (2002) 'Overseas groups get on the UK utility map', *Financial Times*, 17 June, p. 4.

Wagstyl, S. (1997) 'Arranged marriages', *Financial Times*, 14 October, p. 21.

Wagstyl, S. (2002a) 'Candidates see red over funds', *Financial Times*, 10 December, p. 10.

Wagstyl, S. (2002b) 'Common past fuels drive to agree biggest EU expansion', *Financial Times*, 10 December, p. 10.

Wolf, M. (2002a) 'GDP per head', *Financial Times*, 10 December, p. 23.

Wolf, M. (2002b) 'Europe risks destruction to widen peace and prosperity', *Financial Times*, 11 December, p. 23.

Yárnoz, C. (2003) 'El 63 per cent de los europeos apoya que la UE tenga su propia Constitución', *El País*, 23 July, p. 7.

RECOMMENDED WEBSITES

http://www.ft.com/europe

http://www.ft.com/brussels

RECOMMENDED FURTHER READING

Antonides, G. and Raaij, W.F. van (1998) *Consumer behaviour: a European perspective,* Chichester: Wiley.

Brown, L. and McDonald, M.H.B. (1994) *Competitive marketing strategy for Europe,* Basingstoke: Macmillan.

Carlsnaes, W. and Smith, S. (eds) (1994) *European foreign policy: the EC and changing perspectives in Europe,* London: Sage.

Crane, R. (2000) *European business cultures,* Harlow: Pearson/Financial Times/Prentice Hall.

El-Agraa, A.M. (1994) *The economics of the European Community,* 4th edn, Hemel Hempstead: Harvester Wheatsheaf.

Harris, P. and McDonald, F. (1994) *European business and marketing strategic issues,* London: Paul Chapman.

Mercado, S., Welford, R. and Prescott, K. (2001) *European business,* 4th edn, Harlow: Pearson Education/Financial Times/Prentice Hall.

Somers, F. (ed.) (1994) *European Community economies: a comparative study*, 2nd edn, London: Pitman.

Chapter 4

International Marketing Information Systems: marketing research

INTRODUCTION

This chapter examines the role of Marketing Information Systems (MISs) incorporating marketing research within international marketing. Marketing research is the activity whereby market information is gathered and analysed to help management reduce the risk associated with decision-making and, as such, marketing research plays an important role within Management Information Systems. International marketing research is the systematic and objective collection of information concerning international markets. It helps management to reach sound decisions concerning the selection and implementation of their international marketing. Marketing research should be used in international marketing to establish the most favoured marketing mix for the product, or service, to use in terms of determining product characteristics, pricing approaches, promotional methods and channels of distribution that will suit the targeted market. Marketing research can assess customer behaviour to provide management with an informed understanding of demand at all stages of the product life cycle. For example, when a new product, or service, is introduced to a new market, test marketing can assess customer demand. Customer satisfaction studies can ensure the product matches customer expectations throughout the growth, mature and decline stages of the product's life cycle. Sales tracking can determine appropriate levels of advertising expenditure. As in the domestic market, marketing research within the international market reduces the chances of marketing mistakes being made.

LEARNING OBJECTIVES

The objectives of this chapter are to:
- show the role of the MIS within international marketing;
- demonstrate sources of information, both secondary and primary, that can be used within the MIS;
- discuss the role and organization of the international marketing research industry;
- identify criteria for selecting an international marketing research agency;
- highlight sources of government help available for international marketing research;
- evaluate approaches to implementing international marketing research.

When you have completed the chapter you should be able to:
- explain how international MISs operate;
- distinguish the contribution that internal reporting, market intelligence and marketing research make to international MISs;
- select appropriate marketing research methods for different international markets;
- use the help that may be available from government bodies for international marketing research;
- specify how to plan and implement an international marketing research programme;
- assess the role of marketing research within international marketing.

MANAGEMENT INFORMATION SYSTEMS

Within every organization management is required to bring together the data gathered through its functional activities and to analyse that data to help management decision-making. The data obtained can come from a range of sources. The MIS (Marketing Information System) concentrates on the provision of the data related to the market being targeted. These marketing data contribute to the overall Management Information System for the organization. An MIS has been defined as being: 'people, equipment and procedures to gather, sort, analyze, evaluate and distribute needed, timely and accurate information to marketing decision makers' (Kotler *et al.*, 1999: 317).

Internal staff within the marketing services function, usually located at, or within close proximity to, the organization's central head office, are expected to manage the MIS. The marketing data is gathered through a combination of formal and informal communication routes using internal and external sources within the organization. It can come from any, or all, of the accounting and finance, research and development, production and personnel functional areas. Formal internal sources of information include sales force reports and sales monitoring, while informal sources could be data gathered through meetings with colleagues and associates. Formal external information comes from a wide range of sources including statistics produced by international bodies such as the United Nations (UN), the World Health Organization (WHO) and the World Bank, national governments and trade associations. More informal external sources of data might be trade experts attending trade exhibitions and seminars, as well as industry experts working within marketing research agencies, advertising agencies and management consultancies.

An MIS is developed from the inter-linkage and analysis of data collected from three types of information gathering (see Figure 4.1). These are internal reporting, marketing intelligence and marketing research.

The three data gathering sources should interact on a continuous basis, e.g. internal reporting sources covering information obtained from within the organization may be used in the preparation of marketing research studies. Similarly, marketing intelligence environmental scanning is used in conjunction with the internal reporting process which, in turn, can feed into the marketing research function. All the data gathered from the internal reporting process, from marketing intelligence and from marketing research should be analysed and assessed to determine market trends. These are used to develop databases for the organization providing market data related to actual and potential customers which, in turn, help management to monitor market activity and ascertain the organization's performance. In this way, a list of customers might detail customer locations, their purchasing patterns and the payment methods that they use and this can help the marketing department to decide on the most appropriate marketing mix to reach the customer. Product characteristics, pricing strategies, promotional approaches, advertising and the sales effort, as well as the appropriate logistics operations, can be determined in conjunction with segmentation, positioning and targeting strategies.

Within the organization, the data gathered for the MIS are analysed and assessed. The findings should be passed upwards from the marketing services function/department through to corporate or strategic planners to help in strategic decision-making. The strategic planners, in the same way, should feed information back into the MIS to direct, or target, market interests within the marketing services department. This information should also be communicated to, and should be received from, the other functional sections of the organization including production, research and development, finance and sales. Within the

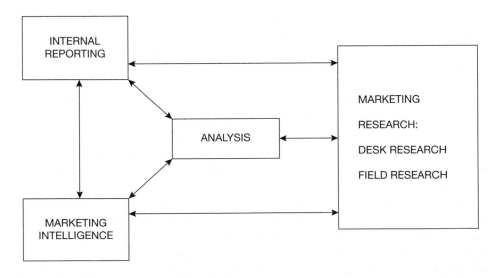

Figure 4.1 Marketing Information System

organization, individual functional departments, company subsidiaries and strategic business units (SBUs) provide marketing data related to their own particular product, or service, for the MIS. The system should take this data, assimilate it with data from outside the organization, analyse the data and feed the findings to the departments for management decision-making.

The data obtained for the MIS will vary in quality and may require careful interpretation in the light of their source. For example, data gained from SBUs within an organization may be delayed or even adjusted before being passed to central marketing services for processing within the MIS. Sales figures may be provided in an incomplete manner to avoid highlighting a drop in sales that might lead to reductions in resources for the SBU concerned. Consequently, close control is required in the collection of data to ensure accurate market assessment.

While the specific objectives of the MIS will differ from organization to organization, generally, such systems monitor the marketing environment and the performance of the organization within a market. The MIS should provide data that brings together the different functions within the organization. It should identify the needs of customers, competitor performance and indicate how well the organization is performing. The MIS should be an effective and reliable decision-making tool to help management satisfy consumer demand.

The process of gathering data for the international MIS is fundamentally the same as that for marketing within a single country, i.e. data are collected, assessed, interpreted and reported upon for management decision-making. The prime difference is that the data collected relate to product, and service, performance in international markets. In the international marketing situation, marketing research can be undertaken at a single or multi-country level, with a wider geographical coverage than for the national marketing organization. It involves collecting data from at least one country other than the domestic country and may use data from several countries, or even global data.

The resources, in terms of finance, personnel and time, necessary for undertaking multi-country marketing research are likely to be greater than for single country research due to the increased geographical spread of collecting the data, as well as the complexities of analysing and reporting on the data. Increased human resources is often required for international marketing research administration for field-force data collection, data processing, analysis and for presentation of the research findings. The number and expertise of the persons required is a function of the type of research undertaken, in the same way as for national marketing research. The researchers involved need to possess an appreciation of the culture as well as the language skills appropriate for the countries being investigated. While data can be collected on a national, or even regional, basis, those persons undertaking international marketing research have to gather and interpret data across all the countries concerned, which can be challenging.

The international MIS gathers market data using three sources – internal records, market intelligence and marketing research – which are brought together, often using databases, analysed and reported to management for marketing decision-making (see Figure 4.1). As would be expected, the international dimension makes the collection process necessarily more complex than in the national situation, but the process used is fundamentally the same as for the domestic MIS.

ROLE OF MARKETING RESEARCH: LINKAGE TO MARKETING DECISION-MAKING

The data collected from the MIS using internal records, market intelligence and marketing research have to be analysed and presented to management in a format suitable for decision-making. These data are brought together, often as databases, to assess market demand. Such databases can relate to sales and profit margins and provide data on customers such as their number, location, industry type, volume of purchases, creditworthiness and purchase decision influencers. In the international arena, management needs to analyse the sales by country and region, as well as the market segmentation criteria considered appropriate.

Clearly, the scale of the analysis required for assessing international markets is greater than for domestic markets. Differences in market data collection procedures and the IT used by marketing research suppliers in different countries can compound difficulties. If at all possible, the same marketing research methods with the same (or complementary) information systems and IT are used, particularly where data are provided through local marketing research agencies rather than subsidiaries of a major agency. But it may not be possible to have the ideal situation. While, theoretically, it can be envisaged that an international marketing research agency such as A.C. Nielsen would use common information systems worldwide, enabling a common approach to market analysis, in practice, different systems may have to be used. Nevertheless, with the increased sophistication in software, the challenges posed for analysis of data can be overcome and the data gathered made compatible. The co-ordinating agency assimilates the data gathered from its associate agencies across the world, requesting that the data be presented in a format that allows for data analysis.

SECONDARY RESEARCH: SOURCES OF MARKET DATA

Desk research

Initial desk research can use both internal and external secondary sources of data that can be maintained internally within the organization to monitor market conditions. They have been collected for general purposes and not specifically for the research that is being conducted.

Internal sources

Internal sources involve the collection of data produced within the organization, e.g. sales reports, customer credit records and Electronic Point of Sale (EPOS) data. For international marketing research the organization can collect sales reports on a country basis, by product type, brand and sales outlet, as well as by region or trading bloc, e.g. the EU, the North American Free Trade Agreement (NAFTA), the Southern Cone Common Market (MERCOSUR) or the Andean Common Market (ANCOM). In this way, sales and profit contribution of goods sold can be assessed on criteria such as the type of product, brand, product colour and size, sales retail outlet as well as by the country, or region, in which the sales occurred. Such analysis provides an assessment of the firm's performance in international markets showing the pattern of its trade and the profitability of the operations concerned, highlighting the markets and countries that offer the favoured growth opportunities.

Generally, internal sources are inexpensive to use, but they relate to market conditions experienced within the organization and, consequently, can be subject to reporting bias. Access to the desirable data may be subject to internal political group dynamics as when a departmental manager prevents full disclosure of sales to protect the sales force. Problems of access to data can become even more challenging within the international arena as culture and geographical distance increase. For these reasons, the researcher may favour using external sources rather than internal sources, despite the data being available within the organization. Certainly, external sources should be used to check the reliability of the internal data.

External sources

Sources of market data available from outside the organization are extensive. They range from the economic indicators published by the UN covering most countries within the world to publications that concentrate on specialist markets such as the European industrial paint market. Some of these data are available only in hard book format but, frequently, they are available on-line through the Internet. Some data are available free or at a nominal charge: others may be expensive to access, being supplied by management consultancies.

Most governments provide services to encourage trade by their national firms. Useful external sources of international market information are government agencies, such as those provided by the Trade Partners UK Information Centre through library and trade regulation services (see pp. 107–9 for more details). Trade associations (see p. 111) also provide market data although usually only to their members. Typically, the market data provided relate to the production of trade association members within national boundaries which, through reciprocal links, can be cumulated across countries. The CBD organization produces international directories of trade associations which can be used to trace the relevant trade association.

Marketing intelligence

As with the domestic market, gathering marketing intelligence from networking is critically important in multi-country marketing. Data can be sourced from persons within the organization or within associated SBUs operating in other divisions or countries. The marketing researcher can contact individuals within the organization to gain advice on trading conditions in a country not personally known to the researcher and can use these contacts to reach other market experts. External sources include trade associations (as discussed above) as well as attendance at trade fairs and trade seminars and so on. Indeed, much market data can be gathered by talking to trade experts, competitors, customers and potential customers at international trade exhibitions where the participants often present their new product developments. The stock market is another useful source of market intelligence, although care has to be taken in interpreting data provided, especially regarding estimates of company performance. Scanning Internet sources also provides useful international market intelligence.

National commercial diplomatic staff can provide useful market intelligence, both formally and informally. For the UK, these data are provided by commercial attachés working at embassies and consulates throughout the world and feeding market data into the services provided by the Trade Partners UK Information Centre (see pp. 107–9). The Chambers of Commerce, funded by industry and commerce, may also provide useful market intelligence (see p. 110). For example, a potential UK exporter of machinery to Brazil could contact the Trade Partners UK Information Centre for advice related to demand for the equipment, competitor activity, trade controls and payment methods as well as for recommendations regarding most favoured market entry methods. Chambers of Commerce can provide additional information on export markets by accessing their international networks.

The advantage of using market intelligence is that it is relatively inexpensive to obtain and relates to current market conditions. The disadvantage is that it may be subject to bias, being based on hearsay and anecdote that require cautious interpretation. Nevertheless, in conjunction with other sources of marketing information, market intelligence can provide useful data for management decision-making.

PRIMARY RESEARCH: FIELD RESEARCH

Marketing research

As with marketing research conducted within one country, decisions have to be taken about the selection of the appropriate primary research methods to gather the desired data to ascertain customer demand. Primary research, often termed 'field research' (and, sometimes, 'fieldwork'), involves the live collection of primary data from external sources by using methods that provide qualitative or quantitative data. This research may be undertaken on an ad hoc or a continuous basis. Ad hoc research is conducted on one particular occasion, e.g. to assess market demand for a new product. Continuous research is defined as being, 'A survey conducted on a regular and frequent basis amongst parallel samples with the same population or a survey in which the interviews are spread over a long time period' (Market Research Society, 2003). It is frequently used to monitor changes in customer demand over time.

Selection of research method

In the same way as for single-country marketing research, the choice of research method depends on issues such as:

- objectives of the research;
- target audience (end-client) for the research;
- type of research question being considered;
- methods used for organizing the research;
- resources available within the organization in terms of:
  - availability of suitable personnel;
  - availability of finance;
  - time constraints;

89

- culture of the country in which the marketing research is to take place;
- previous experience in conducting international marketing research;
- who will conduct the research – staff from within the organization or from a marketing research agency.

Primary research methods

Once the secondary (or desk) research has been completed, gaps in the information gathered can be filled through field research, i.e. by using marketing researchers to collect information from persons in the market. Such persons can be customers, or potential customers, as well as market influencers, or intermediaries, within the supply chain such as retailers, wholesalers and sales agents. Within multi-country marketing research, as with domestic marketing research, both qualitative and quantitative research techniques are used or, more commonly, a combination of both methods. Qualitative research involves studying a smaller number of persons to gain an in-depth understanding of the issues being investigated, while quantitative research involves a larger number to enable measurement and statistical analysis. It should be appreciated that both qualitative and quantitative research are susceptible to bias through the influence of culture.

Qualitative research methods

As with domestic marketing research, qualitative research techniques are used as an exploratory approach to gain insights into potential and actual consumer perception and behaviour towards products, and services. Qualitative research techniques use 'a body of research techniques which seek insights through loosely structured, mainly verbal data rather than measurements. Analysis is interpretative, subjective, impressionistic and diagnostic' (Market Research Society, 2003). Qualitative research allows marketing researchers to delve more deeply into consumer behaviour patterns than traditional quantitative research methods. However, qualitative research is labour intensive, involving a high input of senior marketing research executive time. Furthermore, the intrinsic subjectivity of the research topics can challenge the understanding and interpretation of findings. Yet this very difference provokes deeper consideration of the research topic, which is particularly helpful to marketing management as is apparent by the extensive use of qualitative research.

Qualitative research usually takes the form of focus (sometimes termed 'intensive') one-to-one personal interviews and group discussions. The latter involves 'eight or nine relevant people [being] brought together for an hour, or perhaps an hour and a half to discuss something – [such as] the new product, the advertisement campaign' (Market Research Society, 2003). Other qualitative methods include brainstorming (sometimes termed 'synectics'), observation and accompanied shopping. When qualitative research is undertaken within different countries, normally a common interview structure is used for each country, with appropriate translation and interpreting to match population requirements.

Qualitative research is used extensively in international marketing research, in particular for new product development. It can be used to:

- define areas for investigation;
- obtain background market information;
- identify and explore concepts as well as undertake preliminary screening processes;
- study sensitive, personal or embarrassing issues;
- identify relevant behaviour patterns;
- conduct post-research investigations;
- develop issues and ideas for questionnaires.

Quantitative research methods

'Quantitative research seeks to make measurements as distinct from qualitative research' (Market Research Society, 2003). In marketing research, quantitative research methods usually involve some form of survey, i.e. the systematic collection, analysis and interpretation of data. It may also cover observation and experimentation techniques. Typically, the term is applied to the collection of data about actual and potential customers, often using sampling to select individuals and organizations to survey. International marketing research uses the same quantitative research methods, with measurements as a base for assessment, as those used for single country research.

Survey methods include questionnaire completion using face-to-face and telephone interviewing as well as the postal services and, increasingly, interactive web-based communication. Other methods such as questionnaire enclosure in a newspaper or magazine, or its placement on a publicity stand, or on a theatre seat, may be used to access potential respondents. Sometimes, if appropriate, the questionnaire may be personally handed to the targeted individual, e.g. customer service questionnaires given to passengers on a train or aeroplane, the customer in a restaurant or bank, or the purchaser of a car.

Observation using 'a non-verbal means of obtaining primary data as an alternative or complement to questioning' may also be used (Market Research Society, 2003). Data collected in this manner may be of a quantitative or qualitative nature and involve the marketing researcher observing the behaviour of targeted actual, or potential, consumers. Quantitative measures such as the number and value of purchases of products are monitored.

Mystery shopping, the 'collection of information from retail outlets, showrooms etc., by people posing as ordinary members of the public' (Market Research Society, 2003), is frequently used to monitor consumer satisfaction within the service sector, especially in banking. It, too, can use both quantitative and qualitative methods to ascertain service performance.

Face-to-face personal interview survey

Face-to-face (or personal) interviews can take various forms with different completion times and are used primarily for gathering quantitative data. Usually a questionnaire is used to guide the interviewing process. The typical street (or shopping mall) interview might last for ten minutes whereas an in-home social survey interview often takes two hours or more. Face-to face interviews are becoming difficult and expensive to effect in Western Europe and the challenges of undertaking these across national borders are obvious. Interviewers face problems in obtaining the participation of the desired interviewees. The personal safety of both the interviewers and interviewees is a concern. While face-to-face interviews can provide rich data for market analysis and remain the most used method of obtaining market data, marketing researchers frequently turn to alternatives, especially telephone interviewing.

Information technology (IT) is used to manage the interviewing process and for collecting and analysing the interview data. Computer Assisted Personal Interviewing (CAPI) uses portable lap-top computers for face-to-face interviewing; Computer Assisted Telephone Interviewing (CATI) uses telephone centres and Computer Assisted Self Interviewing (CASI) involves self-completion of a questionnaire on a lap-top computer or a disk sent by post. Computer Assisted Web Interviewing (CAWI) is conducted over the Internet rather than face-to-face. Recent developments have led to the introduction of multi-media methods to enable personal interviewing in the home or office without the physical presence of the interviewer, but these are still at an early stage of development.

CAPI, CATI, CASI and CAWI all help to improve the efficiency of the survey through closer monitoring of the interviewing process. An additional benefit of using CASI has been that self completion on a lap-top computer leads to greater accuracy in response to sensitive issues such as crime, drugs, sex, etc. due to greater confidentiality than pen and paper recording methods. Obviously, such benefits have to be put against the high costs of investing in hardware provision for the field interviewers, although most major market research agencies have this facility.

Telephone interview survey

Telephone interviewing may be conducted through a CATI centre based in the UK or within the country where the study is being completed. CATI techniques are used at all stages of the interviewing process:

- for selecting the sample of interviews using random selection methods, quota controls and automatic dialling;
- for conducting the interview, whereby the questionnaire is shown on a monitor screen and the interviewer inputs respondent answers directly for computer analysis;
- for analysis of findings, both during and after the interview.

In this way, the process can be controlled through almost simultaneous interviews and results. This form of collecting marketing research data is increasing.

The choice of location of the telephone centre depends on factors such as:

- targeted sample for interviewing;
- sample size;
- interview length;
- access to mother-tongue interviewers;
- costs of undertaking the interviews.

Typically, Business-to-Business (B-to-B) international telephone interviewing is conducted in the marketing research agency CATI centres in the host country (say, the UK), and directed at businesses in the targeted countries. For example, a survey of business training managers could be conducted from the UK directed at firms operating across Europe. Lists of the firms to contact would be obtained from telephone directories such as *Yellow Pages* that cover most developed countries. With the move towards outsourcing telephone centres to lower-cost countries, in particular to India, it is possible that marketing research CATI centres are likely to follow. However, time differences between continents pose challenges, with six or more hours between Europe and the US, and even more between Europe and Japan or Australia. The use of voice mail to filter telephone calls also poses a major challenge.

A telephone interview survey targeted towards B-to-B, individual consumers or households in different countries, using an UK-based CATI centre can pose difficulties. It is important for the interviewer to communicate effectively with the potential respondent, so language skills with the appropriate accents are required, which is challenging. Consequently, national CATI centres with interviewers with accents familiar to, and accepted by, the interviewees are favoured. It is not sufficient for the interviewer to speak the respondent's language; the interviewer's dialect and accent must also be acceptable. For example, it is not appropriate to use Dutch interviewers for interviewing in Belgium, despite the close proximity, because local accents are required. In the same way, certain regional accents are more acceptable than others are, e.g. interviewers with Scottish accents are considered more honest and financially astute than those with other British accents.

The costs of telephone calls encourages CATI centres in close proximity to potential respondents but other factors such as lower running costs are encouraging CATI centres to be located outside country boundaries. Telephone interviewing can be administered from within a country, or across country borders.

The move away from using land telephones towards mobile phones poses challenges for telephone interviewing. There is no comprehensive listing of mobile phone users. The conventional telephone directory excludes mobile phones. Many people, especially the younger age group, exclusively use mobile phones, landlines being used for linking to the Internet. At an international level, this situation presents difficulties in finding a suitable sample frame for telephone interviewing. Issues such as the right to privacy exacerbate these problems with more than 30 per cent of UK telephone users choosing to keep their details 'ex-directory', i.e. out of the conventional telephone directory. In addition, in some countries low telephone penetration is also an issue.

Internet

Increasingly, the Internet is used as a medium for international marketing research. It has the benefit that it can cross national boundaries at relatively low cost and with very rapid response times. However, the Internet has the disadvantage of only being used by persons with access to computers and supporting software who predominantly live within the developed economies. Internet users are biased towards the younger age groups, especially the under 50s. Another problem associated with using the Internet for marketing research purposes is that of obtaining a satisfactory sample frame listing of e-mail addresses. Potential respondents can make mistakes in providing their addresses. One solution is to ask the potential respondents to e-mail the initiator of the study and then to use the address list provided as the sample frame, but obviously this requires the support of the potential respondent and takes time to implement.

Nevertheless, the Internet is used successfully for marketing research covering topical issues and sensitive matters, with results obtained quickly and at low cost. The Internet route to questioning targeted persons may provide adequate findings to answer the marketing problem on its own or it may be used for preliminary research as an aid to more extensive study using conventional research methods. Most certainly, the use of the Internet for international research is increasing as access to, and familiarity with, personal computers is extended.

BOX 4.1 MARKETING RESEARCH IN DANGEROUS ENVIRONS

Marketing research is conducted across the world, even in the world's trouble spots where special measures have to be taken to protect fieldworkers to ensure they interview a representative sample of the population.

In Argentina, where the economic crisis has led to a rise in crime, police or fire officers sometimes accompany field workers into the most dangerous neighbourhoods. As only about 60 per cent of households have a telephone, face-to-face interviews are necessary according to Anibal Cantarian, managing director of Taylor Nelson Sofres (hereafter TNS) Gallup Argentina. Some of his 300 field workers have been robbed. They are advised not to wear jewellery or expensive clothes and to carry a small amount of money that can be handed over if threatened with physical assault. They endeavour to interview only in daylight hours. With the increase in refusal rates in high socio-economic areas, householders are encouraged to telephone the TNS Gallup office to verify the identity of interviewers and to confirm that responses will be anonymous. Face-to-face interviewing remains the norm in Argentina.

Despite formidable obstacles, only in one case has TNS had to postpone a study; this was in December 2001, when President Fernando de la Rúa resigned and the country defaulted on US $95bn (£60bn) of commercial debt. Riots and police tear gas trapped field workers who were testing a healthcare concept in Buenos Aires. The research was completed several days later.

In place of traditional marketing research there has been a move towards new types of research in Argentina, e.g. testing attitudes to lower-cost packaging, rising prices, job cuts and tracking consumer trends such as the return to bartering. According to Cantarian (quoted in Maitland, 2003), 'There is more interest in political matters because companies are conscious they need this information to plan. The concept of corporate social responsibility is becoming more relevant. Also foreign interest in Argentina's [economic] crisis has increased, translating itself in research projects.'

In Israel, where 95 per cent of homes have telephones, there has been a rapid shift towards telephone interviewing according to Dori Shadmon, managing director of TNS/ Teleseeker in Tel Aviv. Hebrew, Arabic and Russian speakers staff the large TNS telephone centre. Only about 20 per cent of interviewing is conducted face to face. Normally some 20 per cent of people decline to answer questions but this can rise to at least 30 per cent on the day of an incident. A larger number of contacts have to be made to produce a given sample of respondents, which takes more time.

Interviewing by telephone, or via the Internet, can act as a buffer against religious or ethnic sensitivities. But it has its limitations, e.g. when interviewers have to show a lengthy questionnaire or a picture or packaging. Face-to-face interviewing is often conducted in shopping malls. However, as more women than men shop in malls, responses have to be weighted to represent the broader population.

Applying a consistent approach to research around the world is important but difficult, according to Richard Asquith, managing director of BMRB Media Services, which runs UK-based Target Group Index (TGI). In the UK it uses a random postal survey conducted throughout the year to monitor consumer consumption and lifestyle to track people's consumption of media, goods and services, as well as attitudes and lifestyle. It has extended operations across 41 countries, including France, Germany, Italy, Spain, Eastern Europe, as well as China, Israel, Japan, Latin America and the US. Important differences between cultures have been found, e.g. the concept of brands, taken for granted in the West, is not readily understood in China. Questions concerning alcohol have to be left out of surveys in Saudi Arabia, and in some countries low literacy levels in developing countries mean respondents need more 'hand-holding' by interviewers.

As is shown in Northern Ireland, in divided communities having the wrong accent can put interviewers at risk, according to Ian McShane, managing director of TNS/MRBI in Dublin. 'The way they pronounce certain words and even their names will identify them as a nationalist Catholic or a unionist Protestant. So an interviewer called Billy Jones knocking on the door of a republican family in Crossmaglen is unlikely to receive any information. If he does, it's likely to be biased, and he's probably putting himself in danger' (Maitland, 2003). TNS/MRBI usually designs its own marketing research studies, but then sub-contracts the interviewing to Northern Ireland-based agencies such as Mori MRC, which employs field workers from the community being surveyed. As people in Northern Ireland are nervous of doorstep interviewers, the more neutral public surroundings of a shopping centre or town hall are normally used. McShane considers 'the vast majority of face-to-face research in the republic [of Ireland] is in the home, but in the north it's on the street or in town halls' (Maitland, 2003). Nonetheless, increasingly in the more normal climate of Northern Ireland, accommodation between communities can be reached with a little sensitivity and tolerance.

(Adapted from Maitland, 2003)

Consumer panel

A consumer panel is a 'permanent representative sample maintained by a market research agency from which information is obtained on more than one occasion either for continuous research or for 'ad hoc' projects' (Market Research Society, 2003). The sample may be made up of individuals, households or firms. They are used to monitor market trends, e.g. food consumption, and to examine issues such as brand switching, repeat buying and media audiences. A range of tools is used to monitor consumer behaviour, including home audits (sometimes involving dustbin checks), diary recording, television set meters and on-line shopping records. Consumer panel members may be given small rewards to encourage their involvement, such as a token voucher for a national retailer or the chance to enter a prize draw. The scale of geographical coverage of the panel depends on access to potential participants, user demand and agency resources. While consumer panels use respondents located in regions within countries and persons using, or consuming, particular goods and services, most provide national coverage, e.g. the UK-based TNS Superpanel covering Fast Moving Consumer Goods (FMCG) purchasing. Similar panels are run in France, Italy, Spain and other countries. Generally, multi-country marketing researchers use national consumer panels which are assimilated to provide comparable international assessments of consumer behaviour. Consumer panels covering more than one country are exceptional due to the difficulties of their implementation.

Examples of consumer panels that have international coverage include:

- Panels targeted at specialist market segments, e.g. the UK-based Carrick James Market Research (CJMR) panels targeted at children, youths and parents in Western Europe, Eastern Europe and the Commonwealth of Independent States (CIS). Media Plus Research runs a dedicated company panel for the Financial Times European newspaper, made up of a representative sample of readers who are asked to complete three questionnaires a year, covering topics of interest to FT advertisers such as reader leisure activities and expenditure on cars.
- Television (TV) audience measurement panels, e.g. TNS has undertaken TV audience measurement in many countries across the world and can provide cross-European audience comparisons.

Access panels

These provide access to consumers willing to participate regularly in marketing research and cover Europe, the US and Canada. With the problem of falling response rates and database marketing, some marketing research agencies have developed their own sample frames, or databases, of consumers recruited as willing to participate in marketing research. In particular, NFO (now part of TNS) has access panels in Denmark, Finland, France, Germany, Italy, the Netherlands, Norway, Spain, Sweden and the UK covering more than 418,000 willing individuals. These can give access to individuals for marketing research using different collection methods, namely on-line (140,000), postal survey (331,000), telephone interview (150,000) and personal face-to-face (58,000). These access panels enable studies to be undertaken across Europe more readily and encourage users to implement cross-country marketing rather than individual country-by-country approaches. For example, by using the database of online individuals it would be feasible to track the effectiveness of a common cross-country promotional campaign across the ten European countries concerned. This is useful for FMCG MNCs such as Procter & Gamble or Gillette operating across Europe.

Omnibus survey

Omnibus surveys cover 'a number of topics, usually for different clients. The samples tend to be nationally representative and composed of types of people for which there is a general demand. Clients are charged by the market research agency on the basis of the questionnaire space or the number of questions required' (Market Research Society, 2003). They use regular ad hoc surveys involving different samples and different clients, whereas consumer panels aim to have the same clients and the same samples. Omnibus surveys use a fresh sample each time the population is surveyed, rather than a permanent sample. Usually the data is collected by personal face-to-face or telephone interview. An example of a typical use of omnibus surveys is where the FMCG producer of a new range of yoghurt wishes to assess the effectiveness of a television advertising campaign. The producer could place one or two questions, alongside other client questions, in the relevant omnibus survey and use the response to gauge advertising awareness before and after the campaign.

Omnibus surveys are run by most of the marketing research agencies that have specialist consumer behaviour panels.

While traditionally omnibus surveys have been based on national samples, some cover more than one country, e.g. the NOP European Telebus Telephone omnibus survey targets adults in France, Germany, Italy and the UK. However, omnibus surveys do not always operate in the same way for all countries and this can pose problems. Within the UK, they are usually conducted on a weekly, fortnightly or monthly time scale whereas elsewhere omnibus surveys may be less frequent. Overseas omnibus surveys may not have national geographical coverage in the countries in which they operate. Some omnibus surveys do not cover the full population age profile; for example, they may only including people up to the age of 65 or 69, and the sample of 'housewives' may only cover females, excluding the male 'housewives' covered in the UK surveys. Care has to be taken in the use and interpretation of data collected through these surveys.

Role of information technology (IT) in consumer panel development

Since the late 1980s Electronic Point of Sale (EPOS) and Electronic Funds Transfer at Point of Sale (EFTPOS) have been used to provide retailers with on-line virtual information regarding customer demand based on scanned purchases at retailer checkout tills. Customer demand data, traditionally used for operations management in stock control and logistics, have been extended into marketing applications. As retailers, especially food retailers, have become ever larger with increased market shares, so, too, have their customer databases more closely represented total demand. The data collected covers customer sales in terms of product, brand, outlet and region as well as customer names, payment method, frequency of visiting the outlet, etc. Customer addresses and postcodes can be matched to customer identifiers such as loyalty scheme membership. The data is then further analysed alongside other marketing databases such as geodemographic databases, e.g. ACORN (A Classification of Residential Neighbourhoods) and MOSAIC in the UK, for supporting marketing decision-making. In this way, the success of a retailer's promotional television campaign can be gauged by the product sales achieved at its outlets in the targeted region for the duration of the campaign. Comparison of these sales with competing brands across the region provides estimates of market share performance. Geodemographic analysis can identify the retailer's customer ACORN or MOSAIC groups and indicate marketing approaches to match their demand.

Traditionally, marketing research agencies developed consumer panels and retail auditing for national market databases within the consumer mass-market producers. As retailers have developed their own databases, marketing research agencies have been obliged to improve theirs. Indeed, some marketing research agencies have begun to buy into retailer databases, placing ever more power in the hands of the retailers concerned. It remains to be seen how the manufacturers will react to this development.

Product clinic

Product clinics are used to ascertain new products for consumer goods and certain industrial products such as new features in cars, leisure cruisers and cabs for commercial vehicles. For these types of products the time required to achieve repeat buying of the product may be too long to enable traditional test marketing. Consequently, potential customers are asked to meet at central locations, such as an exhibition hall in a large city, where the product (or at least the product prototype) is presented for their comment. Representatives of the persons, such as retailers and distributors, and others in the supply chain who are influential in the purchasing decision may also be invited to assess the proposed product. The participants are questioned concerning their opinion of the product proposals and may be asked to make comparisons between the new product and other competing products. Interviewees may spend two to three hours evaluating the product designs through a combination of completing lengthy self-completion questionnaires, participating in group discussion and individual unstructured interviews.

Hall testing

Hall tests involve recruiting individuals to attend a location, often a large room or hall, to respond to a set of stimuli such as samples of food or beverage. The individual participates in various product tests such as tasting trials and sips tests and is questioned on attributes of the product. Sometimes, where it is considered that the household rather than an individual makes the buying decision, home trials are undertaken. Then the product is delivered to the selected houses and the household members are asked to comment on its performance. A new range of detergent or a soya-based food product might be tested in this way rather than by using a hall test.

BOX 4.2 CAR INDUSTRY USE OF PRODUCT CLINICS

The car industry uses marketing research extensively to test prototypes. The automotive MNCs spend millions both on running internal marketing research departments and on buying in marketing research from marketing research agencies using extensive desk and field research. Desk research is used to monitor sales worldwide; field research helps to fill gaps in market data for marketing decisions. Each MNC makes extensive use of market intelligence, attending trade exhibitions, research seminars and the like to ascertain market trends. Field research can be conducted over a lengthy period. For example, a new car design may take upwards of five years to move from the concept stage to ultimate completion when it reaches the consumer. As part of this process, car product clinics are used with prototypes of new car designs being shown to potential consumers for their comment. Seidler (1976) and Smith and Molloy (1976) describe early use of these techniques relating to the development of Ford's Fiesta car.

In the case of a multinational study, product clinics are usually undertaken by marketing research agencies with control being given to the co-ordinating agency, which might, if appropriate, sub-contract to other supplier agencies to complete the research. The product clinic is usually located at central geographical locations such as: a capital city, Paris or London; a major industrial city, Sao Paolo in Brazil or Los Angeles in the US; or geograph-ically central, as for Lausanne in Switzerland. The participants are brought to the location, usually in homogeneous groups, i.e. in national groups, or influencer groups. For cars, the people questioned are likely to include actual and potential purchasers of different demo-graphic profiles – male and female, age groups, ethnic groups, etc. – as well as car dealers, industry experts and press critics.

A combination of both qualitative and quantitative research techniques is used to ascer-tain consumer reaction to proposed car designs. Initially, the participants might be asked to view alternative designs for the cars as depicted by polystyrene prototypes and pho-tographs of parts of the car, e.g. the front and back lighting configuration. As they proceed around the exhibition, the participants are asked to complete a questionnaire expressing their opinions on favoured designs. The questions elicit both qualitative and quantitative responses to the exhibits and are similar to those used for national marketing research. The questionnaire is translated into different languages to take account of the various national groups participating in the study. Some adaptation of the new product display and ques-tionnaire might be required to match the different country populations being targeted.

After the initial questionnaire completion, which might take up to two hours, some of the participants could be asked to join a group discussion of eight to ten persons. A moder-ator leads the discussion into areas of interest to the client such as the image portrayed by given car designs and associations of the car designs with given car producers. The data gathered from the series of product clinics across the targeted countries are assimilated by the co-ordinating agency. The results are presented to the client, who, in turn, incor-porates the findings with its other marketing research into the MIS for further management decision-making.

The geographical coverage of hall tests can be extended across national borders using the same research methods in each country although sometimes methods will need modification to take account of different conditions, e.g. climate.

Further discussion on marketing research methodology can be found in Craig and Douglas (2000) and Chisnall (2001) for international marketing research, Burns and Bush (2003) for online marketing research applications and McGivern (2003) for market and social research practice.

ROLE AND ORGANIZATION OF INTERNATIONAL MARKETING RESEARCH

Whether the services of a marketing research agency should be brought in, or whether staff from within the organization should conduct the marketing research, depends on the research to be undertaken. For B-to-B, or industrial marketing research, the firm's internal staff such as sales engineers and industrial marketing researchers may have the skills and expertise to undertake the marketing research. For example, firms such as Motorola or Hewlett Packard investigating the demand for a new product, perhaps mobile telephones or printers, may use their own sales engineers to report on trade opinion across the countries in which they operate. Sometimes, the same individual sales engineer moving from country to country undertakes the research; sometimes, different individuals using the same research techniques assess the situation, for example where a sales team investigates customer reaction to a new product. The scale of the research and the resource implications influence the choice of whether to use internal staff or an outside marketing research agency.

Within consumer marketing research the services of marketing research agencies are most frequently sought for international marketing research. Usually one marketing research agency is selected to take responsibility for the research programme and it sub-contracts (or buys in) research from local agencies in the countries concerned. The chosen marketing research agency should have expertise in co-ordinating other marketing research agencies in the targeted countries, or regions. These may be the co-ordinating agency's own sister agencies or separate local agencies that have associations with it.

Marketing research agencies use a combination of organization structures to implement international marketing research. The larger organizations have separate national operations managed through a central controlling head office base, usually in the home country. In this way, A.C. Nielsen, the largest international marketing research agency, has its main base in the US, while its European operations are managed through Oxford in the UK. The UK-based TNS, ranked fourth in the global market in 1998, has its headquarters in the UK. Through its growth by acquisition, taking over NFO in 2003, it has substantial operations across Europe, Asia and South America. These large marketing research agencies have networks of subsidiaries and strategic alliances operating across international markets to support their large customers. However, control of a marketing research programme depends on where research is commissioned, not necessarily where head office is located.

Whatever combination of marketing research agencies is used, the co-ordinator of the research should match the objectives set down within the marketing research brief with the expertise and resources available to decide the most appropriate way to obtain the data.

The co-ordinating agency needs to ensure the data are gathered by using common, or comparable, research procedures.

Pre-buying research/currency

The co-ordinating agency may face uncertainty over currency fluctuations, which, not surprisingly, are more prevalent for long-term contracts than for short-term ones. It has to minimize any adverse effects of currency fluctuations, usually by buying currency for the contract in advance of the work being completed. Local agencies bidding for the research contract are required to quote either in the local currency or in GB pounds sterling, euros and US dollars (or the currency used by the co-ordinating agency). If the quote is in the agency's local currency, the co-ordinating agency is likely to buy that currency in advance of completing the contract, thereby covering itself for adverse currency fluctuation. This situation is eased within the EU Eurozone where the euro currency is used across 12 member countries.

Price variations between countries

In 2003 the European Society for Opinion and Marketing Research (ESOMAR) study of 407 research companies from across the world found that there are wide variations in prices quoted for research projects in different countries (ESOMAR, 2003). Respondents were asked to give quotes for a national usage and attitude survey, a tracking study on washing powders, a computer assisted advertising pre-test, four group discussions, a customer satisfaction web survey and a B-to-B telephone survey. It was found that the price range between the highest and lowest quotations showed a typical survey costing more than a third extra in the US and Japan than in the UK, France and Germany (see Table 4.1) (Tarran, 2003).

Table 4.1 *Research price overall index, 2003*

Country	Average index
US	242
Japan	230
Sweden	180
UK	170
Australia	166
France	158
South Africa	157
Germany	152
Belgium	138
Netherlands	137

Source: ESOMAR (2003)

Choice of marketing research method

The choice of marketing research method depends on the country markets being studied. Over time the research methods used in different markets are becoming more similar and standardized, and more like those used in the UK. Leading marketing research agencies have expanded internationally through joint venture and acquisitions of local marketing research agencies. Similar research methods to those used in the established marketing research agencies have become common practices in these operations. Furthermore, research methods that have proven effective in one country have been taken to other countries. For example, where qualitative group discussions have been shown to provide insights into customer behaviour for a MNC car manufacturer investigating a promotional campaign in the UK, the MNC management is likely to investigate consumer demand in other countries using the same, or similar, research methods. Those countries with similar cultures will be receptive to using similar marketing research methods.

The research methods used may have to be adjusted to suit the conditions of a particular market, e.g. where telephone interviewing is appropriate for one country but inappropriate in another. In these situations adaptation of the research method would occur, perhaps, using personal face-to-face interviewing in place of telephone interviewing. The data collected for the research from the different countries should be produced in a format that is comparable so that the co-ordinating agency can re-format it, using software, into a compatible form for analysis.

However, in some cases, the physical constraints such as geography, transport availability and associated climatic conditions of the country may themselves determine the favoured marketing research methods to use. For example, in Scandinavia street interviews for marketing research are uncommon due to the high costs involved and the high percentage of working women, necessitating interviews being conducted in the evenings and at weekends. The cold winters also hinder such activities. Increasingly, market studies are conducted by telephone rather than through face-to-face interviewing. In this way, while all the marketing research methods used in the UK can be used in Scandinavia, the pattern of usage is not the same as in the UK. Marketing research methods evolve to suit the requirements for investigating the consumer representatives of each country.

STRUCTURE OF MARKETING RESEARCH AGENCIES INDUSTRY

In 1998, the total market research worldwide market was estimated at €12bn of which the EU accounted for 40 per cent and Europe as a whole for 44 per cent, while the US had a 37 per cent share (ESOMAR, 1998) (see Table 4.2). The fastest rate of growth was in the US (13 per cent) followed by the EU (12 per cent). The difficult economic situation faced by the Japanese led to a 9 per cent fall in marketing research in Japan in 1998, at a time when the EU market grew by 12 per cent, and the US by 13 per cent. By 2000, the marketing research market was estimated to be US $15.5bn and in 2001 it was about US $15.9bn.

In 2002, the world's 25 largest marketing research agencies had revenues of US $9.7bn, up 6.3 per cent on the previous year which, with worldwide inflation rate estimated at 2.2 per cent, was a real growth rate of 4.1 per cent (Honomichl, 2002). However, the top 25

Table 4.2 *World market research industry, 1998*

Turnover	US $m	€m	%	1998 increase over 1997 %
Europe	5,838	5,213	43.5	11.2
EU15	5,416	4,837	40.4	12.1
North America	5,180	4,625	38.6	n/a
US	4,935	4,406	36.8	12.0
Central/South America	735	656	5.5	n/a
Asia Pacific	1,582	1,413	11.8	n/a
Japan	884	798	6.7	−8.8
Other	75	69	0.6	n/a
World total	13,410	11,976	100.0	10.1

Source: ESOMAR (1998)

organizations are atypical of the research services industry. The large syndicated service firms, such as A.C. Nielsen, IMS, Information Resources Inc and Arbitron, have most of their business under contract and as such are not as susceptible to economic downturns. The revenues of the leading research firms are heavily weighted by syndicated/contract revenues, making it likely that the group performed better in 2001 than the rest of the market. Industry leaders are increasingly global with 63 per cent (US $6.2bn) of the top 25's total revenue of US $9.7bn coming from operations outside their home countries. Collectively they employ about 89,000 full-time employees across the world.

In 2002, the leading marketing research company, VNU NV, the Netherlands-based marketing information industry conglomerate which acquired the US A.C. Nielsen in 2001, had a global research revenue of US $2,400m accounting for a 25 per cent market share (see Table 4.3).

The larger marketing research agencies concentrate on providing services for the mass consumer markets. For example, within VNU NV, the A.C. Nielsen group concentrates on the consumer product and services industries. It provides marketing research services in over 80 countries with strengths in:

- retail measurement, tracking product movement through food, pharmaceutical and other retail stores in more than 80 countries;
- consumer panel research, tracking the buying behaviour of more than 155,000 demographically balanced households in 21 countries indicating who is buying, what they are buying and where they shop;
- customized research services, providing information services about consumer attitudes and behaviour in more than 60 countries.

Within Europe, the UK, Germany and France marketing research industries dominate, accounting for 67 per cent of gross turnover of €5bn in 1998 (see Table 4.4). Of this,

103

Table 4.3 *World top marketing research companies, 2002*

	Marketing research agency	Revenues (in US $m)
1	VNU NV (including A.C. Nielsen)	2,400
2	IMS Health Inc.	1,171
3	WPP plc (Kantar Group including Millward Brown Group and BMRB)	1,007
4	Taylor Nelson Sofres plc (TNS)	813
5	Information Resources Inc (IRI)	556
6	GfK Group	480
7	NFO WorldGroup Inc.	453
8	Ipsos Group SA	423
9	NOP World	325
10	Westat Inc.	286
Total top 10 global research companies		7,914
Total top 25 global research companies		9,744

Source: adapted from Honomichl (2002)

72 per cent was classified as consumer research (the remainder being industrial and commercial research), and within the consumer research, 53 per cent was on ad hoc surveys while 47 per cent was from continuous research (see Table 4.5).

UK marketing research industry

In 2002, in the UK the major marketing research agencies, comprising around 36 members of the British Market Research Association (BMRA), had a turnover of £1,176m (see Table 4.6). The UK domestic market accounted for 75 per cent (£884m) and the overseas market for the remaining 25 per cent (£292m). However, there are more than 800 marketing research agencies that are not members of BMRA and some firms use their own internal staff rather than marketing research agencies, so the total UK marketing research industry turnover is somewhat higher than the BMRA estimates. UK marketing research agencies have about 10 per cent of the worldwide market and 25 per cent of the EU market.

Consolidation in the marketing research industry is continuing with the industry market leaders becoming ever more dominant (see Table 4.6). In particular, the largest UK-based marketing research group, TNS plc, the world's fourth largest market information company, dominates in the UK with a strong presence in European consumer research, both qualitative and quantitative, especially research associated with consumer panels. TNS has grown from Taylor Nelson's acquisition of the UK company Audits of Great Britain (AGB), in 1992, the French Sofrès agency in 1998 and, in July 2003, the NFO WorldGroup. Further consolidation in the UK is likely, especially with MORI coming onto the market and seeking a buyer.

104

Table 4.4 *Market research turnover in Europe, 1998*

Country (in order of turnover)	Turnover (1998) €m	1998 increase over 1997 %
UK	1,362	8
Germany	1,184	14
France	809	7
Italy	370	8
Spain	245	2
Netherlands	231	8
Sweden	208	10
Switzerland	105	13
Belgium	102	8
Austria	81	2
Denmark	77	15
Norway	60	10
Turkey	60	14
Finland	56	16
Poland	49	10
Total	4,999	n/a

Source: ESOMAR (1998)

Table 4.5 *Expenditure on consumer research in Europe by research method, 1998*

Type of research	Average expenditure across all countries %
Ad hoc quantitative research	43
Ad hoc qualitative research	10
Total ad hoc research	**53**
Omnibus surveys	5
Panels	28
Other continuous research	14
Total continuous research	**47**

Source: ESOMAR (1998)

Market Research Society (MRS) – http://www.mrs.org.uk

In the UK, the Market Research Society (MRS) is the professional body for marketing researchers which, in 2003, has more than 8,000 members working in more than 50 countries in marketing research agencies, industry and commerce. MRS is the world's largest international membership organization for professional researchers. It liaises with members, users of marketing research, the public and government to develop the marketing research industry. It has lists of marketing research agencies and marketing researchers

Table 4.6 *Estimate of UK marketing research agency turnover, 2002*

UK rank	British Market Research Association (BMRA) members*	Turnover £m	Growth 2002 over 2001 %
1	TNS plc	113.2	−5.4
2	NOP Research Group	77.2	3.4
3	NFO WorldGroup	47.0	4.2
4	Ipsos (UK)	44.1	0.3
5	MORI	35.8	5.8
6	Information Resources	34.7	2.2
7	Maritz/TRBI	25.1	3.2
8	Martin Hamilton GFK	19.3	11.7
9	ISIS Research	17.3	27.8
10	Synovate	15.6	27.4
Estimated industry size		1,176.0	2.6
UK domestic sector		884.0 (75.2%)	2.3
UK international sector		292.0 (24.8%)	3.5

Source: adapted from BMRA (2003) quoted in Mackenzie (2003)
* excludes A.C. Nielsen and research companies within the WPP Group

together with profiles of their expertise to help in agency and/or market researcher selection. The MRS operates a Code of Conduct, which all its members agree to follow, that regulates the industry concerning the confidentiality of market research findings, the ways in which marketing research interviews are obtained and conducted and the use of the data found (Market Research Society, 1998). The MRS has guidelines for handling databases which supplement the Data Protection Act (1998) regulation to protect the confidentiality of individual personal information (Market Research Society, 2002).

British Market Research Association (BMRA) – http://www.bmra.org.uk

The British Market Research Association (BMRA), formed in 1998, represents the UK marketing research industry. Unfortunately, although it has 36 or so members, it does not include some major players such as A.C. Nielsen and consequently is not as strong a voice for the industry as might be desirable.

European Society for Opinion and Marketing Research (ESOMAR) – http://www.esomar.org

ESOMAR, the traditional representative of the European marketing research industry, is facing competition from the European Federation of Associations of Market Research Organisations (EFAMRO) which represents major national marketing research supplier associations in France, Germany, the Netherlands, Spain, Italy and the UK. It promotes the role and value of research to European governments and the European Commission. Both ESOMAR and EFAMRO monitor the rules, regulations and directives that control European marketing research. For example, ESOMAR has introduced a guideline for Internet research to show legislators ways in which the marketing research industry can regulate itself on the Web.

GOVERNMENT HELP FOR INTERNATIONAL MARKETING RESEARCH

Trade Partners UK – http://www.tradepartners.gov.uk

Typical of government agencies that encourage exports is the Trade Partners UK Information Centre. It provides a library providing trade statistics, Country Help Desks, market prospect reporting and export intelligence services. It gives exporters financial support in various ways including export insurance through the Export Credits Guarantee Department (ECGD) (see p. 110 and Chapter 6: International pricing) and international promotional activities such as trade missions, overseas trade fairs and store promotions. It also contributes towards international marketing research. In 1992 (latest available data) overseas trade fairs took the largest share of the net expenditure on these services (£14m) with 7,000 participants attending 335 exhibitions. Outward trade missions took £0.8m to support 2,000 participants in 120 missions, while £1.5m was spent on the Export Marketing Research Scheme (EMRS) which was used by 205 firms to support their international marketing research (see details on pp. 109–10).

Library: Trade Partners UK Information Centre (formerly Export Market Information Centre)

The Trade Partners UK Information Centre brings together the government library service and the microfilm database of product information. It has a self-help reference library and research facility including foreign statistics, country profiles, directories, marketing research reports, mail order catalogues, development plans, overseas investment information, visitor guides and street plans, export opportunities and sales leads. Access to, and personal use of, the Information Centre is free of charge. However, charges are made for staff research services.

Foreign statistics

The library has an extensive collection of national government statistics equivalent to the UK government publications, especially covering publications giving economic indicators and trade (import and export) statistics. These publications are necessarily published in the national language with statistics given in national currencies. Sometimes, for convenience, a commonly used language or currency is also provided, e.g. English or French language and the US dollar currency. Care is required in the interpretation of the data provided for market assessments, especially if they are used for inter-country comparisons. In particular, discrepancies can occur when comparing product classifications and value of goods in terms of currencies.

107

Consequently, for the purposes of inter-country comparison economic indicator statistics provided by the UN or the Organisation for Economic Co-operation and Development (OECD) can be used. These are derived from individual country statistics that provide greater detail than general inter-country comparison publications, so it may be preferable to use individual country statistics. Many of these data are available on-line.

Development plans

The library holds copies of country development plans that are useful for providing an indication of the current state of the economy and the future strategic projections for the country in question. These are three to five year plans prepared by governments, often to gain financial support from bodies such as the International Monetary Fund (IMF). Usually, they provide statistics showing the country's economic development over the previous five years or so and predictions for the ensuing five years. While, in practice, the plans may not be fully implemented within the specified time scale, they show economic growth expectations as well capital investment infrastructure proposals. Development plans detail the types of investment a country's government wishes to promote and provide evidence of the products (and services) likely to be demanded from international business.

Technical Help to Exporters section

The Technical Help to Exporters section provides information regarding the technical standards required for products being exported to a country. It provides advice on foreign requirements including:

- national laws, particularly in relation to safety and environmental protection;
- technical standards and the certification process in relation to customer needs.

Country Help Desks

The officers at the specialist Country Help Desks, which target the smaller firm with limited resources wishing to export manufactured goods, should be among the first government help services to be contacted when initiating export activity. There are 55 Country Desks covering nearly 200 markets based with staff working closely with export promoters and the Foreign and Commonwealth Office diplomatic staff (particularly embassy and consular commercial attachés). Much of the information provided is free of charge. The Country Desk staff provides country-specific export advice related to:

- political and economic conditions;
- local business conditions, such as legislation and methods of doing business;
- market prospects and product suitability;
- local tariffs and import regulations;
- business contacts.

Market Information Enquiry Service

The Trade Partners UK Information Centre also has a range of sources and services to help exporters to determine market opportunities. In particular, staff in the relevant diplomatic office, such as the commercial attachés within embassies and consulates can undertake marketing research on behalf of individual firms for a competitive fee. Such information might include:

- assessment of market prospects (sometimes termed 'overseas status reports') for a particular product or service;
- checking lists of potential sales contacts;
- reporting on potential sales agents or distributors through the export representative service;
- making recommendations for future marketing activity;
- providing information on tariffs and legislation.

Overseas Investment Enquiry Service

Advice regarding overseas investment is also given, again for the appropriate payment.

Export intelligence service

In conjunction with the Foreign and Commonwealth Office diplomatic staff, Trade Partners UK Information Centre operates a computerized information service to match incoming market intelligence against subscriber interests. It covers leads such as enquiries from overseas buyers, overseas agents seeking to represent British companies, invitations to tender from public sector bodies, information on forthcoming projects, aid and loan arrangements.

Implementation of international trade promotion

Other international trade support includes:

Export Promoter Initiative Through this service senior business executives from British firms provide specialist market knowledge and experience in key export markets and advice on methods of implementing exporting.

National Business Language Information Service A database of language training providers, translators and interpreters is available from the Centre for Information on Language Teaching and Research to promote exporting.

Language in Export Advisory Scheme Grants are available to encourage language skills to help exporting for:

- a UK company of two years' standing with up to 250 employees;
- a company already exporting, or considering exporting, into non-English speaking markets;
- a first-time user of the scheme.

Trade missions Trade Partners UK Information Centre organizes and supports attending overseas and inward trade missions, trade fairs and store promotions through subsidies for travel fares, exhibition stands and interpreter expenses.

Export Marketing Research Scheme

The Export Marketing Research Scheme (EMRS) is managed through the British Chambers of Commerce (see http://www.britishchambers.org.uk/exportzone). It provides financial help for international marketing research to UK-based firms with fewer than 500 employees producing goods or services with export potential. Trade associations are eligible to apply on behalf of their members where their membership comprises at least ten companies with less than 500 employees. The scheme allows up to ten successful applications, or a maximum grant per company of £60,000, whichever is reached first. However, only three of these may be for markets within the EU or English-speaking North America. Where financial help is provided, part of the marketing research costs may be paid as follows:

- If independent consultants are commissioned to undertake marketing research, the EMRS can support up to half the cost subject to a maximum contribution of £20,000 per project.
- If a firm's internal staff with the appropriate professional ability and experience is used for overseas marketing, research support is available for up to half of the eligible costs (including travel costs) and interpreter fees. There is a daily allowance for one researcher for time necessarily spent overseas conducting field research. This facility does not extend to research relating to the EU.
- Support is available for purchasing published marketing research, such as that undertaken by marketing research agencies and management consultancies, but does not include directories, marketing research overviews or updating subscriptions.

Export Credits Guarantee Department

The Export Credits Guarantee Department (ECGD) provides businesses with export credit help and the related documentation in accordance with inter-government agreements on international trade. Goods exported must have British content to qualify for the credit (see Chapter 6: International pricing, p. 149 for further related discussion).

Training Enterprise Companies

Exporters may also obtain help from the appropriate local Training Enterprise Company network, which gives advice to promote business within the regions and to encourage inward investment.

Chambers of Commerce – http://www.britishchambers.org.uk/exportzone

There is a network of Chambers of Commerce throughout the UK supported by industry and commerce offering support services to encourage international marketing. The services offered vary but often include support for trade seminars and trade missions as well as promoting links with Chambers of Commerce in other countries.

Trade associations

As with Chambers of Commerce, some trade associations provide services to support international marketing activity among their members. Apart from providing domestic and, sometimes, international trade statistics, they may organize trade missions, targeting attractive markets, e.g. the British Wool Marketing Board could decide to lead a trade mission to the US. Usually such trade missions will give members access to potential buyers within the targeted market and provide opportunities to research a potential market at a competitive cost. Such trade missions can benefit from financial support from the government-backed Trade Partners UK Information Centre (see p. 110).

IMPLEMENTATION OF INTERNATIONAL MARKETING RESEARCH

Defining the client

It is important to be clear as to who the client is and who may be influencing the judgement of the client. Within a small firm, the managing director may sign the marketing research contract. However, someone else may be the prime user of the research, perhaps the sales director or the new product development manager. The small firm may be eligible for financial support for the marketing research from the government (see EMRS on p. 110) in which case the appropriate government advisers will examine the research undertaken. The marketing research will have to satisfy all these people if repeat contracts are to be obtained.

In the case of the MNC, the contract may be negotiated through the organization's headquarters located in its home market while the marketing research will be undertaken in another country. Negotiations may also be with the subsidiary, SBU, or a division of the MNC located geographically close to the marketing research agency co-ordinating the study (within the same country). Each situation poses different challenges for the co-ordinating marketing research agency which needs to be clear as to the person, or persons, to whom its executive is answerable and to whom the research will be targeted.

Setting objectives

A brief for the marketing research project is prepared by the client and sent out to selected marketing research agencies. Often this brief is generalized, being little more than a page in length, outlining the research topic. It does not usually state the research methods to be used. Interested marketing research agencies respond with a research proposal which is prepared by the marketing research co-ordinator. The proposal details the research objectives, e.g. to support new product development, to increase awareness of social health issues, to investigate the influence of price on image, to examine the changing use of the Internet for purchasing, etc. The proposal specifies the research methods to be used such as the sampling methods, field-force availability, length of interview and questionnaire construction if required (see pp. 90–100), as well as the lines of communication, authority and reporting methods, timetables, logistical support and quality controls. For international marketing special attention has to be paid to the culture, language and population profile of the target market. Other issues to be considered include any physical constraints (see pp. 94–100), the laws governing data protection and advertising, telephone penetration levels, retail trade structure, competitor activity and brand history, which may be influential. The proposal also specifies the format in which the findings will be presented at the end of the project.

Most critically, the proposal quotes a price of the proposed research based on projected costs including the possible use of incentives. It is important to indicate what is, and is not, included in the costs associated with the contract (Coutts, 1988). It can be that there are hidden expenses not considered in the initial proposal quote as was shown in an instance where a hall test was contracted to a local marketing research agency in Jamaica. The final bill included an additional charge for the hire of chairs and tables, which was unexpected and surprisingly expensive.

The proposal is taken as the base for the research contract, which is signed between the client and the marketing research agency.

Communications

Once the contract is agreed, it is necessary for the co-ordinating marketing research agency executive leading the investigation to brief the local market research agency to ensure that all concerned appreciate what is required of them. If an overseas marketing research agency is involved, ideally, and assuming the client will pay the expense, the executive should visit the local marketing research agency to meet the marketing researchers. The executive should brief the local agency regarding the marketing research to be undertaken and should observe at least the start of the research to ensure that the designated research procedures are followed. Usually national researchers with 'mother-tongue' language skills and dedi-cated to each country's interviewing programme are used. The executive from the co-ordinating agency may require an interpreter for language communication; a translator can be used for any questionnaire preparation. If the proposal is being sent to a local agency, without a personal face-to-face meeting, it will need to contain the additional detail which might otherwise have been explained personally.

The lines of communication between the providers of the marketing research can become complex, as is shown in the example in Figure 4.2. In the case where an FMCG MNC wants marketing research to assess reactions to an advertising campaign being run in Belgium, France, Italy and the UK, various communication routes might be used. Typically, the co-ordinating marketing research agency, say TNS, based in the UK, would manage the communication between the client, based in Belgium, its subsidiary associates operating in France and Italy and those of independent local suppliers. The UK-based group could obtain its marketing research data through its own subsidiaries and from independent local suppliers. The local suppliers would be marketing research agencies working in conjunc-tion with the co-ordinating agency. As can be seen from Figure 4.2, there are numerous lines of communication between the marketing research providers and the co-ordinating marketing research agency which demand considerable management skills. Nevertheless, such marketing research can be, and is, successfully conducted across national borders.

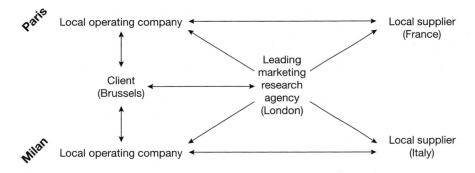

Figure 4.2 *Communication with clients*

Resource constraints

Once the research objectives have been agreed, the resources allocated for the study should be determined.

Finance

Details of the financial resources should indicate how much is to be spent on the marketing research, who will pay it and the currency in which it will be paid. In particular, it should be determined whether the client will pay through a central organizing administrative office or through the relevant SBU for each country. The client's management may raise sensitive internal political issues related to control which have to be clarified so that all concerned are aware of the responsibilities associated with successfully completing the research.

The absolute expenditure on international marketing research will differ from organization to organization. It is likely to be higher for research covering more than one country than for research covering only one country. Costs can vary immensely. Some countries have higher research costs than others (ESOMAR, 2003 and Table 4.1). Additional expenses such as incentives (not normally given in the UK) may have to be included.

Timing

Ideally, marketing research should form an integral part of the management decision-making process and should be incorporated into the planning process. However, all too often, it is relegated to a secondary 'after thought' position. Frequently, management can fail to allocate adequate resources, especially time, for the marketing research to be conducted effectively, posing many problems including ethical considerations as to whether the proposed marketing research should be undertaken at all. There can be a supposition that reliable results can be conjured up from minimal research. In such circumstances, marketing research management needs to produce the best market data within the time constraints imposed, which may not be ideal for effective marketing research. Clearly, there are few circumstances when marketing researchers can be given total time flexibility to complete their studies. Nevertheless, they must have sufficient time to ensure that reliable data are

113

collected for decision-making. Contracts should be refused if it is not feasible to complete the research to an acceptable standard.

In general, it is advisable to allow more time for the completion of a multi-country marketing research project than for a similar project in the UK to account for the extra stages involved in translation and checking. Allowances must be made for conditions specific to the particular market being investigated, especially for local holidays, climate and work practices.

Personnel

Decisions are needed regarding who should undertake the marketing research. The number of researchers to use will relate to the scale of the study, i.e. the number of countries to be covered and the geographical spread of the population. The skills of the researchers required will depend on the culture and language of the markets being investigated and the research method to be used. For example, telephone interviewing will require persons able to communicate with the targeted respondent, with native language speakers being preferable (see pp. 86, 96, 99 and 102).

Other choices to consider are whether to use internal staff, or to sub-contract the research to external agencies. The use of internal staff to undertake marketing research can be advantageous for B-to-B research where the product being researched has high technical attributes and requires engineering expertise to appreciate its operational complexities. Sometimes, sales engineers in organizations producing such goods undertake the marketing research. However, such a choice may lead to bias in the interpretation of the research findings. Furthermore, the time pressures on internal staff and the conflict of interest, with the research being subsumed within other job responsibilities, may lead to the marketing research being less than effectively performed. Nevertheless, in appropriate circumstances and with suitable management control, internal staff can be used to undertake international market-

BOX 4.3 DIFFERENT LOCAL HOLIDAYS IN DIFFERENT COUNTRIES

The marketing research co-ordinator has to take account of holidays that influence working time in different countries. For example, the Chinese New Year in China, Hong Kong and other Far Eastern countries and Thanksgiving in the US introduce different holidays to those commonly considered in the UK. Similarly, it is difficult to conduct field research during the August summer holiday in continental Europe, especially in France, Italy and Spain.

Time zone differences also pose problems for the marketing research co-ordinator. Telephone calls from the UK to some parts of Asia need to be made before 10 a.m. (UK time) to contact the local agency researchers. Climate and the associated seasons can be challenging for field research, e.g. in Hong Kong during a period of typhoon warnings, it will be difficult to undertake street interviews.

ing research, assuming the individuals concerned have the required expertise and time to complete the task. The alternative, as with domestic marketing research, is to sub-contract the research to external agencies, which may be marketing research agencies or management consultants (for discussion on selection of marketing research agencies see pp. 100–7).

Research methodology

Decisions have to be made regarding the implementation of the selected research approach. Typically, some desk research will be conducted, assessing market data that have been obtained from earlier research, or for another research programme. If the research has been defined as being 'to search for a new country market into which to expand', at the early stages the desk research may cover a large number of potential markets which can be reduced as the study progresses. It could be that, in the first instance, up to ten potential countries are examined. Through filtering desk research data, these can be reduced to the favoured one or two countries.

In the early stages of the desk research, published statistics produced by world bodies such as the UN and the OECD can provide country economic indicators for comparing the potential of countries. Such indicators include country Gross National Product (GNP), inflation rates, population size and growth rates, employment levels and house building rates and show the countries with the more favoured economies for the product (or service). See also the Purchasing Power Parity comparison on pp. 7–9.

At the same time, it is useful to examine the statistics relevant to foreign trade. In particular, measures should be made of:

■   import statistics of the target country;
■   exports from the home country;
■   any re-export activity;
■   targeted country's product demand.

Import statistics of the target country

The pattern of imports to the targeted country gives an indication of the type and volume (or value) of products that are readily imported and are within the favoured category of goods to import. Individual country trade statistics provide details but they can be difficult to interpret and to compare with other countries, due to differences in the collection and measurement of such statistics. The value of imports will usually be quoted in national currency. Volume statistics are not always available or relevant.

Exports from home country

Another useful measure is the home country's own record of trade statistics (provided by the Customs and Excise department in the UK). These trade statistics show the value (and sometimes volume) of exports sent from the UK to the countries of destination. They are given in UK currency, i.e. GB pounds (or equivalent units of volume) and can be used for

115

comparison of export values for different product groups being sent from the UK to the destination countries. However, if the product considered is new to this export activity, or has not previously been exported to the targeted countries, then the trade statistics will not be available. A further complication is that trade values for exports from one country are quoted at Free-on-Board (FOB) prices, whereas imports are quoted at Cost, insurance and freight (CIF) prices (see Table 6.1 on p. 146 for explanation of the terms used). This makes a small difference in the values of trade comparison calculations.

Re-export activity

Sometimes the goods that are imported to a country are not actually consumed within that country, e.g. oil production equipment imported to France may be re-exported for use in the Gulf of Mexico, the North Sea or elsewhere. Yet the statistics indicate that these products are imported to France. This can cause misinterpretation of the trade statistics.

Targeted country's product demand

At this early stage, it is important to assess the likely demand for the imports within the targeted country. Where the product is produced in the country concerned, e.g. wine in France, the country's own production statistics can be used and supplemented by allowance for any import, or export, activity on consumption estimates. However, where there is little or no domestic production, e.g. wine in the UK, domestic consumption can be estimated by using import statistics. Other sources of data could include government statistical surveys, marketing research agency consumer panels and retail audits which provide details of market segment consumption and the buying seasons for the product. It is advisable to assess competitor activity to determine the structure of the market, the viability of a newcomer entering the market and to indicate areas where problems may be encountered. Determining competitor market shares in volume (or value) terms is useful.

Information on import restrictions

If it is proposed that the product is to be exported from one country A to another country B, the regulations governing such exports (or imports to the country B) should be examined. Details of quantitative import restrictions can be obtained from the relevant government body. These import restrictions include:

- import licences and quotas;
- tariffs, import levies and excise duties;
- foreign exchange controls including deposit schemes;
- anti-dumping minimum price control;
- official, or unofficial, boycotts;
- legislation governing packaging;
- trade marks.

In the UK, the Trade Partners UK Information Centre, through its Country Help Desk service, provides details of import restrictions that UK exporters might face (see p. 108). General information regarding language and documentation requirements for exports is also available.

Favoured import areas

In some instances, imports are encouraged by favourable fiscal treatment, as where they are imported to free ports and free trade zones. Usually no import duties or equivalents are imposed while the goods remain within these areas where local manufacture is promoted. Within the drinks and tobacco industries, the location and management of bonded warehouses can be important in the selection of trade markets. These may be located within the free trade zone areas. Once again, the relevant Country Help Desk officer can provide this information.

Summary of desk research contribution to field research

After the preliminary desk research data have been obtained and assessments made that show the countries with potential for export trade opportunities, the marketer has to consider the marketing approach to use in the new market. Some details of product specifications, pricing (and profits), promotional methods and channels of distribution: logistics support; transport, storage and warehousing may be provided through the Country Help Desk officers.

Then, by gathering all the market data through the desk research, gaps in the information may indicate any field (or primary) research that is necessary. Once again, some of the Trade Partners UK Information Centre services discussed above can be used but, ultimately, field research directed at the potential consumer within the targeted country might be required. Decisions have to be made concerning who should undertake the research, the resource implications and the research methodology to use.

CONCLUSION

International marketing research involves using an effective MIS to assess demand in targeted country markets. The MIS uses a range of sources of information which fit into the categories of internal reporting, market intelligence and marketing research. The process of collecting, analysing and using data is usually continuous with inter-linkage between the source data, e.g. the use of sales reports (internal reporting) may include information gained from sales force attendance at trade seminars (marketing intelligence) with both types of information contributing to marketing research studies. All three types of data can be assimilated for analysis to develop appropriate marketing databases to support management decision-making.

Marketing research may use either qualitative or quantitative research methods, or a combination of both. Qualitative research methods include in-depth focus interviews and focus group discussions. Quantitative research methods cover the various types of surveys, including using personal face-to-face and telephone interviewing as well as the post. Throughout the marketing research process, the resource constraints of finance, staff expertise and availability, as well as time, have to be considered. These constraints encourage users to contract out their needs to marketing research agencies rather than to undertake these services internally themselves. Increasingly, the marketing research role within the organization is one of monitoring the research process, rather than that of actually undertaking the research.

Internal and external sources are used for desk research. Internal sources range from statistics on export sales to sales force reports. External sources are extensive, frequently covering those that are available from government export promoting bodies such as the Trade Partners UK Information Centre. After the secondary sources have been examined, gaps in market data are likely to be obtained through marketing research (or field research) generating primary data. Sometimes, as in the case of small businesses starting to export, financial help is available from government bodies for marketing research. Firms that have established international marketing operations use international marketing research to reduce the risks associated with international marketing by improving decision-making related to the marketing mix.

Decisions need to be made concerning the marketing research to be undertaken. These relate to:

- Who should undertake the research: internal staff or external marketing research agency staff?
- What research methodology should be used?
- What resource allocation is required, in terms of finance, staff and time?

These issues have been discussed in the chapter, together with suggestions on how they can be solved.

REVIEW QUESTIONS

4.1 Giving examples, discuss the contribution that can be made by internal reporting, marketing intelligence and marketing research in developing an international Marketing Information System (MIS).

4.2 Explain the ways in which qualitative and quantitative marketing research can be assimilated within an international marketing research programme aimed at assessing demand across national borders.

4.3 What challenges have to be addressed when undertaking personal interview surveys in more than one country?

4.4 How useful are consumer panels in determining consumer demand across national borders?

4.5 Examine the role that government bodies can make towards supporting international marketing research.

REFERENCES

Burns, A.C. and Bush, R.F. (2003) *Marketing research: online research applications,* 4th edn, Upper Saddle River, NJ: Prentice Hall.

Chisnall, P.M. (2001) *Marketing research,* 6th edn, London: McGraw-Hill.

Coutts, C. (1988) *International research: making it work,* London: Research Business International.

Craig, C.S. and Douglas, S.P. (2000) *International marketing research,* 2nd edn, Chichester: John Wiley.

ESOMAR (1998) 'Survey of world market research', *Research World,* April and www.inra.com/info/researchworld.htm.

ESOMAR (2003) 'Research prices study', *Research World,* Amsterdam: Netherlands.

Honomichl, J. (2002) 'Honomichl global top 25: 2002 report on the global research industry', *Marketing News,* American Marketing Association, Vol. 36, No. 17, 19 August, pp. H3-H27.

Kotler, P., Armstrong, G., Saunders, J. and Wong, V. (1999) *Principles of Marketing,* 2nd European edn, Upper Saddle River, NJ: Prentice Hall.

McGivern, Y. (2003) *The practice of market and social research,* Harlow: Financial Times/ Prentice Hall.

Mackenzie, Y. (2003) 'Reassessing the figures', *Research,* Market Research Society, June, Issue 445, p. 11.

Maitland, A. (2003) 'Market research: when the word on the street is danger', *Financial Times,* 5 March, p. 16.

Market Research Society (1998) 'Code of conduct', pamphlet issued by Market Research Society, April.

Market Research Society (2002) 'A basic guide to the Data Protection Act 1998', pamphlet issued by Market Research Society, February.

Market Research Society (2003) *The research buyer's guide UK & Ireland 2003,* London: MRS, pp. 42–43.

Seidler, E. (1976) *Let's call it Fiesta: the auto-biography of Ford's project Bobcat,* Cambridge: Patrick Stephens.

Smith, R.P. and Molloy, C.A. (1976) 'Fiesta: the marketing research contribution to the development of Ford's small car for Europe', *ESOMAR Conference,* pp. 195–210.

Tarran, B. (2003) 'Price variations still exist in mature markets, says study', *Research,* Issue 446, July, p. 9.

RECOMMENDED WEBSITES

http://www.bmra.org.uk

http://www.britishchambers.org.uk/exportzone

http://www.dti.gov.uk/for_business.html

http://www.esomar.org

http://www.inra.com/info/researchworld.htm

http://www.mrs.org.uk

http://www.tradepartners.gov.uk

Chapter 5

International product development

INTRODUCTION

In this chapter the traditional term 'product' is used for the product, or service, which an organization is offering. Products and services have long been treated separately, but increasingly it is being recognized that all products have an element of service, as for example, where capital equipment is sold with a long-term credit package, commissioning by a service engineer and the provision of training for operatives. More and more, the change over time has led to specialized products becoming general ones. For example, computers which are sold in all kinds of outlets rather than specialized ones have become generic commodities that can only be distinguished from similar products by the services which are provided with them. Conversely, services may be provided but be reliant on products for their execution as in the provision of insurance-cover. This involves the production of a policy and can involve the use of the telephone, the fax machine and the Internet. In this way air transport service involves more than the provision of transport, it also includes the issue of tickets, baggage facilities and conveyance, the seat on the aircraft and, sometimes, the serving of food. One or other element, product or service, is likely to dominate to varying degrees depending on the nature of the offering.

Irrespective of the dominant element, there persists a belief that there is a classic dilemma for the international marketer in deciding whether to standardize the product/service to reduce costs or to adapt the marketing mix to meet the specific needs of smaller segments of the market. The area of the product is suitable for an examination of this problem since it is surrounded by factors like economies of scale, international standards and consumer mobility across countries which reduce costs and create savings in production, research and development (R&D) and marketing. Conversely, other issues such as government regulations with regard to standards, packaging and labelling, the widening gap between rich and poor countries, different conditions of product use, the plunging cost of computer memory and the growing fragmentation of markets and concentration of buying power push companies towards product adaptation. This gives a significant boost to sales with the closer match between product and market demand as well as increased sensitivity to markets in general. The international marketer has to resolve this dilemma in a global setting.

The core product, or benefit, has important attributes which aim to differentiate it from other generic products on the market. The most important of these is the brand, which is arguably the most significant of the attributes for a number of important classes of product. Consumers do not just buy the brand name; they buy branded products which are an amalgamation of the tangible and intangible benefits created by the efforts of the company. In people's minds, the brand is synonymous with consumer expectations. It is the ambition of every chief executive concerned with brands to make heterogeneous brands into global ones if at all possible so that cost economies can be achieved. Advances in technology are making it possible to create new cost economies through economies of scope.

LEARNING OBJECTIVES

The objectives of this chapter are to:

- show the importance of the product as the key element of the marketing mix;
- demonstrate various alternatives within the standardization/adaptation continuum;
- underscore the significance of the brand;
- identify attributes complementary to the product or brand;
- illustrate the contribution of technology to the resolution of product problems.

When you have completed the chapter you should be able to:

- recognize the factors which determine the degree of standardization of a product;
- establish the determinants of brand internationalization;
- show awareness of the means by which mass customization can be achieved;
- distinguish the importance of intellectual property as an attribute of a product or brand;
- take account of different kinds of market segmentation in matching products to international markets.

The product-service mix

As noted above, products and services are a mixture of the two elements depending on the kind of offering. A useful perspective on these is in the continuum of Shostack (1982), which is seen in Figure 5.1. It shows that tangibility (ability to touch, see, smell and hear prior to purchase) decreases, moving from left to right. Every organization on the continuum delivers some degree of service as part of its total offering. However, it is the organizations to the right which deliver most in the way of services. Each may add value by the further service it offers and so try to distinguish itself from the offerings of others. A classic example of a service-dominant organization distinguishing its offering by additional service is the pensions provided by phone by Scottish Widows. Its promotional message features an attractive widow in her weeds to indicate that even younger people anywhere can be bereaved by the loss of a partner but they can easily make provision for such a contingency by taking their mobile phone out of a pocket and dialling the number given.

The growing importance of services in the economies of developed countries and many developing ones is related to information and communication technology (ICT) applications, convergence of technologies and the break-up of government monopolies in many parts of the world. In an era when many products are becoming commoditized, organizations have to obtain competitive advantage by creating added value with the services they provide (Vandermerwe, 1993a). The mix of product/service and the increasingly important value-added service element represent the total 'offering' of an organization.

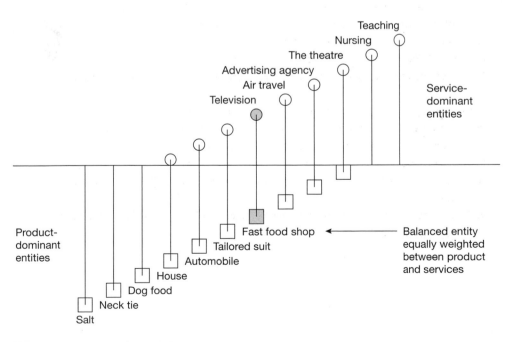

Figure 5.1 Shostack's 'scale of elemental dominance' (Shostack, 1982; reprinted courtesy of Emerald, www.emeraldinsight.com)

Mass customization

As innovation advances, markets fragment and emphasize that customers as individuals and organizations are not part of a homogeneous market but have their own unique problems to resolve. Using this as his point of departure, Pine (1993) has developed the concept of *mass customization*. This apparently contradictory term is given to what is claimed as a new frontier in business competition. It is made possible by the ability of microprocessors to embed intelligence in a wide range of products which, when allied to the plummeting costs of computer memory, facilitates the expansion of the service element in the product-service mix.

BOX 5.1 MAKING SHOES AND THE CONTRIBUTION OF COMPUTER TECHNOLOGY

The making of shoes is a basic manufacturing activity all over the world. It is labour intensive. The introduction of automation has been difficult for a number of reasons including the flexible nature of the materials used and the enormous range of styles and sizes required. Add to this the limited life of fashions and the large number of permutations involved in meeting needs in a heterogeneous and fast-changing market, survival in the shoe production industry is challenging. Mechatronics is the discipline which brings the power of the computer to assist in adapting the process of production to achieve the production variety needed at minimum cost to satisfy demand. Its adoption is assisted by the dramatic fall in the cost of computer memory enabling the profitable use of the computer in the manufacturing process.

The upper part of the shoe is assembled from a number of separate components which have not proved amenable to the automation process. Traditionally, it has been carried out on a batch production basis in a workplace characterized by freestanding work stations together with large amounts of work-in-progress and a throughput time which could take weeks to complete. In identifying typical shoe upper operations and applying mechatronics to some of the problems, research found solutions that dramatically reduced the work-in-progress and the throughput times. It solved the problem of working with limp, non-homogeneous materials, so assisting in the creation of manufacturing flexibility. These solutions included:

- automation of the shoe component stitch marking and thinning of tapered edges which had been a manual operation, to assist in the correct alignment of these components when sewn together;
- developing a new operation using computer-assisted applications to the process of lock stitching in joining leather components.

All these new automated activities dramatically accelerated the production process.

(The information in this box was adapted from Preece *et al.*, 1994)

Technology applications have been, and are being, introduced and developed across many product ranges in the Americas, Asia, Australasia and Europe, providing the basis for flexible and cheap production. In the process, economies of scale which were created by standardized products are being complemented, or replaced, by economies of scope in the more flexible system. In the latter, the application of a single process can produce a greater variety of products, often more cheaply and more quickly, than mass production methods.

Pine (1993) established five means of achieving mass customization, namely:

1   Customize services around standardized products and services;
2   Create customizable products and services;
3   Provide point-of-delivery customization;
4   Provide quick response throughout the value chain;
5   Modularize components to customize end-products and services.

Customize services around standardized products and services

Marketing and delivery can still customize completely standardized products before being sent to customers. For example, in the car rental industry, Hertz has added customized services around its standard car hire. It has for a long time had an express service to enable its most valued customers to access a car with minimum wait. It added its Club Gold service to individualize the car rental experience by keeping records of customer preferences and tracking incoming flights to make sure the right mix of vehicles is available to service demand. When a customer arrives, the car is taken to a weather-protected stall, the key is put in the ignition, the engine is run to warm the car when it is cold and the customer's name and stall number are displayed on a computer-controlled directory board. Services can be performed on standard information which include personalizing, categorizing, repackaging, integrating, facilitating, monitoring, filtering and matching, when and where a customer wants a service. Similarly, Dow Jones News/Retrieval, which provides on-line access to news data, business journal articles, financial reports, *Financial Times* and *Wall Street Journal* articles, share prices, sport and weather reports and so on, automatically searches all incoming news and provides its customers with only the information they want to see.

Create customizable products and services

An alternative to customizing services in the delivery function is to create offerings in the development function that are essentially mass-produced but are customizable to, and often by, each customer. Companies and individuals put computers and their associated software to many different uses to customize to specific needs. People use Excel, for example, for numerous purposes in Microsoft Office, the common factor being the need to set out data in columnar form, compute and keep track of independent data and automatically generate illustrative 'what if' conditions. Normann and Ramirez (1993), who examined interactive strategy as systematic social innovation, have expressed this in a different way. They consider the consumer creates his/her own value as a result of companies perpetually re-inventing value by re-configuring roles, relationships and structures. There is dialogue between competencies and customers. They connect the specific knowledge of organizations directly to their relationships.

125

Provide point-of-delivery customization

The point-of-delivery method of customization is used when the customer's preference, or at least the final customizing step, is produced where the product is sold. Companies like Vision Express and Eyelab within the optician/vision sector, can produce the humble spectacles (or eye glasses) in an hour on location, a product that at one time had to be made in a central factory and took weeks to deliver. The same principle has been applied to shoe repairs, printing, copying and dry-cleaning as well as photographic developing. Technology, however, has caught up with Pine (1993) in connection with the last-mentioned process as noted below.

BOX 5.2 PHOTOPRINTS WITHOUT LEAVING HOME

It will no longer be necessary to take your holiday snapshots to a shop to be processed. Fujitsu, a Japanese company aiming to become a leading Internet Service Provider (ISP), has recruited Fuji Film Co. to provide digital imaging services for its ISP subscribers. Consumers are able to transmit their digital images to Fuji for processing into prints and then take delivery of them without moving from the comfort of their own homes.

(Adapted from *Business Week*, 1999)

Provide quick response throughout the value chain

Providing a swift, even instant, response to customer desires is an even better way of incorporating mass customization. The example of Custom Vêtement Associates and its use of satellite and Minitel (see Chapter 1) is a case in point. Other examples come from the retail and textile manufacturing industries as shown by Levi Strauss and Du Pont. Each organization throughout the value chain is linking together through these technologies so that all members of the value chain know what is selling at the retail level and what to produce and distribute at each preceding level in the chain. Major progress has been accomplished in the replenishment cycle to reduce the time from 25 weeks to less than 6, which means that retailers no longer have to guess and purchase for the season and hope for the best. At six weeks, and even more so at the aimed-for ideal of two weeks, retailers can order smaller amounts of many more styles, then re-order what customers really want most.

Modularize components to customize end-products and services

This is a popular method for achieving mass customization. Economies of scale are achieved through the components rather than the products. Economies of scope are gained by using the modular components time and time again in different products. The wide range of products that can be configured gains customization. American Express can identify lifestyle changes like marriage, or moving house, or match projected travel plans, to the specific buying habits of its customers.

BOX 5.3 HOW BENETTON MEETS THE NEEDS OF INDIVIDUAL CUSTOMERS

Benetton, the Italian design-led producer of textiles that combine value and style, is a leader in the field of fast replenishment of worldwide stocks centralized on Italy, with international production locations to reduce costs. It sub-contracts nearly 95 per cent of its production to more than 700 small producers, so creating a flexible response to a change in market mood. By centralizing the purchase of raw materials, it obtains considerable cost advantages. The only activities kept in-house are those where expensive high technology can be used which benefits from economies of scale such as complex chemical processes for making colours and Computer Assisted Design and Manufacture (CAD/CAM), which deliver quality and efficiency in the cutting of materials while delivering variety. An automated warehouse provides economies of scale in logistics. Through information linkage to its franchisees, its sales agents, its supplier network (with short-cycle networked production techniques) and to international customers, Benetton can deliver to franchisees in less than one week from receipt of order.

Sales are to franchisees using the Benetton name. Their owners operate the shops. They are highly motivated to identify accurately market needs because they buy all their stock from Benetton and are not allowed to return any stock. The links between the company and the shop owners are the sales agents, of whom there are about 80 worldwide. They set up the retail network in each country and become the country experts, providing Benetton with feedback on market preferences and reactions. They are free to own their own shops, which gives them the first-hand knowledge of consumers and the problems of the shop owners.

(Adapted from Ketelhöhn, 1993)

These different approaches to mass customization are not mutually exclusive. The Italian company, Benetton, uses at least three of them and a short account of its operations through its network of suppliers and retail outlets is instructive as to how it tailors its products to customer needs and relates them to other marketing approaches.

INTERNATIONAL MARKET SEGMENTATION

For those organizations unable, for reasons of product inflexibility, or unwilling to embrace mass customization, there are other alternatives. They can enter niche markets, or segment their market, to serve their customers by adapting as circumstances require. There are various approaches as noted below.

Segmentation by market clusters

By identifying market clusters across the world, companies can reduce the number of product variations, and the number of marketing mixes, to make the necessary penetration using, in essence, a market portfolio approach. Segmentation by clustering markets can be classified by:

- *Stage of economic development*: for example, by developing markets, or by geography where markets of reasonable homogeneity exist as in the Scandinavian countries or in countries where the product is generic and does not need adaptation;
- *Language*: where the product and its attributes are aimed at, say, the Spanish-speaking areas;
- *Lifestyles*: as in the case of people who see motor cars as an extension of their personalities;
- *Product attributes*: like umbrellas doubling as parasols for use in the tropics with handles of a design that can hook over the shoulder for the convenience of the many cyclists;
- *Usage rates*: as in the case of the number of landings an aircraft tyre makes.

An associated factor is whether a company wants to standardize its offering to different segments in these countries. Canon re-positioned its auto-exposure, single-lens reflex camera to appeal to up-market first-time buyers in the US, and to older, technically knowledgeable buyers in Germany, after aiming it at re-placement buyers in Japan.

Segmentation across country borders

In order to obtain the benefits of mass production, a company can target a market segment across national borders, which creates cost savings while responding to the specific market needs. For example, the German brewer König has found a niche across countries in the supply of cask beer which keeps cool for days after chilling and which is aimed at the market for outside events where it is difficult to keep beer cool. Radio Finland identified a narrow market segment in its 'News in Latin' programme, aimed at people who had studied Latin and have a continuing interest in the application of the language to current situations, requiring creativity and imagination both in translating into and from the language. Examples include situations such as the use of *essedarium caelarum* meaning an aeroplane or 'chariot of the skies'.

British Airways traditionally focused on the top end of the business traveller market within the otherwise highly competitive transatlantic routes. In Europe, while targeting the business traveller, British Airways also developed its subsidiary Go aimed at the low-cost fare customers on intra-European routes. This was later hived off as a management buyout (MBO) and subsequently, in 2002, it was taken over by UK-based easyJet. British Airways could probably have benefited from the lessons of this segmentation and the mindset underlying it, judging from the financial success of low-cost, no-frills airlines, in particular, easyJet and Ryanair in the UK, operating in Europe.

Segmentation by clusters across markets

An unusual approach is taken by Vandermerwe (1993b) in identifying a European system. Instead of one market of similar preferences as in the case of a market cluster, or a collection of small specialized markets as in international market segments, she envisages a market system consisting of regional Euro-clusters across markets. In each of these Euro-clusters across markets, new markets grow out of:

- groups of regional mass clusters, made up of consumers with common needs;
- groups of regional niche clusters, made up of consumers with similar but differentiated needs;
- groups of local and specialized clusters.

The targets are no longer citizens of a given country but rather a specific group of individuals across a number of countries, all sharing similar economic, demographic or lifestyle characteristics.

Designing and adapting the product to specific segments/markets

Organizations would prefer to have a standard product aimed at the segment being targeted because of cost, which encourages them to look for markets where there is no need for product modification. This entails basing the design on a benchmark market which usually is the home market if that market is large enough to justify this step. If the home market is small, then a larger market may be selected. As long as the US remains the major country enabling international economic growth, then that market would be a reasonable one on which to build a product and move out into US-type markets. The US market for 60Hz electricity supply motors is the largest. Consequently, the majority of countries in the Americas copies that frequency. On the other hand, most of Europe is on a 50Hz electricity supply. Local regulations in countries like Canada differ in substance from US regulations, e.g. in relation to insulation. The high costs of building a centrifuge motor to Canadian specifications (individual states sometimes have their own regulations) led to an English supplier, Thomas Broadbent and Sons Ltd, declining to design centrifuges for the Canadian chemical industry as the small market size did not warrant the expense.

Sometimes, the additional variable costs of modification are minimal, e.g. labelling or translation of foreign language terms. In these circumstances, a company may decide not to be disadvantaged in a particular country and include that country in its market portfolio. If the product has an edge in terms of what it is designed to do, then other markets may want the product and the portfolio becomes more extensive. If, as a result of foreign direct investment (FDI), the product can be produced in the market it is intended to serve, then the company will not have to confront tariff barriers to which exporting companies may be exposed. Of course, should it decide to export from that base it may face tariff barriers, if they are applicable.

It is in a company's interest to ensure that its product is matched to the market concerned. The factors bearing on that adaptation can be classified under two categories, namely, prescriptive and discretionary factors.

1   *Prescriptive factors* These include the laws of a country and any regulations made under them. For instance, it is not permitted to use certain colourants in Belgium, among

129

them one used by the makers of Rose's Lime Juice, which prevented the company marketing in Belgium although its product was acceptable in other European countries. Marking and labelling can sometimes be required to be specific to a country. The EU has harmonized a number of standards and these have to be complied with, even when goods are supplied from outside the Union. Individual countries have their own product standards and these also have to be complied with, e.g. within the insurance industry there is a plethora of rules for each country which will take time to deregulate within the Single European Market. The International Standards Organization (ISO) has published standards to which producers supplying member countries must adhere. ISO 9000, or its local equivalent, is the quality standard which firms seek to acquire as a prized indication of superior performance. Product-specific quality seals testify that a given product meets a set of characteristics, usually prescribed in association with public authorities, producers and consumers, so distinguishing the product from similar products. Certification of origin, e.g. real Scotch whisky, is intended to protect products whose quality is located in a special location or know-how. Health and safety are prime concerns in advanced economies and are surrounded with all sorts of restrictions on products. Consumers have to be informed of any risks associated with products as in prescription drugs or rotating equipment; high-risk products need particular attention. Importers, not makers, are held responsible in some jurisdictions for the safety of products produced abroad. Since product liability laws (whole books have been written on the subject) are swingeing in their application, makers have to be aware of them to ensure they are not violated.

2   *Discretionary factors* While prescriptive factors are based on awareness and should be part of the general international marketing intelligence system of a company, discretionary factors are not so obvious and require information of a higher order. The 'six honest serving men' of marketing research can tell much about markets in the search to match the product to them. How a product is used, what determines its use, who uses it, and where, when, why and how it is bought can highlight the features which should be incorporated in it. Computers may be offered through intermediaries who provide all kinds of hold-your-hand service. They may provide low price outlets with contracted connection service, telephone support and optional long-term guarantees (on which many companies rely for their end-of-year profits), companies specializing in 'pick and mix' systems and specialized offerings for the technologically wise aficionado. Similarly, grains of sugar can be combined in a number of ways, e.g. as lumps, as free-flowing granules, as cones or as special sugars with particular taste in coffee or confectionery. In Norway, it is the custom to drink coffee through a sugar lump. Free-flowing sugar (like granulated or caster) is used for baking as well as used by the spoonful, packet or tube to sweeten drinks, cereals and other foods particularly in retail catering. Cones of sugar which can be chopped into customers' preferred lengths have long been made for North African markets where transport is hazardous and multiple handling a possible source of loss of free-flowing grains: sugar shares with gunpowder a tendency to seek the minutest hole in a container. Special sugars have been created to impart a special taste to whatever it is added. Demerara sugar is

a combination of refined sugar and molasses, according to a learned judge who was asked to decide whether the description of a special sugar as 'London Demerara' was legitimate, as discussed in Box 5.4.

BOX 5.4 FROM SPECIALIZED PRODUCT TO A GENERIC ONE

The example of Tate & Lyle Ltd shows that environmental change encourages change in product strategy which may itself be highly innovative and can have an influence on product development. This company specialized in refining 'raw' or 'cargo' sugar imported from the cane sugar producing areas and marketed it in its domestic and export markets. Much of its sugar was originally imported under the Commonwealth Sugar Agreement whereby producers from certain British Commonwealth countries were paid prices well above the, then low, world price. Refiners received an agreed price per ton for refining this raw sugar and could only increase profitability by reducing their costs, which was exceedingly difficult. Only on special sugars could more attractive profit margins be generated.

Tate & Lyle sugar specialists identified an opportunity to make a sugar similar in appearance to Demerara sugar, a special sugar made and sold by a small company in Guyana called the Demerara Sugar Company (part of the Guyana Sugar Corporation). Combining refined white sugar with molasses, the residue left after sugar has been separated from its mother liquor, did this. It was put on the market under the name of 'London Demerara'. The name was challenged in court by an individual and defended by lawyers representing Tate & Lyle. The court ruled that Demerara sugar and London Demerara were no different in kind, as both were a combination of sugar and molasses, albeit made by different processes, and decided in favour of the refiners.

After some 20 years the 'London' was dropped from the name. It had become a generic product as a result of the court's decision and its legitimization as Demerara sugar by use over time. Tate & Lyle retains a strong market share through being the first company to make it on a large scale, despite others making Demerara sugar, and gaining the advantage of the experience curve in a growing market due in large part to the reliable Tate & Lyle brand name.

There were those in the industry who believed the Court erred in its judgment. The original Demerara was a premium-priced, unrefined sugar with a unique flavour and was in demand, particularly for sweetening coffee, in more discriminating circles. It was made by a sulphitation process as distinct from the carbonatation process used by the refiners and current makers of unrefined brown sugars. It also had another unique characteristic at the time – when a spoonful was taken from a bowl, the sugar left in it 'crawled'. Anybody can test to establish whether they are experiencing the real thing or the equivalent version by taking a few grains on a spoon, dipping it into a cup of coffee and then draining the liquid. If the grains go white, it is the refiner-made Demerara. By contrast, the original Demerara has 80 per cent of its colour locked up in the crystal and will not lose its colour. Tate & Lyle has done its research well and has developed and modified a successful product strategy in the light of changing conditions.

Environmental conditions have to be examined to match products to markets to determine the core product and the attributes with which it is surrounded or augmented. Geography and climate have to be taken into account as in the case of a manufacturer of sundials, which are enjoying a renewed popularity. It has to be known that south of the equator sundials have to be calibrated in the reverse direction from that which is customary north of it, as the sun appears to move from west to east rather than from east to west. Forage harvesters designed for the Finnish market have to be modified for use in Ireland where ground conditions are wetter and the machinery does not perform as in Finland. In the economic and socio-cultural context, commodities in a poor country like Benin or Myanmar have of necessity to be the cheapest. For example, sweets have to be within a suitable price range and packaged in quantities that can be broken down into very small amounts. The successful middleman will have the enterprise to break down packets of, say, 100 sweets into lots of five or ten for sale or into a number appropriate to the smallest denomination of coin.

At the technical and educational level, before sophisticated office systems are offered to markets without the education system to support their use and maintenance, they may need to be re-designed more simply for them. This echoes Juran's classic definition of quality as 'fitness for purpose' (Evans and Lindsay, 1989). The mechanically operated 'wind-up' radio is a classic model of a product designed to meet needs where the infrastructure does not give appropriate support. In this case the technological environment concerns the lack of electricity provision to millions and the economic one relates to the perceived prohibitive cost of batteries.

The above examples lead to consideration of the physical properties of the product. The categories can overlap. Size, as pointed out, has to be suited to the market, as has design. More and more materials are specially made for particular purposes. Examples of weight being reduced to extend the market are shown through the miniaturization of electronic products such as with the transistor radio, the laptop computer and the mobile telephone. The last-mentioned is enjoying a boom in Europe as a result of 'pay-and-talk' agreements which are widening the market to ever younger people to suit their needs. It is possible to buy mobile telephones the size of Mars bars (slips easily into a pocket or bag) available in a range of attractive colours aimed at this segment of the market. The matching of product to market is an on-going and ever-changing activity. The international marketer has to keep in touch through a Marketing Information System (MIS) (see Chapter 4) especially monitoring the marketing intelligence contribution concerning all these market and environment conditions, possible applications of the physical properties of the product as well as government and related regulations.

TEST MARKETING

Examples of failures in new product introduction are extensive with well quoted cases including Ford losing over US $350m on its Edsel model, RCA US $580m on its SelectaVision and Texas Instruments US $660m on home computers (Kotler and Armstrong, 1996). An instant mash potato product failed when it was first introduced initially due to culture tastes not suiting consumer practices at the time of introduction.

McDonald's introduced a McPloughman's lunch and fried chicken products which were failures (Dibb *et al.*, 1997 and *US Today*, 1989). Green Giant introduced Oven Crock baked beans but found that 'Our beans were terrific, but they were a solution to no known problem', according to John M. Stafford, vice-president of Pillsbury. On the other hand, test marketing of 'After Eight' mints in Scotland suggested that they would fail in the market but when management decided to proceed with the product it became an international success.

Test marketing is one method of reducing the risk of product failure. The product or service is introduced to a small part of the market so that the reaction of consumers and intermediaries within the supply chain is assessed prior to the product being fully launched. At an international level, products may be introduced to one country and then 'rolled out' across borders to the international and global market as appropriate. Nevertheless, care is required at the introductory stages in the assessment of market demand in the different countries, as demands may well differ according to the cultures of each country or region.

INTERNATIONAL BRANDING: POSITIONING AND TARGETING

Brands endow products with purpose. Traditionally, marketing textbooks have focused on launching new products where marketing the brand is considered merely as a tactical and final decision which is developed through communication such as advertising, packaging and the logo. Today, marketers are forced to think whether or not growth should come about through existing brands by developing their sphere of activity, or through new brands whether created or bought. The brand gives the product meaning and defines its identity in both time and space. It has to be managed, nourished and controlled. Brands become credible through persistency and repetition. One acknowledged brand expert has said that, by creating satisfaction and loyalty, a brand eventually creates a kind of quasi-contract which binds it to the market (Kapferer, 1997) as was the case with the Gillette Sensor razor and the expensively researched successor Mach 3.

A brand has to explore fresh avenues to sustain its competitive edge in terms of economies of scale and productivity. It is aided in this by geographic extension being built into the brand concept. The growth of a brand, and the reduction of unit costs that stem from it, depend on international expansion. If the brand is to remain competitive, it must be offered immediately to all at the lowest possible price. It is no longer possible to delay the full effect of a new brand by initially offering it to a minority at a high price and then gradually extending its market; the marginal cost of each progressive feature rises day by day. A global product does not necessarily signify a global brand; the same product, however, can be marketed under different brand names in different countries, e.g. the soap powder is Ariel in Europe, Tide in the US and Cheer in Japan.

Opportunities for the single brand

The single, or global brand, is essential whenever the clients are themselves operating on a worldwide basis. Companies using Packard Bell computers in New York would think it sensible to have the same brand in their offices in Mexico City or Caracas. The same applies to companies in most technological industries such as 3M, Matsushita, Monsanto, Alcatel, Caterpillar, Unilever and Hewlett Packard, quite apart from their being global enterprises. The global brand is a necessity. It is also necessary to retain a single brand when that brand corresponds to the signature of its original creator, e.g. Yves St Laurent. Even if the creator is dead, it remains true that from a single source comes a single name.

The global, or single brand, enables a product to adapt to new international opportunities. Travellers abroad, whether businessmen or tourists, are more likely to buy a brand they know and trust as it reduces the risk of the purchase. The greater the development of international media, the greater the opportunities for the single brand. The advent of Sky television and the increasing international coverage of satellite transmissions are examples of this widening reach. When a brand goes international, it can attract the interest of large retailers involved worldwide like Wal-Mart and Carrefour that derive benefit from centralized purchasing or through using strategic alliances with foreign retailers. The global brand, having acquired a wider international presence and awareness, provides a lever for entering other markets.

Developing strategies for globalization

While one option is to introduce a brand to foreign markets by proceeding cautiously from market to market, this alerts competitors as to what a company is seeking to do. There are two main alternatives to this:

1   The company can launch the brand simultaneously in a number of countries. Local adaptations of product or advertising may be incorporated as the product is fine-tuned to the emerging needs of the market.
2   Acquired local brands can be unified. The Nestlé take-over of Rowntree (UK), Buitoni (Italy) and Perrier (France) relates to the need to acquire strong brands. A step towards unification of these brands is the inclusion of the Nestlé logo in light typescript under all of these acquired brands. In some instances, the original brand

BOX 5.5 THE IMPORTANCE OF PRODUCTS IS BEING REPLACED RAPIDLY BY THAT OF BRANDS

Kapferer (1997) illustrates the growing importance of brands with the example of Essilor, a leading international manufacturer of spectacle lenses, which is being challenged by companies like Nikon and Seiko. These latter companies have entered the market on the back of Nikon's reputation in optics (not far removed from eyesight) and Seiko's in watch making (yielding an image of precision and reliability). All of a sudden, brand awareness is a key factor in the consumer buying decision in this market.

134

owner names have been dropped as where Rowntree's KitKat only uses the Nestlé family brand name, no longer referring to Rowntree.

The company as a brand has been around for decades. It has been expanded to include industrial firms, banks, insurance companies, service industries and retailers selling their own brands. Axa, the French-based insurance giant with acquisitions in Europe and beyond, is using its own name to advertise the products of the acquired companies, as is evidenced by their television advertising messages and international sporting events. Both Nestlé and Axa intend that over time their brands will convey qualities and differences. It is not the registered trademark as such which creates value. It is the policy of brand management conducted by the company. Its central concept is brand identity, not brand image, which must be carefully managed.

Closely associated with identity is the name of the brand. There are product names of which their originators did not realize the international implications. What may sound inspirational in one language may translate into something amusing, irrelevant, bawdy or offensive in another. A Finnish brand marketed in Europe to unfreeze frozen locks on car doors was called 'Piss'. It was superseded by an improved version 'Super Piss'. This brand name would not be acceptable when using the English language.

In seeking to illustrate the features of a strong service brand, Kasper *et al.* (1999) quote from Berry *et al.* (1988). A 'strong' service (dominant) brand (and presumably a product-dominant offering) should possess some, if not all, of the characteristics of distinctiveness, relevance, memorability and flexibility:

1   *Distinctiveness*: immediately identifies the supplier and distinguishes it from competitors;
2   *Relevance*: conveys the nature of the service offering or the service benefit;
3   *Memorability*: can be understood, used and recalled with ease;
4   *Flexibility*: should be broad enough to cover the organization's current business and the need for foreseeable expansion.

In short, a cohesive branding programme requires effective blending of all communication elements, using them consistently and imaginatively across services and media. The bottom line remains that the quality of the service determines the success of the image. If customers are not satisfied, the name will not help. But, of course, if good performance is combined with a good name, the more powerful branding effect can be generated for the product or service.

When the global approach is frustrated

Sometimes, products are embedded in a particular culture and it is impossible to give an international identity to them. Kapferer (1993), an international authority on brands, showed that food brands are more likely to be standardized in Germany and the UK than in France and Italy, this difference being attributed to the greater importance given to eating in the Latin culture than in the British and German ones. Kapferer's interesting Europe-wide survey was conducted to determine whether the concept of a European brand was a reality, or about to become one. Isolating four types of European manager and their sensitivity to differences between countries, he found wide variations in the ways they centralized or localized aspects of the marketing mix. These include the degree of control exercised by head offices over their affiliates, the kinds of competitive practices adopted, power-related factors and the advocacy of international and local advertising agencies, all of which may influence policy in relation to the Europeanization of the brand.

Another industry which is strongly influenced by national culture is retail financial services. As yet, they do not serve the Single European Market, but are slowly moving in that direction. Currently, regulations, buying habits and distribution patterns vary from country to country. Even when retail investors buy foreign assets, they mostly do so through domestic stockbrokers or fund managers who handle the crossing of borders on their behalf. These barriers are as much related to personal mindsets as in law or regulation. If this fragmented market could be approached globally, it could become a high growth market with changing patterns of demand to which companies would have to bring new added value.

Distributor own brands

In all developed countries, as markets come to maturity, manufacturer brands face fierce competition from distributor own brands (DOBs), which are usually termed private brands. Competition arises not only in the food and consumer goods industries, but also in sectors such as those for sporting goods, kitchen appliances, televisions and video recorders, clothing and banking services. Manufacturers are being put under pressure from large international retailers buying direct from them, often to specified standards, and selling direct to the public under their own brand name like Safeway (UK), Ahold (the Netherlands) and Delhaize (Belgium) in foods, IKEA (Sweden) in furniture, and Super Club (Belgium) in video rentals. Many own label brands sold by these and similar organizations are marketing innovations as distinct from the 'second best' image of the traditional, cheaper, private brand or own-label. Changes in international retail distribution are making the position of the retailers stronger as acquisition and merger across countries result in larger units with the power to commission ever better innovations and put more pressure on manufacturers and their brands.

INTELLECTUAL PROPERTY AS A PRODUCT ATTRIBUTE

A patent is a device whereby a company or individual receives protection for a limited period from those who would otherwise copy an innovative product. It is protected in law in nearly all countries, the traditional Arab countries being the exception. Without this protection, there would be little incentive to fund research and development to produce new and socially useful products, and international trade would be inhibited, too. A similar protection applies to registered trade marks as well as to copyright. Together these represent intellectual property. A granted patent, or copyright or registered trademark or brand is an attribute of a product which adds value to it and enhances it in the eyes of a purchaser.

Patents

As indicated in Chapter 1, different governments have different approaches to the question of patents. Local laws and practices vary in respect of what is defined as patentable, the period of protection, the rights of third parties and the cover afforded by patenting. For example, under revised Mexican laws, the concept of Certificates of Invention has been adopted. This is a means, still favoured in Russia, whereby processes for making mixtures of chemicals, and for making alloys not subject to the protection of patents, can be protected. In some countries, such as Thailand, there is no patent protection for pharmaceutical products, allowing pharmaceutical products manufactured there to compete at much lower prices than those manufactured by companies which have incurred the expense of developing them. The international marketer takes account of these factors and seeks to harness them to advantage.

The globalization of markets, advances in ICT enabling easier transfer of technology, trading blocs and progressive tariff abolition have rendered inadequate patents covering only the country of origin. The selection of markets in which patent cover is sought is a critical marketing decision. The product decision, and its ultimate profitablity, is bound up closely with the manner and speed with which patent cover is acquired to take account of the variations in local laws and the period of monopoly conferred by the patent.

Different countries, different interpretations

In most countries certain inventions are barred by statute from being patentable, e.g. in Japan and Russia chemical compounds *per se* cannot be patented. The only method of protection available is patenting the process for making the product since claims to the process are held to extend to the products made by that process. Additionally, in Japan, if there is only one known method of producing a product, all such products are assumed to have been made by that process and the onus is on the infringer to prove otherwise. In a number of countries, claims to a pharmaceutical compound are not acceptable. In Italy and Turkey, neither the process for making the pharmaceutical goods, nor the product itself, is patentable if used in the treatment of mankind.

Managing the patentability factor

One important limiting factor governing what may, or may not, be patented in any country is the definition of what constitutes 'prior art'. This varies from (1) the practice that considers anything previously known or used anywhere in the world to (2) the practice which accepts as prior art only prior publication or use in the country concerned. France, Italy, the Netherlands, Sweden, Argentina and Mexico are the major exponents of the former approach (1). The UK and Australia are the only countries of note pursuing the latter approach (2). The remainder generally require the prior art to be local but allow the prior publication to be anywhere. 'Prior' in this context means before the earliest effective application date for the patent which is not necessarily the date when the patent application was filed. There is a long-standing international convention on patents whereby, in signatory countries, foreign nationals are extended the same rights as locals in major aspects of patent law. For example, if an applicant files the patent application in another convention country within one year of filing the originating application, the second application is given the same effective application filing date as the original application. The international marketer is likely to make such decisions under professional advice, which does not excuse him/her from being aware of the importance of managing internationally the relationship of the product and patents.

Patented products and processes in most cases cannot be readily manufactured without the disclosure of know-how if the product is to be made as in the case of a licensee. This know-how may consist of secret information, drawings, formulae and technical data, and may be associated with a trade mark. With the rapid advance of technology, some companies prefer to communicate as know-how all, or part, of new products and processes developed by their research and development departments, rather than have them patented and disclosed to competitors.

Trade marks and copyright

Copyright is not as widely applicable to manufacturing and service-dominant firms as are patents and trade marks. Nevertheless, it is of considerable importance for organizations producing items such as compact discs, books and software which are all billion-euro markets.

Trade marks, which include registered brands, have significance in global markets, not least because they are protection against 'brand piracy' provided there is support from the government of the country in which the piracy is taking place. Such counterfeiting of brands, as well as infringement of copyright, has been a serious feature since the 1980s.

Intellectual property and the European Union

Patent, trade mark and copyright owners and possessors of un-patented know-how have rights in the EU which have been established as the result of landmark cases in the European Court. These demonstrate how product policy relates to company strategy. It is not possible to apply national trademark laws to an agreement if it is in violation of Article 85 of the Treaty of Rome. This means that tariff barriers removed under EU auspices will not be replaced by private barriers in the form of restrictive agreements that distort EU competition. It is known as the prohibition in Article 85 and includes agreements expressly forbidding sales by a distributor outside his own territory. The Treaty guarantees only the existence of national property rights but not the exercise of them. A description of a seminal case, which established a guiding principle and from which other important judgments have stemmed, is given in Box 5.6.

- It is not possible by virtue of trade mark right to prevent the import of products originating in other member states bearing the same mark if the owners have acquired the right to use it.
- Import restrictions based on intellectual property rights violate the Treaty of Rome once a product has been lawfully sold in another member EU country.
- National copyright cannot be invoked to prevent imports by a manufacturer which has itself sold them in another EU member country. This rule also applies in respect of parallel patents.

138

BOX 5.6 GRUNDIG CONSTEN CASE

The European Court held it inconsistent with the principles and aim of the competition system of the Treaty of Rome if the rights granted under national trade mark laws of the member states could be abused for purposes in conflict with EU competition law. It arose from the agreement which Grundig, the German manufacturers of tape recorders, etc., had made with its distributor, Consten SA in France. Having imposed an export prohibition on its German distributors, it created a supplementary trade mark, GINT, which it assigned to national distributors. Grundig's pricing policy was to charge a higher price in the export market than in the domestic market. A French wholesaler, Unef, had imported tape recorders from a wholesaler in Germany and sold them to French dealers. Consten sued Unef for unfair competition and trade mark infringement. Unef appealed to the European Commission which ruled that the agreement between Grundig and Consten violated Article 85, a ruling affirmed by the European Court (OJEC, 1996).

■ Where a brand is being sold more cheaply in a country outside the European Economic Area (EEA), an EU retailer, for example, can no longer get supplies from there. This was the surprise ruling of the European Court concerning the EU trade mark directive overriding member state laws on parallel imports.

Did the European Court undermine EU competition policy?

The ruling imparted in the judgment contained in the OJEC (1998) supports the opposite of what happens within the EU where Single European Market watchdogs are strongly committed to encouraging parallel imports between the EU and associated countries to stimulate competition and efficiency. The implication is that manufacturers of branded goods are encouraged to 'milk' the EU market for profits which they can use to subsidise lower prices in markets where there is not the same purchasing power.

The above decision has been condemned by commentators. Retailers and wholesalers of branded products both inside and outside the EU should be alert to this concern as a decision reversal could influence their product planning. The long-run profitability of the product is affected by the way in which intellectual property is handled at the planning stage (see McCall and Warrington (1989) Chapter 6 for further discussion on how European law impinges on product decisions).

Threats to the 'status quo' from new technology

Product counterfeiting has been a problem for many years as it is difficult to manage and depends on the active and willing participation of the authorities policing possible infringements. It takes many forms (Paliwoda and Thomas, 1998). It is evidenced most strongly in compact discs which can be copied easily and represent an ongoing menace for software manufacturers who can see the expected fruits of their expensive labour being sucked by others who have not contributed to their creation. Similarly, in sports or leisure wear and for luxury goods where the logo or design associated with the product is readily reproducible, there is the temptation to cash in on obvious profitability.

Internet fraud is a recent development in which the security of the system is paramount for people who buy or do their banking transactions on it. The Microsoft system on which many of the Internet service providers rely, has been shown to be less than 100 per cent secure even with encryption protection. As hackers become more sophisticated, so product systems have to become more complex to keep them at bay.

On the positive side, the boom in cellular phones referred to earlier in this chapter is promising to give Europe a lead in the new technology. Europe is becoming the biggest laboratory for introducing advanced Internet services. Nokia of Finland has become a leader in connecting mobile phones to the Internet, and Vodafone of the UK has become the first global cell-phone provider. The US has been held back by a market fractured by competing wireless standards. In a few years the number of cell phones tied to the Internet could be far in excess of that of on-line PCs. Experiments are proceeding in a laboratory outside Paris by Matsushita of Japan, in association with Nortel, a Canadian telecommunications company, to develop cell phones that offer video-conferencing, video game playing and music downloading.

WARRANTIES

There are no economies of scale in standardizing warranties compared to those which product, packaging or branding offer. As the firm can expect little cost reduction from international standardization, there is limited expectation of serious efforts in that direction although some factors encourage warranty standardization:

- International customers and customers buying centrally want warranties to be standardized.
- High risk products are likely to be standardized as the basic needs of purchasers across the world are the same.
- Where worldwide service backing is available, standardized warranties will be in demand.

Adaptation of the warranties to individual markets is encouraged by the following:

- There are no economic advantages to be won by standardizing.
- Differing conditions for use across markets can be costly in terms of warranty unless matched to market conditions, e.g. extreme temperatures, particularly in the course of a day, or high humidity, dust or salty sea-affected air, can cause breakdowns that arise from adverse use conditions rather than defects in the product. Furthermore, in some developing countries a product may be subjected to more stress and abuse than in others.

140

■ A warranty matched to competitive conditions in the market means adaptation to bring it in line with competing products. A standard warranty may be too expensive to introduce.

In the EU, it has been established in law that even if an item has been bought as a parallel import, it still carries the same warranty rights from the manufacturer as if bought from an authorized dealer in the country concerned.

LABELLING AND PACKAGING

The protection needs of products may vary from market to market depending on mode(s) of transport and handling, length of distribution channels, preferences of consumers and channel members, shopping habits and package size. The determination of national preferences, or regional niches or local clusters, is a step in deciding the package appropriate for a market. There will also be a need to co-ordinate the package with overall promotion policy.

Labelling is an associated concern. The decision to standardize, or adapt, can be simple since governments often require country-specific information, which excludes standardization. Even when labels are standardized, the language usually varies. Some suppliers, especially pharmaceutical and photographic film producers, use multi-lingual labels but may need to have more detailed information in the language of the customer country.

CONCLUSION

It has been shown that, increasingly, there is a movement towards differentiation through service across the spectrum of product-dominant to service-dominant industries. Such innovations have resulted in the fragmentation of markets and emergence of mass customization as a response to it. Where mass customization is not possible, international market segmentation is the means by which suppliers adapt their products to the needs of the market across countries. Brands are essential elements of many company offerings which sometimes take on a significance greater than that of the product itself. Classic strategic models discuss product portfolios, whereas in reality many companies have to manage their brand portfolios. The product/brand has to be managed within the restrictions and opportunities provided by the law as it is applied under different legal systems, and in the case of transnational law, across countries.

What emerges is a situation more complex than the 'costs versus special needs of the market debate'. In some service-dominant organizations and with some manufacturers of luxury consumer goods, production costs are typically a small proportion of total costs and do not create scale economies. Some products do not lend themselves to globalization; others may be global in their nature but need to be adapted to markets due to constraints imposed by government and trade regulations as well as to culture and economic circumstances. Mass customization brings the advantages of standardization and adaptation together, creating economies of scale and scope that may outstrip the benefits of either extreme. The Internet remains in a fluid state as innovation is piled on innovation, with the changes taking place in cellular telephony being the most far-reaching. Test marketing plays a role in ensuring the ultimate success of the international product, or service, expansion across borders.

REVIEW QUESTIONS

5.1 To what extent can a product be standardized?

5.2 Examine the ways in which a product can be made more acceptable to a target market by the attributes with which it is surrounded.

5.3 Discuss the functions performed by brands for the consumer and supplier of products and examine the barriers to the achievement of these functions through a global brand.

5.4 Yours is an American-owned company which manufactures high-quality video systems in Ireland for industrial use. A large claim has been made by an Italian purchaser in respect of a warranty. Investigations have shown that the equipment was not purchased through your authorized distributor in Italy but had been purchased from your distributor in Greece (where, for reasons of company policy, you sell at a cheaper relative price than in Italy). Your company's systems have patent and trade mark cover in Italy and it is felt that this import infringes the patent and trademark cover. There is a strong feeling in top management that the warranty claim should not be met. Advise them.

5.5 Distinguish between prescriptive and discretionary factors in matching a product to a particular market.

5.6 Consider the role that test marketing can play in supporting product development across international markets.

REFERENCES

Berry, L.L., Lefkowith, E.F. and Clark, T. (1988) 'In services, what's in a name?', *Harvard Business Review*, September–October pp. 28–30.

Business Week (1999) 'The behemoth of the net? Fujitsu cuts a slew of e-deals in a bid to become a cyberpower', 16 August, p. 27.

Dibb, S., Simkin, L., Pride, W.M. and Ferrell, O.C. (1997) *Marketing concepts and strategies*, 3rd edn, Boston, Mass.: Houghton Mifflin.

Evans, J.R. and Lindsay, W.M. (1989) *The management and control of quality*, St. Paul, Minn.: West Publishing, Chapter 1, p. 23.

Kapferer, J.-N. (1993) 'La marque européenne: état des lieux', *Revue française de gestion*, No. 93, pp. 55–60.

Kapferer, J.-N. (1997) *Strategic brand management: creating and sustaining brand equity long term*, London: Kogan Page.

Kasper, H., Van Helsdingen, P. and De Vries, W. (1999) *Services marketing management: an international perspective*, Chichester: John Wiley.

Ketelhöhn, W. (1993) 'An interview with Aldo Palmeri of Benetton', *European Management Journal*, Vol. 11, Nos. 3 and 4.

Kotler, P. and Armstrong, G. (1996) *Principles of marketing*, 7th edn, Englewood Cliffs, NJ: Prentice Hall.

McCall, J.B. and Warrington, M.B. (1989) *Marketing by agreement: a cross-cultural approach to business negotiations*, Chichester: John Wiley.

Normann, R. and Ramirez, R. (1993) 'From value chain to value constellation: designing interactive strategy', *Harvard Business Review*, July–August, pp. 65–77.

OJEC (1996) *The Official Journal of the European Community* incorporating Common Market Law Report 489/64, 25 January.

OJEC (1998) 'Silhouette International Schmied vs Hartlauer Handelsgesellschaft', Case 355/96, *The Official Journal of the European Community*, 16 July.

Paliwoda, S.J. and Thomas, M.J. (1998) *International marketing*, 3rd edn, Oxford: Butterworth-Heinemann.

Pine, B.J. II (1993) *Mass customization*, Boston, Mass.: Harvard Business School Press.

Preece, C., Simmons, J.E.L. and Reedman, D.C. (1994) 'Mechatronics, the basis for new industrial development', *Computational Mechanics Publications*, pp. 109–14.

Shostack, G.L. (1982) 'How to design a service', *European Journal of Marketing*, Vol. 16, No. 1, pp. 49–64.

US Today (1989) 'Winging it at McDonald's', 5 September, p. 1b.

Vandermerwe, S. (1993a) *From tin soldiers to Russian dolls: creating added value through services*, Oxford: Butterworth-Heinemann.

Vandermerwe, S. (1993b) 'A framework for constructing Euro-networks', *European Management Journal*, Vol. 11, No. 1, pp. 55–61.

143

Chapter 6

International pricing

INTRODUCTION

In international marketing there are factors which bear on the pricing decisions a marketer must take that do not exist in domestic markets, or that differ in some crucial dimension from domestic practice. They are brought about by the institutions and commercial customs that have evolved to facilitate the delivery and payment of goods and services across national borders as well as by factors in the environment very often specific to a given country. How marketers respond to these and how they use the different approaches available to them will also bear on pricing decisions made. As markets have become ferociously competitive, driven by globalization, so the need has grown to understand these factors that affect price in this still developing scenario. There is a grand experiment ongoing in the European Union (EU) in terms of the European and Monetary Union (EMU) which economists refer to as an 'optimal currency area'. The theory of this makes the proposition that there are gains to be had from sharing a currency across borders, which also has considerable implications for pricing in the international market. Prices are often subject to negotiation and special skills are needed in negotiating across cultures.

LEARNING OBJECTIVES

The objectives of this chapter are to:

■ illustrate the factors that escalate price to the foreign consumer;
■ examine the implications of quoting in the domestic currency and in the customer country currency;
■ identify the effects on pricing of the EMU in the EU;
■ evaluate the different approaches to pricing in an international context;
■ underline the importance of the negotiated price.

When you have completed the chapter you should be able to:

■ take account of the special factors that increase price in the foreign market in making pricing decisions;

■ demonstrate how to incorporate in these decisions the means by which exchange risk is mitigated;

■ make informed judgements in relation to pricing in the EU;

■ use pricing approaches appropriate to the market(s) concerned;

■ show awareness of the cross-cultural skills required in international price negotiations;

■ build up a price from a known cost to the consumer price in a market;

■ establish whether an acceptable price in a market can be met by working back from that price to production cost.

COMMERCIAL FACTORS

Price decisions have to be made in relation to known commercial factors. There are certain assumptions a marketer has to make first. People in the target market must be able to buy and want what is on offer. Demand in a target market depends on the sales volume that can be made at given price levels because there is a cost/volume relationship. These price levels, in turn, are influenced strongly by factors unique to the international market.

Margins in the channels

It is highly unlikely that margins in distribution channels will be identical in any two countries. Consequently, they will differ from the margins in the domestic market. They will depend on the nature of the channels themselves, the power structure within them and the functions performed by channel members. For example, in the UK, the motor vehicle industry is one in which the form of reimbursement to the dealer has changed several times. As the UK laws have to comply with the EU European Commission product liability directives, and responsibility for product defects rests with the manufacturer rather than the seller, new agreements have been entered into between manufacturers and distributors. Basic functions and rewards have been re-negotiated. These have had to reflect the new responsibilities undertaken by dealers together with the resulting reduction in distributor margins related to the greater bargaining power of the automotive manufacturers.

Insurance and freight costs

Many countries export by sea but, irrespective of whether export is by land, sea or in combination, these costs are normally greater than in the domestic trade. There are obvious exceptions as where delivery costs by land across the US can exceed the costs of sea-borne export from the east coast to Haiti or Jamaica. These costs, like all others related to

145

commercial factors, normally are recovered in the price of the product. Sometimes, they are passed on to the buyer in a separate contract of affreightment depending on the basis of the contract (see Table 6.1).

Tariffs and taxes

Tariffs and taxes vary from market to market. Some countries impose a tax on sales to the final consumer; others have a 'value added tax' where the tax is added at each stage of a product build-up from the raw material through the intermediate products to the final article. Within the EU, value added tax (VAT) can vary from over 30 per cent on luxury products in Ireland and Italy to a maximum of 12 per cent in Luxembourg. In common markets, imports of a similar category from outside the market attract a similar tariff in each member country. Outside the EU other special taxes may be levied.

Table 6.1 *International trade terms*

Term	Seller responsibility	Buyer responsibility	Comments
Ex Works (EXW) named place	Fulfils obligation to deliver when he/she has made goods available at his/her place. Not responsible for loading goods on vehicle provided by buyer.	Buyer bears all costs and risks from seller premises onwards.	Minimum obligation for seller.
Free-on-Board (FOB) named shipment port	Fulfils obligation to deliver when goods have passed over ship's rail. Seller has to clear goods for export.	Has to bear risks and costs of loss or damage from FOB point on.	Only used for sea/waterway transport. FCA* used for RoRo* and container traffic.
Cost, insurance and freight (CIF) named port of destination	Pays the costs and freight to named port of destination and marine insurance against buyer's risk of loss or damage.	Requires to pay any extra over and above the minimum coverage.	Sea and waterway only. CIP* is used for RoRo* and containers.
Delivered duty paid (DDP) named port of destination	Fulfils obligation when goods have been made available at named place in country of destination. Has to bear all risks and costs including duties, taxes and other charges of delivering goods cleared for import.	No responsibility	Maximum obligation for seller.

* RoRo refers to 'Roll on – Roll off' as for containers being transported by ferry; FCA means free carrier (named place) related to RoRo; CIP means Carriage and insurance paid to (named port of destination). Less used terms can be found by entering 'Incoterms' on search engines like AltaVista and Google. Practising managers should never be without a copy of *Incoterms 2000* on their bookshelves

International trade terms

The international business community has built up a set of rules based on its joint experience over the years for the interpretation of the most commonly used trade terms to accommodate differences between business practices in different countries. These rules are the *Incoterms 2000* published by the International Chamber of Commerce (ICC) and are an updated version of earlier *Incoterms 1990*. Table 6.1 shows some of the more commonly used terms. Most search engines give all the terms including those that are only occasionally used.

All these factors increase the price in foreign markets. Marketers must be aware of the implications of each factor in the final price and be able to vary an offer. If a prospective buyer expresses such a wish in the course of a transaction, e.g. if the buyer wants a DDP price rather than a FOB one, then that base has to be used for pricing.

In making quotations, the currency and amount are stated, followed by the appropriate term with '(*Incoterms 2000*)' at the end, e.g. 'Price DDP New York . . . $60,400 (*Incoterms 2000*)'. This spells out unequivocally the conditions under which an offer is made and the associated responsibilities of buyer and seller. It is preferable that at the early negotiation stage it should be agreed that *Incoterms 2000* be used, which ensures there is no misunderstanding, whether deliberate or otherwise, of what the duties are for the parties involved. It enabled the supplier in the case given below to negotiate further from a position of relative strength.

BOX 6.1 THE RUSSIAN CONTRACT

A recently privatized Russian company has sent to a small specialist British supplier a contract for signature for additional capital items and spares to a value of £250,000 for equipment originally supplied as a sub-contractor. It was on the company's standard contract form for such items, which included provision for the contract to be made under English law. The British company's original quotation was for the supply of equipment 'delivered FOB Hull £250,000 (*Incoterms 1990*)'. The commercial manager would not sign the contract which contained a clause stating that the contract superseded all earlier exchanges whereby a contract is made on the basis of 'offer and acceptance'. If the contract had been acceptable, that would not have presented a problem. What made him seek to negotiate changes in the contract was the number of clauses which could result in considerable erosion of the company's profit margin.

Consequently, the company faxed the Russian organization that it could not accept the contract as it stood and requested a meeting. Its request was based on three principal objections to the contract document:

1   The company's original quotation on which the price was calculated was for delivery to Hull which was the nearest port for shipment. The Russians wanted to deliver to Hull or Southampton to take advantage of the availability of Russian ships to avoid

the costs in foreign currency for a foreign vessel, foreign currency being very costly. If Southampton was chosen, the British company would incur an additional expense of £3,500.

2   The original quotation based on Incoterms included a responsibility for costs to the FOB point which ceased when the goods crossed the ship's rail. The Russians had a definition of FOB that included stowage in the vessel, passing on the stevedoring costs to the supplier. This was a tactic originally used by the Union of Soviet Socialist Republics (USSR) state buying organizations to save on foreign currency which, if accepted, would involve another £2,000 in costs to the British supplier.

3   Due to delays by the Russians in providing details that would allow manufacture to proceed, it would no longer be possible to provide 'November Bills of Lading' as required by the contract, which was conveniently ignored by the Russian drafters of the contract. A 'Bill of Lading' is the document of title to the goods shipped; if November bills are part of the contract, then the goods have to be on board the ship in November). Acceptance of the contract would mean four weeks delay in delivery exposing the British company to 'liquidated damages' which is the English legal expression for a penalty. English law differs from continental laws in that liquidated damages must include a genuine pre-estimate of the loss. These damages were stipulated in the contract as 1½ per cent of the contract value for every week the delivery was late.

There were other less important, but still possible, profit-eroding points for discussion. In particular, concerning where arbitration should take place, the contract stated it should be the All Union Chamber of Commerce in Moscow, while the original quotation included arbitration in London. In conclusion, the British company had made a critical error by assuming that the Russian company did business in the same way as other European companies. Its management would have to negotiate, and presumably make some concessions, to claw back some of the likely losses.

This case underlines how price is affected by commercial terms and other factors. The asking price is not necessarily the price of the final contract.

(This is a shortened version of 'The Russian contract' in McCall *et al.,* 1990)

Methods of payment

Most international transactions are paid under *open account* which implies a degree of trust between seller and buyer and usually results from a course of dealing that has been established between the parties. In the EU, particularly, it has become the norm. The seller sends the invoice with the goods and, normally, is paid within the period stipulated in his conditions. Increasingly electronic transfer is used to implement such transactions.

In a seller's market it may be possible for the supplier of goods or services to receive payment in advance. In the current environment there are not many of these opportunities. Therefore, there is recourse to the other principal forms of obtaining payment when the degree of trust implicit in open account trading is not present, i.e. by *documentary credit* and *documentary collection*. It is useful to explain these terms by considering how the banks provide an international infrastructure for payments to be effected through their overseas branches or correspondent banks. The contracting parties are allowed to try for their preferred terms as it is unlikely seller and buyer will see the situation in the same light. The seller, particularly with an unknown prospective customer, will want to see the 'colour' of the buyer's money before he releases the goods. On the other hand, the buyer will want to ensure he has delivery of the goods before releasing his money. Trade across borders only becomes possible when one of the parties is prepared to ease his grip on either the money, or the goods, to receive constructive delivery or payment instead. If power in the situation resides with the buyer, it will be the seller who eases his grip and draws a bill of exchange on his bank for the contracted amount. The seller attaches the documents giving title to the goods to it (which together are known as the documentary collection) and forwards them to the buyer for acceptance. These bills are either *sight* bills or *tenour* bills, i.e. either payable on delivery (sight) or at a tenour (time allowed to pay) of usually 60 or 90 days. This means that credit is extended to the buyer and is a cost to be recovered in the price. Usually the cost is based on the interest the amount of credit extended to the buyer could have earned if it had been lodged in an interest-earning bank account.

A documentary credit, more usually referred to as a *letter of credit*, is a common means of reflecting a situation where power resides with the seller. The buyer raises the letter of credit with his/her own bank. Normally it is payable against production of documents at the time of the shipment. It replaces the creditworthiness of the buyer with that of the buyer's bank. It is usually 'irrevocable' in that it can only be altered, or cancelled, with the agreement of all the parties concerned. As if this was not sufficient guarantee, it is sometimes 'confirmed irrevocable', i.e. confirmed by a first class bank in the seller's country, thereby replacing the creditworthiness of the issuing bank with that of a local bank. This is costly to the buyer and anathema to the buyer's bank which sees itself classified as a business risk. The crowning insult is for the seller to ask for an extension to the letter of credit due to the inability of the seller to deliver the goods in time. This not only means there can be unacceptable delay but it also incurs high additional costs for the buyer.

A growing means of payment is *counter-trade*. It originated in the former Eastern Bloc countries because of shortage of foreign exchange over the years of inconvertibility of their currencies. It has been extended worldwide to many other countries as a political, as well as economic, means of doing business. It also ensures local employment and export opportunities in return for the buyer's patronage. In its different forms counter-trade enables payment to be made in whole, or in part, in related or unrelated goods. It usually entails the involvement of a third party specializing in the goods concerned who is in a position to determine the value of these goods on the open market as well as to arrange for their purchase and disposal. Exceptionally, it is used under 'buyback' arrangements whereby a licensor or seller contracts to buy goods made by the licensee or by equipment bought as part of a licensing deal. Usually, the third party is engaged in the contractual arrangements at the preparatory stages prior to the actual negotiations.

Other means of payment include the following:

Factoring Typically, in this arrangement, the client debits all his/her sales to the factor and can draw cash up to about 80 per cent of their value, considerably increasing his/her cash flow. The factor takes over complete responsibility for retrieving the debts due from the client's customers and protects the client from bad debts. Through international factoring companies, most of them set up by the banks, the factor can offer a service to exporters by protecting his customer from bad debts overseas and by giving his client expert advice on foreign exchange transactions. Such transactions apply to trade for most forms of plant and machinery, vehicles or office equipment.

Leasing In the leasing of goods which are exported, the leasing company (the lessor), usually an associate company of the banks, buys the goods outright from the supplier. They are then leased to the ultimate buyer who has the use of the goods for an agreed period subject to payment of the agreed rent to the lessor. The system can operate in one of two ways:

1   by 'cross-border leasing' where a lessor in the exporter's country arranges to buy the goods and to lease them to the overseas buyer;
2   by arranging for a lessor in the buyer's country to act, benefiting the exporting manufacturer with, in effect, a cash sale without recourse to the client unless he defaults on commercial contracts.

Bonding The main types of bonds are 'tender' or 'bid' bonds which are usually 2 to 5 per cent of the tender value and guarantee that the exporter will take up the contract if it is awarded. Failure to take up the contract results in a penalty for the amount of the bond. Usually, the tender bond commits the exporter to join in a performance bond if the contract is awarded. The tender bond serves to prevent the submission of frivolous tenders. The performance bond guarantees that the goods or services will be of the required standard and a stated penalty is payable if they are not. Usually, the amount payable can be up to 10 per cent of the contract value although in special circumstance it can be more.

Forfaiting Under this system of obtaining payment for an export sale, the importer finds a bank, or other first class institution, which is willing to guarantee the liabilities. Normally, the institution is resident in the importer's country. The form of guarantee can be the result of the guarantor endorsing the bills of exchange drawn on the importer who becomes liable for them. It can be a separate guarantee of the importer's liabilities and usually applies when promissory notes rather than bills of exchange are used. When the guarantor is a bank in the US, the guarantee takes the form of a standby letter of credit. The form of the guarantee is unimportant as long as it is legally binding with a reputable guarantor institution.

BUSINESS ENVIRONMENTAL FACTORS

Currency of quotations and exchange rate risk

A most important decision is whether to use one's own currency or that of the buyer's country when quoting. Some companies consider that to quote in one's own currency is good careful management. In practice, it shifts the exchange risk from the seller to the buyer, which is a denial of customer orientation and makes it hard for the customer to compare the seller's quotation with competitors' offers made in his own country currency. While it is desirable to quote in a customer's own currency and to deliver to a customer's premises duty paid, there will be occasions when the supplier's or a third currency may be preferred. For example, for some products it is the custom of the trade to quote in the currency of the supplier's country. Payment is made in dollars when trading in hydro-carbon fuels or aircraft, or in a third country currency by agreement of the parties to suit their purposes.

Risk is removed by the use of forward contracts which enables an exporter to receive, at the time of the contract with the bank, payment in his own currency. The bank, using its knowledge of offsetting risk, recovers the sales contract value when the money is realized at a future date. In this way, the bank carries the exchange risk and the exporter obtains funds at a cost which, normally, will be taken into account when setting a price. Larger global marketing organizations with substantial operations in a number of countries usually have arrangements in place to cover exchange rate variations such as centralized global hedging and swap.

There is a technology available to all those involved in exchange transactions to protect them against adverse exchange movements and help them profit from this specialist knowledge (Edwards, 1990). When the interest rates of country A are noticeably greater than those in country B, it is possible for a company in country A to invoice in the currency of country B. By doing this and either (1) earning the premium by selling forward the country B money, or (2) funding the sale by way of borrowing country B foreign holdings of a country's currency available for purchase at the lower interest rate, it brings the cost of money to the country B level. It might be difficult to do this form of invoicing in countries where customers are reluctant to accept quotations and invoices in their own currency. Such was the case in Germany and Japan when their currencies had been appreciating over the years. It had become a rule of thumb for organizations to ask for quotation and invoice in the supplier country currency which gave them the advantage of any reduction in the value of the supplier country's currency as the Deutschmark and the yen became stronger and stronger over the years. A common currency with common interest rates as in the case of the euro in the EU reduces the necessity of doing this between member countries.

Inflation rates

When price conditions are unstable in the supply market and longer term contracts are envisaged, it is necessary to insure against increases in production/purchasing and labour costs. Providing an adjustment of the contract price as shown in the Rolls Royce aero engine example below can do this:

151

The following is the formula agreed by Rolls Royce and Lockheed for the supply of RB211 engines specially designed for the Tristar passenger aircraft:

$$P_s = P_o \left[\left(0.10 + 0.55 \frac{L}{L_o} + 0.35 \frac{M}{M_o} \right) - 0.06121 \right]$$

All the formula means is that the final contract price P_s would be made up of:

- 10 per cent of the original contract price P_o;
- 55 per cent of a factor L/L_o which allows for increases in labour costs after the signing of the contract;
- 35 per cent of a factor M/M_o which allows for increases in labour costs after the signing of the contract minus just over 6 per cent so that Rolls Royce would not get the benefit of inflation in their profit margin.

Figures for labour (L) and materials (M) come from national cost indices.

However good a contract price adjustment clause, it will not be sufficient protection if the starting price is too low. Rolls Royce aero engine division nearly did not survive because of three factors that made nonsense of its calculations:

1   Lockheed failed to sell as many aircraft as it had hoped and Rolls Royce had calculated to recover its development costs over the projected sales of the aircraft.
2   Carbon fibre fan blades, which were used to give the engine a technical edge over competitors, failed to stand up to requirements in practice. More costly and heavier material was incorporated which gave a poorer power to weight ratio and exposed the company to performance penalties.
3   Rolls Royce engineers failed to solve the problems of an entirely new engine design in the almost impossibly short time agreed in the contract. They failed to meet delivery commitments and further exposed the company to liquidated damages (McCall and Warrington, 1989).

If the quoted price is not always the contract price, neither is the contract price necessarily the price of settlement. Not every product is sold on extended terms when a price adjustment clause, as in the case above, may be included. On goods sold on shorter terms, a limit – say 30 days – is sometimes put on the validity of an offer, which means the price offered may legitimately be adjusted after that time. This may be an important consideration when costs are volatile.

FINANCE-RELATED COSTS

Costs of finance, credit and interest have also to be recouped in the final price. For consumer goods sold on short-term credit and insured through normal commercial processes, the price has to recover not only the cost of insurance but preferably also the interest that could have been earned at commercial rates had the money not been used for export shipment. For longer-term contracts the cost of finance is tied to obtaining insurance for extending of credit to customers and varies according to the type of credit. Countries have their own institutions for providing this insurance through their banking systems and/or special organizations set up for the purpose. These include Compagnie Française d'Assurance pour le Commerce Extérieur (COFACE) in France, Euler Hermes Kreditversicherungs-AG (HERMES) in Germany, Export-Import Bank of the United States (EX-IM Bank) in the US and the Export Credits Guarantee Department (ECGD) in the UK (although the latter does not provide short-term cover).

In the US and the UK, the administration of credit insurance is undertaken by civil servants, either as a government agency in the US or as a department within the Ministry of Trade and Industry in the UK. Both provide credit insurance against non-payment by foreign buyers on contracts which extend credit for three to five years to the customer. These organizations aim to supplement, not to compete with, private capital. They assume risks that private finance cannot accept as they are self-financing. The objective is to boost economies by encouraging trade with developing countries and others previously operating in a command economy. The contracts involved are normally for substantial amounts. The larger the contract the longer the period for which credit is normally extended. These organizations have close relationships with banks which often make funds available only when they know credit insurance will be forthcoming.

In France and Germany, companies specializing in credit insurance look after the state interest. COFACE and HERMES differ from the US and British organizations in that they operate in addition throughout the world with country offices. They have forged affiliations with finance firms through which they work, even in the US and Britain. They have strategic alliances with banks, Business-to-Business service providers and Chambers of Commerce. Both claim to be world leaders in their sphere and supply other services such as factoring to provide their customers with appropriate solutions to their needs. They claim that they have adjusted to the needs of globalization, the implication being that the insurers insuring the credit risk for exports from the home country only have not. What the four organizations have in common in their relationship with exporters is the percentage that must be added to the exporter's price to be tendered which represents their fee for managing the credit risk. They also dictate the terms under which interest is charged and the way in which repayments are scheduled.

MANAGERIAL DECISION FACTORS

Marketers are largely in control of their own destinies despite the vagaries of commercial and environmental factors. Pricing is no exception. There are various approaches at their disposal for making pricing decisions, some of which are more appropriate than others in an international context. The marketing decision-maker has an important role to play.

Cost-based pricing

Usually cost-based pricing is taken to mean starting to price from known fixed costs and adding all variable costs as well as the costs of getting the goods to the customer. This is

referred to as 'parallel imports'. Parallel exporters may then undermine formal agreements and companies will seek to mitigate the harm by, for example, requiring their distributors in the relevant countries not to respond to foreign approaches, or by insisting that any breach of trade mark registration is pursued through the courts. A trade mark cannot be used in the EU to prevent parallel imports if associated with a restrictive agreement. The same is true for patents and copyright. (See Chapter 5: International product development for details of patents and copyright issues).

Transfer pricing

A special case of differential pricing is the company that is its own customer. A sizeable pro-portion (30–40 per cent) of export shipments in the developed countries takes place between company affiliates. A large international company may find it advantageous in terms of over-all company profits to charge internally a price different from one it charges customers out-side the firm. It may transfer at manufacturing cost, minimizing the profit of the producing company, or at 'cost-plus' to reach an equitable profit between the producing company and the affiliate responsible for international operations. Very often the variations are calculated to pay the minimum of tax, in an overall company context, in a country where the rate is low. Customs authorities in the receiving country and, sometimes, revenue authorities in the dispatching country guard against avoidance of duty or tax through low transfer prices.

Standardized pricing

Discriminatory pricing in different national markets invites entrepreneurs to look for parallel export opportunities. 'Grey' markets emerge and suppliers fight to contain them. But, even if the management of a company claims to sell at the same price to all markets – and the idea is seductive from the view of savings in time and money – in practice they do not sell at the same price in these markets.

If value added tax and sales tax levels differ, if wholesale and retail margins vary, if exchange rates are volatile, if countries have dissimilar inflation rates or have different perceptions of value, the impossibility of eliminating parallel imports is evident. Where subsidiaries have the authority to determine price, and have adapted to the practices of the country they are established in, normally the standardization of prices cannot be considered in the majority of markets. Industrial markets are more suited to standardization than consumer products, although often consumer products considered essential are good candi-dates for the standardized approach. It is a cost-based approach that does not take account of the particular nature of the markets such as the preferences of potential buyers, the struc-ture of the industries as well as the tariffs and taxes levied.

Nevertheless, there is pressure on consumer goods manufacturers to standardize prices in the face of the growing number of centrally purchasing retailers and parallel imports. The dilemma these manufacturers have to confront is the pressure to standardize on the one hand, and the apparent attention to country-specific prices to maximize the local company's profits on the other which is reinforced by these companies having adapted to host country norms.

Demand-based pricing

Demand varies with price for offerings that have a high price elasticity of demand. If an estimated volume of sales based on marketing research for different levels of price has been made with details of variable costs, it is possible to calculate the combination of price and volume that will yield the greatest profit contribution. Of course, a company must recover variable *and* fixed costs in the long run if it is to stay in business. But this has no logical bearing on price decisions *after* a company has assumed fixed cost burdens which are shown below in Table 6.3 for a national target market.

In Table 6.3, it is assumed there are variable manufacturing costs of €300 per unit and variable marketing costs (including freight and handling charges) of €200 per unit. There is also a distributor's margin calculated at 40 per cent of the unit selling price and entry costs (tariffs, etc.) equal to 10 per cent of the unit selling price. Although these assumptions greatly simplify the costing job, they serve to indicate the nature of costing for an export sale.

Given these cost assumptions and the projected sales at the different price levels shown, the price that returns the highest profit contribution is €1,500. This may not be the optimum price for the entire planning period envisaged. Another price, or a sequence of prices, may promise the highest contribution because of changes in labour and materials costs, change in consumer preference induced perhaps by an innovative competing model, changes in tariffs and the use of the channels of distribution.

Such a price might well be dropped for another combination of price and volume depending on the objectives set, e.g. a stable pricing policy, a given return on investment or a target market share. It may also be affected by the strategy employed to achieve an objective such as a skimming price or a penetration price. A penetration price strategy implies a future advantage like a growing market in which the benefits of the experience curve apply where costs could drop by between 20 and 30 per cent every time sales double. It subsumes the learning curve, which is the reduction in costs as operatives become more skilled and faster at a particular operation.

There is much written about the Japanese use of the experience curve which in reality is largely coincidental. Generally, Japanese pricing strategies emphasize size and long term vision. Initial prices are set at a level identified as good value by the market and sufficiently low to preclude competition entry. As market share builds up and volume increases, the

Table 6.3 *Demand-based pricing example*

Retail price in euros (€)	950	1,100	1,250	1,500	1,750
Unit sales	500	475	450	250	100
Sales revenue	475,000	522,500	562,500	375,000	175,000
Total variable costs	487,500	498,750	506,250	312,500	137,500
Contribution	(12,500)	23,750	56,250	62,500	37,500

typical cost savings of 20–30 per cent every time volume doubles are not passed on in full to the consumer, and considerable profits are created in the later stages of the PLC. This strategy is facilitated by an ability to carry the delayed profitability due to the advantage inherent in the concentration of overseas trade in the hands of a few conglomerate companies associated with finance houses, banks and shipping and insurance companies (McCall and Warrington, 1989).

The contribution approach may be useful for an overseas manufacturing subsidiary seeking to maximize its own performance so that it does not have to cope with varying exchange rates as does the exporting company. Widely varying rates can invalidate data which, under these conditions, can be considered a snapshot in time not applicable at any other time. In these circumstances the international marketer has to seek another way.

GLOBALIZATION PRICING

The move to globalization has been progressive but, so far, has failed to be matched by global competition. As a result, consumers have not had the benefit that price competition on a global scale is expected to deliver. Neither the WTO, nor its predecessor the General Agreement on Tariffs and Trade (GATT), has come close to addressing the problem.

EUROPEAN UNION PRICING

One of the acknowledged successes of the EU has been its competition law, which has sought by the Articles, particularly 85 and 86, of the Treaty of Rome and the regulations made under them to facilitate the free circulation of goods within its member countries. An interpretation of the intention of the founding fathers is applied to each issue to come before the European Commission and the cases referred to the European Court of Justice by it and domestic courts. These maintain a prohibition on any agreement which might restrict this 'free circulation of goods'. Exceptions are made where there is little likelihood that an agreement will restrict trade or where small companies are concerned. Small companies can get together to be more competitive and agree on prices to be charged where large companies would be in breach of the law. The EU is still far from solving all its competition problems but it has achieved a great deal.

European Union and intellectual property rights

It has been seen that maintaining prices in a market by placing import restrictions based on intellectual property rights is not permitted in the EU (see Chapter 5: International product development). The principle of parallel imports is well and truly entrenched as entrepreneurial parallel exporters identify low-cost countries for certain products and are able to buy them there and re-sell in countries where the prices are higher. This tends to drive prices down and presents organizations whose competitiveness is tied up with research and development, such as pharmaceutical and IT companies, with a problem of generating the profits needed to keep ahead.

BOX 6.3 PRICE RIGGING IN BRITAIN?

In a perfectly free market, the same product, net of transaction costs, will sell everywhere for the same price. If this is so, why should the British consumer pay much more in GB pounds for a lap-top computer or a compact disc or a dishwasher than does the American consumer in US dollars? Why should he, or she, pay over the odds for a British or continental motor car compared to other European consumers?

While, sometimes, consumption taxes, shipping costs and duties can explain such a difference, this represents only a small part of the difference. Britain has much weaker anti-trust laws than the US and a stronger tradition of price maintenance which other European and American manufacturers are pleased to accept. Yet they scream blue murder when price maintenance by foreign distribution systems has the effect of keeping out their products, for example, in Japan.

Entrepreneurial companies have tried to take advantage of buying items like jeans at the US wholesale price and shipping them to a discount warehouse in Britain. The US manufacturers have refused to sell to them. Retail groups such as Tesco were rebuffed by the manufacturers when they tried to discount Calvin Klein and Nike brands. The British Office of Fair Trading (OFT) sided with the manufacturers in such situations. Even if they were to buy retail in the US for sale into a higher-priced foreign market, they could be infringing someone's exclusive distribution rights or the manufacturer's trade mark or copyright (Kuttner, 1998).

The globalization of price competition is lagging behind the globalization of commerce. Price-rigging is a form of non-tariff barrier. The WTO is not handling the problem at all effectively. The Single European Market (SEM) still displays surprising differences although these are not so marked within the Eurozone countries that have adopted the euro. In the EU competition law has more power than national laws of the member countries in that it is not possible to call on patents, trade marks and copyright if these are associated with restrictive agreements. However, that position has been undermined by a decision of the European Court which upheld the right of an Austrian eyeglass manufacturer to sell its products more cheaply outside the EU, and to take legal action against anyone who tried to re-import the discounted eyeglasses for resale within the EU. Nevertheless, the competition law is relentlessly being applied despite setbacks in the courts. It is significant that in a recent business section of a Scottish Sunday newspaper, new Rover 75 cars were advertised at prices below some second-hand ones.

European Union and industry dominance

There is nothing in EU law against achieving a dominant position in an industry, but its abuse is prohibited and abuse can be interpreted as an attempt to expand from an already powerful base. This can also be seen in predatory pricing where prices are set at levels below cost to punish a competitor. A non-dominant company may sell at a loss, but a dominant company may find that to do so infringes Article 86 of the Treaty of Rome. Akzo, a

Netherlands based company which merged with the Swedish company, Nobel, was fined heavily by the European Court for forcing a much smaller new company out of the market for the production of benzoyl peroxide. Akzo claimed that its prices could not be predatory since they were above average variable cost, but the court rejected any cost-based rule as a test for predation and based its findings on predatory intent. Another classic case is that of the Swedish/Swiss firm, Tetra Pak, which was fined 75m European Currency Units (ECUs = euros (€)) for using cross-subsidies, i.e. profits from another part of the organization, to force a competing company out of the business of making cartons for containing liquids (OJEC, 1992).

Euro and its effect on pricing

With the introduction of the euro in parallel with local currencies in 1999 and the abolition of national currencies among the participating states in 2001, the founding member countries became part of what is called the Eurozone. They have the advantage of the removal of the transaction costs involved in changing one currency into another when doing business with each other. Apart from not having that advantage, EU companies in countries outside the 'inner core' countries lose out by being exposed to losses brought about by exchange rate variations. However, this exposure is only to the divergence limit of any band in any new exchange rate mechanism in which they may be required to participate. Countries remaining outside the new exchange rate mechanism have the added disadvantage of having to hedge if they want to cover exchange risk on transactions with organizations in the inner core countries. The additional costs involved result in the erosion of the profit margin. Also, with currency risks gone in the EU countries within the Eurozone, there is no need to operate in as many countries as before. This is leading to the concentration of production in European locations with lower tax and labour costs, which is placing the firms in the countries outside the inner core at a further disadvantage in terms of the costs that have to be recovered in the price.

The introduction of the euro has already increased the transparency of price and highlights pricing disparities, resulting in companies grabbing markets from less competitive rivals. The consequent squeeze on margins is beginning to force companies to slash prices and trim supplier costs to the benefit of consumers. How one Japanese company has sought to adjust to the new currency is illustrated in Box 6.4.

NEGOTIATED PRICE

Despite the different approaches to setting price, each transaction based on price has the possibility of being negotiated. Galbraith (1975) underlined the idea of the central importance of negotiation between organizations. Wroe Alderson, the doyen of marketing writers, saw the fully negotiated transaction as the prototype of all exchange transactions (Alderson, 1971). He viewed it as representing a matching of segments of supply and demand after canvassing all the other factors which might affect the decision on either side. It does not mean that a contract that is more of a routine nature such as the re-ordering of consumables, is not subject to negotiation. On the contrary, many routine transactions contain an element of negotiation. It lies at the heart of marketing as an economic process.

BOX 6.4 HOW A JAPANESE COMPANY ADJUSTED TO THE EURO

Matsushita, the Japanese electronics giant with manufacturing facilities in a number of EU countries, anticipated the introduction of the euro. Matsushita embraced euros throughout its operations for internal use and for dealing with intermediaries in the supply chain. All cash flow from its operations in the Eurozone was centrally managed in euros, even to the extent of making payment for goods supplied by the Japanese parent in euros. When dual pricing was introduced in 1999, it was ready with sales catalogues for its industrial products giving prices in euros as well as in the local currencies for the eleven member countries who originally adopted the single currency. Before this, its prices across Europe had varied by as much as 15 per cent, whereas with the new system the variation was about 5 per cent.

Consumer electronics, which constituted nearly 70 per cent of Matsushita's output, were sold under brand names like Panasonic, which were bought by dealers or large European retail chains such as Kingfisher. At first there was a great reluctance to effect payment in euros among distributors of consumer products and, in the case of industrial products the idea of being invoiced and making payment in euros was taken up even more slowly. The company's years of preparation paid off as gradually the customers accepted the new mode of operation. It has become a widely accepted practice not only in the Eurozone area but also among firms operating in other European countries including the UK, Sweden and Denmark.

Matsushita's success was based on careful study over a period of years of the differences between the European countries in which it does business. Before harmonizing prices, it was necessary to look at the various dealers, importers and chain stores in each country and to address the ingrained habits of the company's local subsidiaries. Under the previous system, an influential customer in one country might conceivably pay more for immediate delivery. Or the local subsidiary might have ordered more than it could sell and, simultaneously, maintain a reasonable cash flow. It would then cut the price to get rid of excess stocks to ease the problem.

Under the new system many of these problems were corrected. The job of ordering products from the group's factories was passed to the European head office which enabled the number of spare parts centres to be reduced from twenty-eight to two. Large parts of internal services, logistics and IT were centralized, too. The question of centrally determined prices was a difficult one and caused some internal resistance due to the loss of autonomy of local staff.

The company would have preferred further rationalization but this presented problems. A traditional Japanese firm, Matsushita was reluctant to put employees out of work and had to balance its ability to create more jobs against putting a limit on the amount of rationalization it could achieve. Re-organization of pricing approaches has a human dimension which involves keeping the work force on side.

(Jackson, 1999)

Interaction and negotiation

Buyer perceptions of value relate to items like product quality, delivery and service support. Sometimes buyers find it difficult to know how the seller might lower costs or improve performance to meet their needs. Faced with these difficulties the buyer infers value from signalling criteria such as company reputation and professionalism of the seller's staff (Porter, 1985). These criteria are developed over a range of episodes in an interacting relationship. The longer a relationship lasts, the more the interacting parties know about each other. Interactions are coloured by what has gone before. If an earlier episode was considered unsatisfactory, then the atmosphere will not be so favourable for an outcome satisfactory to both parties. If the relationship is good, then a solution is likely to be found through mutually established processes. The International Marketing and Purchasing (IMP) Group examined the interaction across national boundaries between buyers and sellers in five different countries. It found that the concept of target market and marketing mix, which assumes a pliant buyer exposed to various stimuli that will elicit the desired response, is not the focus in international business (Ford, 1990). The buyer is likely to have as much influence on outcomes as the seller.

With the move from international organizations through multinational and global organizations to transnational organizations (Bartlett and Ghoshal, 1989), there is a manifold increase in the number of interactions across borders, compounded by the growth of foreign acquisitions, mergers and alliances. The perspective is very much one in which the development of relationships with other organizations is a necessary condition for the harnessing of resources across organizations. Networks emerge. These are value-adding systems within which suppliers, business partners, allies and customers work together to co-produce value. Their underlying role is to create an ever-improving fit between competencies and customers (Normann and Ramirez, 1993). Negotiation is a key activity in making these arrangements work.

Negotiation framework

Wise sellers will have established their costs and set a minimum price below which they will not go, although that price may well be determined by circumstances such as long-term aspirations, contractual risk, contingency amounts and existing relationship if any. Buyers for their part will have taken account of their own cost structures and other factors like how badly they need the product and services. Neither knows exactly what is in the other's mind. Hence the saying that the range within which the parties will settle is 'the buyer's estimate of the seller's minimum and the seller's estimate of the buyer's maximum', that is, where these estimates overlap. Cultural differences have been observed. A Swede or Israeli, coming from consensual cultures, will expect the offer to be close to the final price. Brazilians, with a history of social conflict, have shown a tendency to inflate prices reflected in their readiness to make concessions on price. The dilemma confronting sellers is to pitch the offer at a level that takes these factors into account but does not shut out the business. The nub of the negotiation process is the information the parties can extract from each other and use for mutual influence which can change the parties' perceptions of what the other will pay or receive and is the strategic function of the face-to-face situation.

CULTURE AND NEGOTIATION SKILLS

In the face-to-face situation, the first offer of the seller will already be known from a quotation or a proposed contract for signature. Negotiations usually open with an attempt by the participants to find the negotiation range. The offers in the first instance are what the parties see as their best outcomes. The language, certainly for Europeans and Americans, will be robust and uncompromising. The negotiators seek to identify if there is a gap between what the other says and is prepared to do. If the other's language is strong and simple, there is a presumption that the commitment is considerable. The object of the exchange is to test this commitment.

Such confrontational means of establishing the negotiation range sit uncomfortably in an East Asian setting. Confrontation threatens face and harmony, and is to be avoided. Similarly, the Latin American or Arab buyer often bases his buying decision on the personality of the salesman and not on the characteristics and benefits of the product. It is the salesman's ability to strike chords in him that makes the buyer decide, and confrontation is not the relationship that aids this decision. When people involved in negotiation take up their positions strongly and reinforce them with unyielding repetitions of their basic position or variations on the same theme, the situation can rapidly deteriorate into what has been called 'attack/defend spirals'. It can be difficult to escape from such situations although agreement is still possible.

Playing the strong negotiator can be overdone. If one of the parties is compelled to withdraw from a position of extreme firmness in the face of an opponent's pressure, the loss of image will be carried over to other issues and subsequent negotiations. A buyer or seller has to strike a balance between firmness and credibility. To escape the 'attack/defend spiral' one of the parties has to signal a willingness to move by a signal encapsulated in the phrase 'to convey without commitment,' e.g. 'If you were prepared to accept a later delivery, we might consider a reduction in price.' A suitable reply might be 'We might consider such a step should you find it possible to . . . .' The possibility of agreement has been created without the parties committing themselves. When one of the parties is of a different culture, the time taken is likely to be longer and cues are likely to be more specific: 'This is what we did in the case of . . . .'

When movement has been initiated, the negotiators can test their opposers' assumptions in relation to the issues on which they appear adamant. The negotiation then seeks progressively to sort out these issues on which the parties are obdurate and those on which they are ready to concede, provided there is an equivalent concession in the overall package eventually agreed. They have entered the stage where they are able to identify common ground. It may not be possible to find concessions of equal worth on individual issues. It is more likely that equitability is obtained by relating the issues to the overall agreement. For this reason, negotiators often reserve their positions until they know the extent of all the issues. In Western Europe and the US in particular, the more precisely a position is defined, the stronger is the definer's commitment likely to be. If an Arab speaks like a person from one of these parts of the world, he is either attuned to Western culture or his commitment is not great. His language, couched as it is on the beautiful style of the Koran, is not perfectly suited to the demands of modern commerce, which leads him to exaggerate

163

and elaborate on it to create meaning. The Chinese do not seek to identify where common ground exists by confrontational means. Rather, to avoid possible loss of face, they set about accumulating information by an apparently endless string of questions to build up a picture of what they feel will be acceptable to both parties. If one party is perceived to be making unfair demands on the other, then the latter may appeal to some form of legitimate power or moral rules related to social norms of equity, need, opportunity or historical precedent. Such appeals are emotional and may be successful if the parties share a culture where people express their positions through appeals to the emotions, as in most Latin American and African countries. A Mexican may find it hard to convince someone from a Germanic or Anglo-Saxon culture whose style of persuasion is more influenced by hard facts or expert opinion.

The process of identifying common ground isolates those areas where there is no common ground and there is a need for conflict to be resolved. The parties proceed to 'trade off', that is, to advance to a bargaining process to bring the sides closer together. A negotiator from a Muslim country might insist on taking disputes to a local court but may be less resistant than Western counterparts on issues of warranty. Some elements traded off are worth more than, or less than, any figure set by an accounting convention. If a buyer in Germany urgently requires a part costing €5,000 for a process producing a single product and a week's delay costs €100,000, he/she might feel justified in paying much more than the €5,000 for immediate delivery. A seller might be able to capitalize on such a possibility, but that could be at the cost of any long-term relationship that had been built up.

There are two forces at work on sellers and buyers. One is the esteem motivation that drives them to get the best possible bargain and provide satisfaction for a job well done. The other is the security motivation to settle when a reasonable bargain is identified, rather than seek a more advantageous outcome at the possible risk of no agreement. When a proposed solution is acceptable, a Western negotiator may look his counterpart in the eye as he speaks and treat the statement with a corresponding seriousness supported by non-verbal language like putting papers in order. The counterpart may reassure himself by summarizing what the other has said to ascertain he has a correct understanding of what has been said. In Eastern cultures signals may not be so apparent. One authority has reported that Chinese negotiators never telegraph their next move through a show of emotions. The level of friendliness, or impersonality, remains the same whether negotiations are approaching agreement or failure. Consequently, there seems to be an element of surprise in negotiating with the Chinese (Pye, 1982).

The final stage is to make the agreement. The possibility of agreement is present. Many negotiators find that summarizing the steps through which they have proceeded is a convincing way of getting agreement. It is often achieved by a final concession. This has to be large enough not to be considered trivial, but small enough to convince an opponent that that there are no more concessions to be had. The opponent may also want something in return. An agreement is about to be made. In the process, the participants will have, knowingly or not, tried to resolve the negotiator's eternal dilemma of whether to go for the best possible deal or settle for an acceptable, but not optimal, outcome. East Asians have less feeling for the drama of agreement than Europeans and Americans, viewing it as the beginning of a relationship rather than the culmination of a commercial process.

'Memorandum of agreement' is a term commonly used for the recorded bargain. A simplified form summarizes what has been agreed under heads of agreement. It emphasizes intent rather than the language of lawyers and makes an eventual contract less threatening for Chinese negotiators used to a family system which has no need of formal legal instruments.

PRICING AND COMMUNICATION TECHNOLOGY

The Internet is a natural medium for international buying and selling. People can bid at electronic auctions and prices in many sales transactions may be negotiated over it often in association with a face-to-face element. An interesting innovation, driven by the world wide web, namely the 'name your own price' system, has turned commercial logic on its head. It proves that, for the right price, people will buy something without knowing the brand or, in the case of airline tickets, without knowing when the flight takes off. In the world of priceline.com, the buyer writes the price tag. There is a competing group of sellers whose prices are matched against it by the company. NexTag.com is a company that has come up with an even better way of setting prices. It appears to be another on-line auction house, albeit a large one featuring more than 150,000 items, but the firm does not let buyers compete by bidding the prices up. It offers the opposite; multiple sellers bid prices down to win a buyer's business. The attraction for sellers is that they can discount products without having to lower prices at their own outlets. NexTag.com also provides sellers with free software to automate their responses to bids, and capture data about potential buyers, which is potentially more enticing. However, if the idea catches on with buyers, the sellers may change their minds. The medium is still in a state of flux.

CONCLUSION

It is clear that pricing in an international context is very different from that in the home market. Developments in the world economy, like globalization, and in the regions, like the EMU in the EU, mean that the world is becoming a more competitive place to work in, which pricing policies and practices have to consider. The international marketer may find one approach to pricing in the competitive economy more appropriate than another, but that does not necessarily invalidate any of these alternative approaches. A cost-based price can be modified to take account of what competitors are charging although a demand-based price is more likely to provide a useful starting point where there is a high price elasticity of demand. Such is the rate of technological innovation that what were luxury products yesterday can be commodities tomorrow and move from being priced at the top end of the pricing spectrum to the point where volume sales at lower prices are the order of the day. Such, too, are the far reaching changes like competence-based strategies that drive down costs and create quality differentiation through strategic alliances in which price agreement is a key element in competitiveness. Irrespective of the approach taken, negotiation is a permanent feature of the pricing scene that takes place across national borders and needs to be supported by cross-cultural skills.

REVIEW QUESTIONS

6.1 Read the short narrative below and answer the questions posed:

> MacBeth's produce single malt Scotch whisky sold under the brand name of
> STEADY. With a fall in demand for brown spirit in relation to white spirit like
> vodka and white rum, MacBeth's found it had laid down too much stock as did
> other whisky producers. To take up this excess stock, management decided to
> market in (among others) Venezuela a secondary brand, GLEN RIVER, which
> would be an immature whisky aimed at the price conscious 'mixer' market for
> mixing with soft drinks like lemonade and cola. It would be used to create cash
> flows to support further the premium brand STEADY. The market for the
> secondary brand was different from that of the premium brand and was sold
> through different distributors because of the distinct segment it served.

 a   What should MacBeth's do if all quotations and invoices are made in GB pounds
     in relation to first, STEADY and second, GLEN RIVER, in the event of the British
     pound falling heavily against the Venezuelan bolivar and the pound rising to a
     considerable premium in relation to the bolivar?
 b   What should MacBeth's do if, due to Venezuela's adverse terms of trade with the
     UK, it became necessary to quote and be paid in US dollars, first for STEADY
     and second for GLEN RIVER in the event of the GB pound falling heavily against
     the US dollar and the GB pound rising to a considerable premium against the
     dollar?
 c   To what extent would the problem differ if the business was being conducted
     with an organization in another European country?

6.2 Read the narrative below and the additional data which follows, and answer the
    questions set out at the end:

> A US manufacturer of crushing and vegetable oil expressing plant has quoted a
> Hawaiian macadamia nut producer a DDP price US $1,050,000 against a six
> month delivery requirement for cracking and screening machinery. Payment is on
> the basis of 10 per cent with order, 80 per cent on delivery and 10 per cent after
> commissioning and performance proving tests. This information has been passed
> to the salesman of the British company by the Hawaiian buyer who has invited the
> salesman to submit a formal offer through his company. From discussions with an
> influential member of the macadamia nut producing firm, the salesman has elicited
> the information that its policy is to buy American unless a saving of at least 15 per
> cent can be made on the capital cost for at least equal performance. The British
> machinery has a reputation at least as good as its American competitor's.

> The British manufacturer knows his costs on present charges for labour, material
> and bought-out components to be £300,500, which includes recovery of

overheads. To this he normally adds one-third which is the margin the company considers a reasonable gross profit. To this figure is added a sum which represents the agent's commission of ½ per cent on the selling price, the total being the ex-works price. The company is prepared to negotiate from this price in certain circumstances, e.g. when the company particularly wishes to make a sale (as it does in this instance to gain a foothold in the Hawaiian market). It is company policy not to reduce its profit margin below 10 per cent on sales on entering new markets in view of the difficulty of raising margins on subsequent business. Other relevant data are:

Transport costs ex works to port of shipment	£1,800
Insurance and freight to Hilo, Hawaii	£14,200
US tariff on CIF value	12½%
Charges Hilo and freight costs to place of delivery	£2,200

a On the basis of the information given, would the British company achieve a margin of profit on sales in excess of the minimum 10 per cent policy stipulation if it decided on a quotation of US $882,000 (assume current rate of exchange is £1 = US $1.60)?

b If the buyer wishes to make payment over three years and to take delivery in eighteen rather than six months, what are the risks involved? What actions should the company take to reduce them?

REFERENCES

Alderson, W. (1971) 'The analytical framework for marketing' in Lawrence, R. J. and Thomas, M.J. (eds) *Modern marketing management*, London: Penguin.

Bartlett, C.A. and Ghoshal, S. (1989) *Managing across borders: the transnational solution*, Boston, Mass.: Harvard Business School Press.

Edwards, A.D.P. (1990) *The exporter's and importer's handbook on foreign currencies*, London: Macmillan Press.

Flynn, P.J. and Kynoch, W.S. (1983) 'Scotpack Developments Ltd (A)', Case Clearing House of Great Britain, Cranfield, England, No. 583–011–1.

Ford, D. (ed.) (1990) *Understanding business markets: interaction, relationships, networks*, London: Academic Press.

Galbraith, J.K. (1975) *Economics and the public purpose*, London: André Deutsch.

International Chamber of Commerce (2000) *Incoterms 2000*, Paris: ICC Publishing.

Jackson, T. (1999) 'How a Japanese company became single-minded', *Financial Times*, 18 May, p. 16.

Kuttner, R. (1998) 'Globalization's dirty little secret', *Business Week*, 7 September, p. 12.

McCall, J.B. and Warrington, M.B. (1989) *Marketing by agreement: a cross-cultural approach to business negotiations*, Chichester: John Wiley.

McCall, J.B., Warrington, M.B. and Drummond, G.S. (1990) 'The Russian contract' in *Instructor's manual to accompany marketing by agreement*, Eyemouth: McCall.

Normann, R. and Ramirez, R. (1993) 'From value chains to value constellations: developing interactive strategy', *Harvard Business Review*, July–August, pp. 58–67.

OJEC (1992) *Official Journal of the European Communities*, 18 March, Case No. L72/1–68.

Porter, M.E. (1985) *Competitive advantage: creating and sustaining superior performance*, New York: Free Press.

Pye, L.W. (1982) *Chinese commercial negotiating style*, New York: Oelgeschlager, Gunn and Hain.

Chapter 7

International promotion

INTRODUCTION

As part of international marketing it is necessary to make customers and potential customers aware of the product, or service, being marketed. Methods of developing this awareness are similar to those used for national marketing. However, within the international context, the methods used for national marketing necessarily become more complex, due to their being applied on a larger geographic scale and across different cultures. It is these issues that will be discussed in this chapter.

LEARNING OBJECTIVES

The objectives of this chapter are that you should be able to:
- demonstrate how international promotion operates;
- examine the contribution that elements of the promotional mix have within international promotion;
- identify appropriate promotional methods for different international markets;
- review the process of planning and implementation of an international promotion programme;
- establish how the effectiveness of an international promotion programme can be ascertained;
- investigate the role of international promotion within international marketing.

When you have completed the chapter you should be able to:
- articulate ways in which promotion supports international marketing;
- evaluate the role of advertising agencies in international promotion;
- apply appropriate promotion methods in different cultures;
- determine the role of marketing research in monitoring the effectiveness of international promotion;
- distinguish how international promotion is implemented for mass consumer and industrial products and services.

NATURE OF INTERNATIONAL PROMOTION

Traditionally, international promotion referred to promotion undertaken beyond a company's domestic market, using a common message to a definable international audience. It was accepted that, within the domestic market, a company's market penetration was greater than in the international arena, its local market was broader, its sales message was more detailed and its advertising was created to match actual or perceived local nuances (Hanger, 1995). 'International' usually meant using different advertising for each country covered so that a multinational corporation (MNC) such as Gillette might have different toothpaste campaigns appearing in Spain, Sweden or Hong Kong, although some of these markets might have a translated version of the same copy line. These campaigns were seen as attacking a 'local' market. With all but a few exceptions, international promotion was limited to products and services that were common across borders and were associated with the frequent traveller, e.g. cigarettes, up-market drinks, expensive luxury goods, hotels and airlines.

As MNCs have extended their product coverage globally, international promotion has evolved more global images and applications, with the same, or similar, messages being promoted worldwide. Such promotion has been dependent on the existence of an international medium that was, and still is, predominantly the published word, using English or English/American. But this has been changing. As the press sector has moved towards providing publications with cross-border coverage so, too, have broadcasting media, both television and radio, extended their services beyond national borders in Europe, the Middle East and Asia. Improved telecommunications with 24-hour computer links, e-mail, Internet and facsimile transmission have all contributed to making international operations more feasible.

The traditional international advertisers have been the Fast Moving Consumer Goods (FMCG) mass market producers, such as Coca-Cola, Heinz, Kodak, Nestlé and Unilever. Over time, as international trading has encompassed other diverse businesses, in particular the financial services, so promotion and media have had to expand across national borders to meet their demands. As more executives have become involved in contacts either within their own MNC, or with their clients in other countries, management strategy and marketing have become more internationalized. International promotion has been evolving to meet the associated demand. However, while promotion has become increasingly internationalized, it is not necessarily global promotion. Hanger (1995) distinguished between international and global promotion in the following way:

- 'Global' implies a universal way of thinking, of acting, a common product and a common message. In that respect, precisely the same promotion campaign is seldom, if ever, used worldwide. Rather, the same image may be used and it is likely to be adjusted to suit the expectations of the populations of the different countries targeted. On occasion, in place of global, some promotion campaigns can be considered to be multinational, covering groups of countries with the same campaign.
- 'Multinational' suggests a common promotion message being used in different countries with different implementation methods for each group of countries and with different languages to match customer demand. For example, Coca-Cola used the

same theme across the core European countries when it showed Coca-Cola consumption against background scenes associated with the major European cities including Barcelona, Paris and London, targeting the fashion-conscious European consumer.

- 'International' promotion implies covering markets beyond the domestic market. Traditionally, this form of promotion used a common message and, often, a single language. International marketing is expanding towards multinational marketing with the goal of achieving global marketing. However, few companies have the resources for global marketing, which places a constraint on reaching this goal. The terms 'global' and 'international' are converging and moving towards multinational geographic coverage, but implementation is dependent on resources. International promotion is used for promotion strategies that are implemented across groups of countries, many of which often coincide with economic groupings such as the EU and ASEAN (discussed in Chapter 1).

Definitions

It is common practice when discussing promotion to interchange the use of the terms 'promotion' and 'advertising'. Frequently, in common parlance 'advertising' is taken to be the general term embracing all forms of creating awareness; however, this is not strictly accurate and causes some confusion. The term 'promotion' is the general term, with advertising being one of the components of the promotion mix, itself bringing together the terms:

- advertising;
- sales promotion;
- personal selling;
- public relations (PR) (sometimes termed 'publicity').

For the purposes of this chapter, 'promotion' will be used to cover the overall activity of conveying awareness of a product, or service: 'advertising' will be part of that activity.

Advertising

Advertising is the most commonly referred to component of the promotion mix. It is the popular element of promotion and has been variously defined as being: 'paid-for communication, addressed to the public (or some of it) with the purpose of influencing the opinion or behaviour of those to whom it is addressed' (Advertising Standards Authority, 1979); and 'any paid form of non-personal presentation and promotion of ideas, goods or services by an individual sponsor' (Kotler *et al*. 1999: 793).

Most advertising is communicated through a range of media; the press, television, radio and cinema, categorized as 'above the line' advertising. 'Above the line' refers to media advertising which earns a commission for the advertising agency from the media, as opposed to 'below the line' promotion expenditure which does not. 'Below the line' promotion includes expenditure on sponsorship, sales promotion, exhibitions and competitions. Direct mail is usually classified as a 'below the line' medium.

Details of international media will be discussed on pp. 180–5.

Sales promotion

Sales promotions are the 'activities that stimulate consumer purchases and improve retailer or middlemen effectiveness and co-operation' (Cateora and Graham, 1999). They include money-off coupons, in-store demonstrations, samples, gifts, product tie-ins, contests and sponsorship of special events such as concerts, fairs and sport competitions. Sales promotions are short-term efforts directed to the consumer and/or retailer to achieve such specific objectives as:

1   consumer-product trial and/or immediate purchase;
2   consumer introduction to the store;
3   gaining retail point-of-purchase displays;
4   encouraging stores to stock the product;
5   supporting and augmenting advertising and personal sales efforts.

(Cateora and Graham, 1999)

Sales promotion can be powerful in supporting general advertising. It is targeted more towards potential consumers and takes place nearer to the actual purchase activity than general advertising. It provides the individual potential purchaser with an impetus to purchase a particular product, or service, rather than other competing products. For example, the purchase of a given number of cans of Heineken lager might give the purchaser a 'free' T-shirt, while the purchase of another brand would give no additional gift. The potential purchaser is encouraged to buy the brand with the potential for the free gift.

Many sales promotion practices are nationally orientated and cannot be readily used for international campaigns. National legislation, as well as cultural expectations, prevents some types of sales promotion. For example, free gifts like plastic gnomes are commonly placed in Kellogg's cereal packets in the UK, but they are not allowed in Norway and Sweden where promotion cannot be targeted towards children under 12 years of age. Some countries use promotional methods not seen in others, as is the case of the use of small aeroplanes to fly along beaches in Spain trailing flags with promotional messages encouraging the purchase of goods such as rice, vitamins and sun cream.

Sponsorship is another sales promotion method. A sponsor may support events, persons or groups of persons (teams) to gain public awareness and purchases of its product or service. The sponsor gains public confidence that encourages brand loyalty and purchase of the sponsor's product. Typically, sponsors have supported events such as the Olympic Games, the Football World Cup, and the World Expo. Major international sponsors include the MNCs Coca-Cola, IBM and Nike, as well as cigarette firms Benson & Hedges and Marlborough, and alcoholic drink producers Guinness (beer) and Glenlivet (whisky). Commonly, persons that are sponsored are successful sportsmen and women with whom the sponsor wishes to be associated. The golf or tennis player agrees to wear, or display, the sponsor's product in public (while playing the game) to encourage the public to purchase the product. Teams of persons that are sponsored include football and rugby teams, Formula 1 racing car teams and so on.

There can be difficulties with sponsorship agreements, especially sponsorship of individuals and teams. The high cost of endorsing contracts and the growing risk of being associated with drugs rows and other scandals involving sports stars have persuaded many sponsors, including Fila, the Italian sportswear group, Reebok and Nike of the US, to sponsor events rather than individuals. For example, although Fila is well known for sponsoring individual players such as Bjorn Borg, Boris Becker, Mark Philippoussis and Jelena Dokic, in 1999 Fila signed a US $12m contract to sponsor the Super 9 tournaments of the Association of Tennis Professionals (ATP) men's tennis tour for the next three years.

Personal selling

As with domestic marketing, personal selling has many roles within international marketing that centre around the intention of effecting a sale through the use of individual sales personnel. Personal selling can take various forms, ranging from the sales assistant in a shop to the sales engineer negotiating product design with the buyer of an industrial organization to the telephone customer service assistant offering special rates for calling family and friends numbers. At an international level, personal selling becomes more complex as it has to be sensitive to the culture and expectations of the potential customer. A sales approach used in one country may not be viable for another and *vice versa*. The resources to support the preferred approach will differ. In this way, in the US, it is common practice to sell books through a door-to-door sales force, but in other countries, it would be impractical and unacceptable to use such an approach. Books are also sold through conventional retail outlets, using shop assistants to encourage sales. However, with the advent of e-commerce Internet selling (through www.amazon.co.uk) increasingly books are sold direct to the consumer without the help of personal selling. For these reasons, despite the same product being sold, the personal selling role differs according to circumstance, the product or service being sold and the consumer targeted.

Traditionally, the international sales role involves the support of more intermediaries than would be expected for the domestic situation. As discussed in Chapter 8: International channels of distribution, international selling may use importing agents as well as other conventional intermediaries to reach the customer. All of these intermediaries require consideration within the personal selling role. The international organization planning its selling has to set up a sales operation that incorporates personal selling at all levels of the supply chain. It must consider the sales agents, the sales intermediaries and the selling activity within the retail outlet that displays the product, or service, to the potential consumer. Achieving a cohesive sales operation across international markets is challenging.

It should be appreciated that, with the advent of e-commerce selling through the Internet, traditional approaches are being questioned. It is likely that both the Internet and the traditional routes will become more integrated over time to the advantage of all concerned.

173

Public relations (PR) (sometimes termed publicity)

Public relations (PR) is a form of 'unpaid' promotion and is used alongside 'above the line' advertising in the media and 'below the line' promotion support. It involves achieving awareness for the product, or service, without undertaking conventional paid advertising. This awareness is gained by persuading persons to mention the product within a public arena for no direct payment, e.g. mentioning the name of the firm, or its products and services, within a television commentary or a magazine editorial. PR sets out to achieve a favourable image for the product, or service, being promoted primarily by using press and television coverage to create influential public awareness. However, the promoter has limited control over the message put forward by the editorial team, which acts independently, so messages can be favourable or unfavourable with considerable influence over the overall promotion campaign. At an international level, it is even more difficult to control the message being portrayed, which makes the achievement of a consistent and favourable PR image across all targeted markets demanding.

Alongside the internal staff, firms often use PR agencies to promote a favourable image for the corporate organization. Such agencies operate through personal networks using their communication skills to maintain good relations with influential persons within the media. Usually, they co-ordinate the provision of publicity material for the organization. They issue press releases covering news items that editors are encouraged to publicize within their media. At an international level, the challenge is increased with the larger number of persons involved. Commonly, country-specific PR agencies are used because their personnel have close ties to the local media. Care has to be taken that all concerned are working to spread the same corporate objective. An incident in one part of the world can have a devastating effect on the whole organization, e.g. the fire at Union Carbide Bhopal production plant in India, or the disposal of the Shell oilrig in the North Sea, which had adverse effects on corporate environmental image and worldwide sales. In these cases, a more concerted PR effort might have reduced the negative results of these situations.

IMPLEMENTATION OF PROMOTION STRATEGY

As can be seen from Table 7.1, large sums are spent on promotion, certainly in Europe, Japan and the US. The US has the highest level of spending at €100,342m, followed by Japan with €26,712m, Germany with €17,862m and the UK with €15,502m in 1998. The challenge in international promotion is to spend across the national boundaries in an effective manner. The critical issues of concern when implementing an international promotion programme relate to:

- setting the objective;
- methods of determining the resource implications;
- selection of persons to undertake the promotion;
- choosing the message;
- media selection;
- evaluating performance.

174

Table 7.1 Total display and classified advertising expenditure in Europe, Japan and the US at current prices and exchange rates (in €m)

Country	1992	1995	1998	1999	2000	2001
Austria	1,091	1,227	1,573	1,814	2,000	1,984
Belgium	1,029	1,252	1,630	1,864	1,893	1,894
Denmark	888	1,143	1,333	1,287	1,315	1,272
Finland	708	819	1,032	1,090	1,172	1,137
France	7,104	7,706	8,272	9,071	10,004	9,904
Germany	13,621	16,155	17,899	18,805	20,237	18,557
Greece	564	992	904	1,097	1,242	1,238
Ireland	365	458	636	726	1,015	1,072
Italy	5,565	4,361	5,873	6,930	8,070	7,823
Japan	22,673	29,617	26,442	35,557	42,415	36,417
Netherlands	2,045	2,508	3,361	3,570	3,887	3,708
Norway	652	813	1,025	1,048	1,242	1,282
Portugal	542	567	875	1,037	1,311	1,484
Spain	5,006	3,541	4,391	4,968	5,413	5,095
Sweden	1,350	1,398	1,743	1,785	2,043	1,660
Switzerland	1,717	2,265	2,210	2,574	2,865	2,760
UK	8,843	9,859	15,711	17,055	20,275	18,842
US	58,086	85,250	106,713	114,081	143,176	132,893

Source: adapted from Advertising Association (2002a), National data sources, NTC and Advertising Association (2002b), Table 25.1, p. 239

Note: Data have been manipulated so that they follow the common format developed by the Advertising Information Group Statistics Committee. These data are net of discounts. They include agency commission and press classified advertising expenditure but exclude production costs

Setting the objective

As for the domestic situation, the international promotion programme should start by defining the objectives and motives to be achieved through the programme. The objectives should be defined in measurable terms, if at all possible, so that progress during, and success after, the promotion can be determined. Quantifiable terms for the objectives might be to achieve specified sales, or a particular television or radio audience rating. Other objectives of a qualitative nature can also be set. Such objectives could include the creation of increased awareness of the firm's products, or services, or a more positive opinion of the corporation from the targeted audience, say shareholders.

The objectives of the promotion could include the achievement of:

- increased sales in terms of volume, or market share;
- improved morale and performance of own staff;

- improved communication among the intermediaries within the channels of distribution (value chain);
- launch and trial of a new product, or service.

Broadbent (1997) discusses how these objectives can be used to monitor the performance of a promotion programme within a domestic market. The same principles can be used for the international environment as shown below.

Increased sales in terms of volume, or market share

The objective should be to achieve a given volume of sales, or market share, within the targeted markets. Such a figure can relate to past sales such as those achieved in the last year in each country targeted. It should consider sales forecasts for the years covering the promotion programme, competitor activity and the influence of any other environmental changes likely to occur. Marketing research may be required, especially for new products, to ascertain the characteristics of targeted consumers in terms of demographics, geographic spread and product usage for sales forecasts.

Improved morale and performance of own staff

An added objective of the promotion programme may be to motivate staff within the organization. Staff feel pride in being associated with a high profile promotion campaign which leads to improvement in their own performance. For this reason, the promotion programme may have the objective of helping the sales teams operating in different countries to bond together to improve morale and corporate effort.

Improved communication among the channels of distribution

Similarly, the promotion programme could have the objective of encouraging closer linkage between intermediaries within the channels of distribution. Intermediaries can be encouraged to feel their importance within the value chain as part of the total effort in moving the goods and services to the ultimate consumer. It is the effectiveness of this linkage that is critical to the success of the international promotion programme.

Launch of a new product or service

The promotion programme can be used to create awareness of the introduction of a new product, or service, among potential customers and encourage them to try the product which, in turn, will be critical to its success. An example of this type of promotion is the fanfare that takes place worldwide some months prior to the launch of a new car or a PC model. The MNCs use promotion to alert potential customers to the forthcoming new product to ensure success of the venture.

Methods of determining promotion resource

Once the promotion planners have ascertained the objectives of the promotion task to be accomplished, they will appreciate the scale of the task to be undertaken. They can then consider the resource implications that, in turn, will influence the selection of the message and media for the campaign. In particular, the budget and time scale for the programme will have to be determined. Various indicators are used to ascertain resource requirements. The expenditure on previous promotion campaigns can be considered. If a budget close to that used in the past is proposed, the financial management is more likely to support the expenditure. A starting point is to take the previous year's budget and to increase this in line with forecast inflation for the period of the promotion programme. Approaches to determine the budget include the following, which are discussed below:

- objectives to be achieved;
- advertising to sales ratio;
- product life cycle.

Objectives to be achieved

The promotion budget should consider the objectives of the promotion and match the costs of achieving these objectives. Usually the promotion brief is prepared and sent to the advertising agencies for them to bid for the work. The favoured promotion programme is selected and matched with the expenditure level quoted by the advertising agency. However, the firm may not have the resources, or be prepared, to fund the proposed promotion programme fully, in which case the proposals will need to be scaled down according to what is acceptable to the client.

In practice, the level of expenditure is influenced by consideration of a number of issues and is usually derived through compromise whereby the various alternatives are considered. Advertising expenditure has to meet corporate budget expectations. There is considerable negotiation between all parties concerned in the determination of the final promotion budget with rational decisions put forward to support the case that is accepted. Marketing management is required to justify the budget which will be scrutinized by all concerned before it is finalized.

Advertising to sales ratio

Management can compare promotion expenditure with sales achieved and use that ratio to budget for the future. Thus, if a promotion budget of £500,000 gave a turnover of £10,000,000, this would give a ratio of 5:100 or 5 per cent. Assuming like conditions would occur in the future (which is far from certain), it can be recommended that if sales are predicted to be £15,000,000 then the promotion budget could justifiably be set at £750,000. However, this approach is simplistic and, in reality, can only act as a baseline guide to determining the budget.

Competitor expenditure on promotion should also be considered. Comparison with industry average expenditures on promotion (see Table 7.2) can be used to gauge competitor spending. These ratios relate to average expenditure for each product group within a particular year and only to expenditure within the UK, or the country in question, so they have to be used with care. They are indicative and not prescriptive: it is not

Table 7.2 UK advertising/sales expenditure and ratios, 2000

Product category	Consumers' expenditure £m	Nielsen media research expenditure £'000	Advertising/ sales ratio %
Cinema	748	162,313	21.7
Shampoos	284	53,497	18.8
Hair colourants	186	29,668	16.0
Internet Service Providers (ISPs)	1,016	120,447	11.9
Sauces (bottled)	135	12,395	9.2
Cold/flu decongestants	158	13,958	8.8
Vitamins and minerals	325	25,076	7.7
Dishwashing liquid	140	10,535	7.5
Razors and blades, disposable	164	12,177	7.4
Bleaches and lavatory cleaners	181	12,443	6.9
Soup (dry and fresh)	131	8,617	6.6
DVD players	95	6,105	6.4
Cereals and breakfast products	1,332	69,219	5.2
Cameras	283	13,580	4.8
Toys, games and hobbies	3,181	88,656	2.8
Dog food	808	19,687	2.4
Ice cream	1,178	21,973	1.9
Kitchen furniture	1,693	25,542	1.5
Greenhouses	37	552	1.5
Motor cars, purchase	54,800	597,097	1.1
Cheese	1,903	15,623	0.8
Rail travel	4,239	22,975	0.5
Condoms	89	466	0.5
Jeans	2,270	8,521	0.4
Menswear	5,632	12,953	0.2
Petrol, diesel and motor lubricants	16,811	7,697	0.1
Cigarettes	11,486	6,154	0.1

Source: adapted from Advertising Association (2002b), Tables 20.1 and 20.2, pp. 218–27

necessary to follow the pattern of expenditure followed by the industry, although it will give an indication of its expected level of expenditure. Frequently, industry brand leaders spend above the average promotion for the industry, suggesting that market leader budgets should exceed the industry average. Taking the example set above, the budget would be probably set above the £750,000, perhaps, at £900,000 (6 per cent level) or more.

Product life cycle (PLC)

Another consideration is the life cycle position of the products and services being promoted. Usually, promotion expenditure is higher when products are first introduced, then as the product is established in the market; expenditure (if not in absolute terms certainly in terms of percentage of sales) may be reduced. It is likely to be increased again in the decline stage of the product life cycle (PLC) to reverse the downward fall in sales. The problem is that seldom is it possible to establish exactly where the product fits within the PLC and, furthermore, the product may be at various stages of the life cycle in different countries. While monitoring the PLC progress is useful in determining promotion expenditure, it only provides an indicator of favoured expenditure and does not provide conclusive direction as to what should be spent.

Selection of persons to undertake the promotion

Another issue that has to be decided regarding the campaign is who will undertake the promotion. While the management within the firm has responsibility overall for the promotion strategy and the effectiveness of its implementation, either the firm's own staff or those of an advertising agency could undertake the promotion. It may be that a combination of both internal staff and agency staff is used. In the case of international promotion, the choice of who will undertake the promotion relates to the objectives of the campaign, the resources of the firm and the market in which the product, or service, is being promoted.

Where a mass consumer product, or service, is considered, as for a MNC, it is probable that an international advertising agency with a network of subsidiaries in the relevant countries is used. Typically, this advertising agency is the one that serves the corporation at its head office location; that is, if the firm were US-based, it would probably use the services of the advertising agency that undertakes the contract in the US. This agency may sub-contract some of the promotion to other independent agencies, but the major advertising agency will take responsibility for the overall contract. The process of selecting advertising agencies is discussed further on pp. 189–90.

In the case of an industrial product, or service, resource constraints may preclude the use of a major advertising agency. It is likely that the corporation would undertake the promotion campaign using its own internal staff. Alternatively, help may be sought from agents and intermediaries within the supply chain, including retailers operating within the different countries concerned. The approach used would be similar to that for industrial promotion targeted at the domestic market, except that it would extend to the international arena. Past experience will influence the choice of who would undertake the promotion. If the system used in the past worked well, it is likely to continue to be used; conversely, if there were problems encountered, changes may be required.

179

Choosing the message

Fundamental to promoting awareness of a product, or service, is determining the message to be portrayed. There is an iterative effect whereby the creative element of portraying the message in itself affects the selection of the media to promote the message. On the other hand, selection of the media does influence the creativity used for the promotion campaign.

Choosing the message to be conveyed relates to the objectives set out for the promotion. Usually, the client and the advertising agent determine the message for the campaign, often in conjunction with marketing research, and this, in turn, links into the media used for reaching the target audience.

Media selection

Various factors influence the selection of the media to convey the promotional message. These include the availability of media, what type of media exists, whether space or time can be bought on the media and whether the media can reach the targeted audience. Data are available to show advertising expenditure by type of media within a country as summa-

Table 7.3 Distribution of advertising expenditure by country, 2001

Country	Newspapers % of total	Magazines % of total	TV % of total	Radio % of total	Cinema % of total	Outdoor % of total
Austria	44.6	18.9	23.0	7.6	0.6	5.3
Belgium	25.9	14.9	41.2	9.9	1.3	6.8
Denmark	60.4	14.9	18.6	2.2	0.5	3.4
Finland	57.2	17.3	19.3	3.2	0.1	2.9
France	25.5	24.4	30.4	7.2	0.8	11.7
Germany	46.4	18.7	25.8	4.0	1.0	4.1
Greece	24.9	28.9	42.8	3.4	n/a	n/a
Ireland	66.4	1.7	19.1	5.4	0.6	6.8
Italy	24.9	16.6	50.7	4.5	0.8	2.5
Japan	28.5	9.9	44.7	4.7	n/a	12.2
Netherlands	45.8	24.2	19.7	6.4	0.3	3.6
Norway	56.0	14.3	22.9	4.1	0.6	2.1
Portugal	16.8	19.0	51.1	5.5	0.6	7.0
Spain	31.3	13.6	42.0	7.4	1.0	4.7
Sweden	54.1	14.6	22.9	3.4	0.5	4.5
Switzerland	52.0	18.1	12.0	3.2	1.0	13.7
US	35.2	12.1	39.0	12.6	n/a	1.1

Source: adapted from Advertising Association (2002a), National data sources, NTC and Advertising Association (2002b), Table 24.2, p. 240

Note: These data are net of discounts. They include agency commission and press classified advertising expenditure but exclude production costs

rized in Table 7.3 for 2001. These data show that countries have different patterns of promotion expenditure relating to differences in regulation of the media, especially in broadcasting, and to national culture, including literacy levels. Differences in media usage between countries can be ascertained from national advertising associations.

From Table 7.3, it can be seen that the major types of media are press (newspapers and magazines), television, radio, cinema and outdoor. There are differences between the relative contribution of media within each country. Usually, the press has the larger share of total promotional expenditure. Denmark, Finland, Norway, Switzerland the Netherlands, Sweden, Ireland, Germany, Austria, the UK, Greece, Canada, France, the US and Spain have higher shares of the total promotion expenditure spent on the press (newspapers and magazines) than on television (or any other media). Portugal, Italy, and Japan spend more on television than on press. It can be assumed that potential consumers in the former countries are more influenced by press advertising than those in the latter group of countries, reflecting the pattern of consumer audiences for these media.

When planning promotion expenditure, differences between countries in their pattern of promotion spending have to be considered. At first sight, from the above data, television expenditure would be favoured in Italy, Japan and Portugal, whilst press expenditure would be more likely to be used in the other countries. Complicating the issue, there are differences in the distribution of promotion expenditure between newspapers and magazines (see Table 7.3). Generally, radio, cinema and outdoor media have lower shares of total promotion expenditure than television and the press, but they can be used for supporting press and television expenditure. They may be appropriate for targeting specific groups of consumers, e.g. the cinema for young adults aged 16 to 25 years.

For an international promotion campaign covering the 17 countries shown in Table 7.3, while the same, or similar, media are available in most countries, usually it is desirable to vary the relative expenditure on each type of media. It is likely that it would be better to spend a higher share of the budget for Italy, Japan and Portugal on television than in Denmark, Finland, the Netherlands, Switzerland or Sweden where press expenditure takes a higher share. Other data should be considered before deciding on the precise level of expenditure, but the principle of different approaches across the countries remains. Detailed statistics on advertising expenditure are published for most countries and these can be used in the decision-making process. For example, *The European advertising and media yearbook* published by the Advertising Association (2002a) is a comprehensive source of European advertising and media data. It has country sections that include data on individual media sectors, advertising expenditure, top advertisers and agencies as well as summary tables to enable international comparisons to be made.

Generally, the media share of total advertising expenditure remains similar from year to year, with changes only occurring over the longer time period. As shown in Table 7.4, generally in the UK, press advertising has dominated (at 52 per cent of advertising expenditure in 2001), followed by television (at 25 per cent). Direct mail has taken about 14 per cent, outdoor media 5 per cent, radio 3 per cent and cinema 1 per cent. The Internet grew its share from 0.1 per cent in 1997 to 1 per cent in 2001, reflecting its increasing influence. Over time, changes occur, as with the move towards growth in promotion in the cinema. In the UK, cinema admissions have doubled since 1984, when the first multiplex opened. An estimated 1,300 cinema screens were added in the UK between 1992 and 2002, giving annual admissions of 185 million persons in 2002 compared to 139 million in 1997 (Rawsthorn, 1998). Similar trends can be discerned for all countries.

The availability of media to promote the same, or similar, message across country borders will influence the selection of the international promotion campaign. The attributes of the major media are discussed below:

- press;
- television;
- direct marketing;
- exhibitions;
- outdoor (out-of-home);
- Internet.

Press

Regarding the press, there are financial newspapers and journals with international coverage that can be used to target potential consumers in particular countries, or regions. They are

Table 7.4 *Total UK advertising expenditure at constant 1995 prices*

Media	1990 £m	1995 £m	2000 £m	2001 £m
Press	6,072	5,979	7,534	7,321
Television	2,747	3,136	4,069	3,566
Direct mail	1,157	1,135	1,794	1,916
Outdoor and transport	333	411	709	677
Radio	193	296	521	465
Cinema	46	69	112	141
Internet	n/a	n/a	135	142
Total	10,548	11,026	14,874	14,229
	% of total	% of total	% of total	% of total
Press	57.6	54.2	50.6	51.4
Television	26.0	28.4	27.4	25.1
Direct mail	11.0	10.3	12.1	13.5
Outdoor and transport	3.2	3.7	4.8	4.8
Radio	1.8	2.7	3.5	3.3
Cinema	0.4	0.7	0.8	1.0
Internet	n/a	n/a	0.8	0.9
Total	100.0	100.0	100.0	100.0

Source: adapted from Advertising Association (2002b), Tables 3.1.2 and 3.1.3, p. 32

published with regional editions, e.g. the *Financial Times* which, in addition to the London edition, is published together with a regional supplement in Frankfurt, Hong Kong, Los Angeles, Madrid, New York, Paris, Stockholm and Tokyo. Advertisements in the regional issues can be directed to the local reader. Other examples of the international financial press include *The Economist*, the *Far Eastern Economic Review*, *Eurobusiness*, *Business Week*, *Fortune* and the *Wall Street Journal*.

Among women's magazines, while most are still nationally orientated, some have been successfully launched in more than one country, especially across Europe, e.g. *Cosmopolitan*, *Vogue* (across Europe and taken to Russia in 1998), *Prima* and the more general *Hola/Hello*. These women's magazines can cover 12 or more countries, produced with the same fundamental editorial but translated and adapted to each country's population. They are useful for cross-country promotion. Gruner and Jahr, the publishers of *Prima*, claim the behaviour patterns of women across Europe are broadly similar, so more and more of the quality women's magazines are becoming transnational, offering the potential for advertisers to target similar market segments in different countries (Hanger, 1995).

Television

While terrestrial and cable television are predominantly national with regional services and associated advertising, some operators overlap national boundaries as in the situation in northern Continental Europe across Belgium, France, the Netherlands, Luxembourg and Switzerland. Using these, it is possible to direct advertising beyond national boundaries. Satellite television has long over-ridden restrictions of national boundaries and offers much scope for an international medium, outside national regulation. The wave of merger activity during the 1990s reduced national influence of television companies, further increasing the potential for promoting across borders, at least in Europe. Nevertheless, fundamentally, the options for television promotion remain national, if only because they use local language, but there is room for achieving degrees of cross-border coverage.

Direct marketing

Direct marketing is the umbrella term for all the different marketing techniques used to elicit direct responses from customers. It includes direct mail, telephone selling and mail order advertising. In the 1990s, the trend towards niche marketing encouraged companies to divert expenditure away from traditional mass marketing techniques to include direct marketing. Advances in IT helped them to become more accurate in identifying targets for campaigns, especially direct mail. The growth of consumer credit and the introduction of '0800' free-phone numbers made it easier for consumers to respond to direct marketing offers.

Direct marketing is usually a national discipline, although some firms such as American Express and the Reader's Digest Association operate international programmes, especially direct mail, to sell their products and services across the world. Firms print copies of the promotional brochures in different languages and mail them from countries with low-cost postal rates such as the Netherlands for Europe or Curaçao in the West Indies for other regions. However, as is often the case with international media, direct mail is subject to some odd and novel quirks. For example, while direct mail is commonplace in many

183

countries, in Chile it is virtually eliminated as an effective medium because the sender pays only part of the mailing fee; the letter carrier must collect additional postage for every item delivered. Obviously, advertisers cannot afford to alienate customers by forcing them to pay for unsolicited advertisements (Stewart-Allen, 1998).

On the other hand, in south-eastern Asian markets, where print media are scarce, direct mail is considered one of the most effective ways to reach those responsible for making industrial goods purchases, despite accurate mailing lists being a problem. Similarly, in Russia, the volume of direct mail increased substantially from 150,000 letters per month to over 500,000 per month in 1996 (*Business Europe*, 1996). While Russian direct mail remains relatively small in terms of European and US direct mail, the response rate in Russia is high at between 10 and 20 per cent, compared to only 3 to 4 per cent in the US. The appeal of direct mail for Russians relates to its novelty which may change as direct mailing becomes more common.

The varying responses to direct marketing, especially direct mail, require consideration to be effectively implemented within the international arena.

Exhibitions

Trade fairs, exhibitions and seminars provide a method of displaying goods and services to influencers in the sales chain. Organizations take an exhibition stand for their produce and encourage potential customers to visit the display. This method of promotion is especially applicable to industrial marketing, where trade fairs bring together competitors and potential customers to see the latest technological developments within a specified industrial sector. In this instance, the trade exhibit can be designed at the headquarters of the organization and then modified to suit the international market in which it is exhibited. Supporting sales literature requires translation and adaptation to match local culture and customer expectations.

Outdoor (out-of-home) advertising

In 1997, outdoor advertising was estimated to account for 6 per cent of total advertising expenditure worldwide, valued at US $18bn (£11bn) (Edgecliffe-Johnson, 1998). This was broken down into four smaller segments:

- billboards, which account for 50 per cent;
- transit, i.e. posters on buses, trains and trams, with 20 per cent;
- street furniture, i.e. bus shelters and news stands, with 5 per cent;
- ambient media such as messages on the back of till receipts, small posters in shop windows and one-off stunts such as PepsiCo's decision to paint Concorde blue have 25 per cent.

As might be expected, there are differences between countries, as shown by the street furniture segment having 40 per cent of outdoor advertising expenditure in Sweden, 19 per cent in the UK, 17 per cent in France and only 5 per cent in the US (Edgecliffe-Johnson, 1998). Nevertheless, this is a promotion medium with potential for expansion.

Internet

The Internet has become an increasingly influential interactive global promotion medium with web advertising offering inexpensive promotion that can be efficiently targeted at favoured market segments. Products and services can be promoted through websites, e.g. the Barbie doll website run by its owner, Mattel, provides the interested party with product details. The medium is self-regulated rather than controlled by legislation, although bodies such as the US Federal Trade Commission, International Chambers of Commerce, the Committee on Advertising Practice (UK) and the European Advertising Standards Alliance have been examining the procedures used, to reduce the possibility of abuse of power (Smith, 1998).

Evaluating performance

As with national promotion, it is necessary to evaluate potential and actual performance of promotion expenditure to make informed decisions for future promotion. This can be undertaken in various ways at different stages of the promotion exercise. It should be appreciated that the costs of reaching potential consumers vary according to the media used, as can be seen from a study conducted in 1998 in the UK. The costs of reaching 1,000 persons through the different media are shown in Table 7.5.

The media can be used in different ways, with varying levels of effectiveness depending on the objectives of the promotion programme. Most promotion programmes use more than one medium. Moreover, although the media may reach the potential consumer, it is not known how receptive the consumer might be to the message being portrayed. While television appears the more expensive medium to use with cost per 1,000 persons reached being about £1,800, much higher than the costs of using the radio or street promotion, television can also be the more effective media (although not necessarily). Consequently, promoters continue to spend heavily on advertising through television, despite the apparent attractions of other media, which frequently are used to supplement expenditure on television promotion.

The measures available to ascertain the effectiveness of international promotion expenditure are similar to those for national promotion (see Chapter 4: International Marketing Information Systems: marketing research for details). The methods of evaluating performance centre on achieving the objectives set out for the promotion (see pp. 175–6).

Table 7.5 Comparison of media costs, 1998

Media	Cost per 1,000 persons reached
Independent commercial television (ITV) viewers	£1,759
Newspaper readership	£1,141
Commercial radio listeners	£446
Persons on the street	£239

Source: adapted from Edgecliffe-Johnson (1998)

Effectiveness can be measured in terms of sales achieved, sales to promotion ratio, awareness levels, change in opinion and so on. As with other aspects of international promotion, it is the complexity of covering more than one country and the different national cultures that has to be overcome when evaluating promotion performance.

Within international markets research methods used in the US and the UK have been adapted to the specifics of the market concerned. For example, UK-based TNS and A.C. Nielsen track television audiences to monitor advertising effectiveness across the US and Europe. They have developed similar TV audience metering services across Europe, in India and beyond (*Research*, 1997). In 2001, Audience Television Research (ATR) took over the Broadcasters' Audience Research Board (BARB) contract in the UK, but TNS still has television panel operations across the world.

General approaches to implementation of international promotion

The development from international to global promotion as discussed by Hanger (1995) comprises six approaches that were identified by Mooij (1997) as shown below:

1   fully standardized: one product or brand, display and no values;
2   semi-standardized: one brand, one advertising format with standard execution;
3   one brand: one format using various methods of implementation;
4   one or different brand names: one advertising format with different executions;
5   one or different brand names: one platform with different executions;
6   multi-local: act global, think local endorsement.

Fully standardized: one product or brand, display and no values

One product, or brand, is sold across the national borders. The product is the message. The advertisement shows the product with appropriate supporting song or background music, using little or no copy or descriptive narrative. It is produced in one language. This strategy is used for umbrella, cross-border campaigns as core advertising which is often supplemented by local advertising and cannot differentiate the product by specific values, as it cannot associate with cultural differences in the countries it is targeting. Examples of this approach are those used for Levi's jeans, as well as for Bacardi and Martini alcoholic beverages.

Semi-standardized: one brand, one advertising format with standard execution

The advertising can use a combination of basic formats such as lifestyle, metaphor or entertainment. Visuals are central to the advertisement. In some countries the original language is used (often English); in others a voice-over is necessary. As not all countries are used to lip-synchronization (usually abbreviated to 'lip-sync'), it is advisable not to show advertising with a person's lips while talking as it can show that the advertising has been introduced from another country, irritating the consumer. Personal care and confectionery brands including Oréal, Gillette, Nivea, Mars and Snickers use this approach.

One brand: one format using various methods of implementation

This strategy uses one advertising theme supported by a number of implementation methods which focus on different values for different cultures. Examples might be variations of 'benefit to the user', 'demonstration of how the product works' or 'focus on detailed product attributes'. The advertising message combines opposing values in one advertisement although focus on the values can vary for different cultures. The cultural specifics are compromised so the promotion appeal may be less effective than separate appeals would be in each country. Examples of such combinations of appeals in pan-European campaigns are toothpaste, shampoo and household products.

In particular, in the UK and Germany, toothpaste advertising has used different approaches for the same brand of toothpaste. Generally, in the UK, the focus is on self-confidence, showing the benefit of using the product through producing white, good-looking teeth for the user. The typical German appeal has been to portray a message that toothpaste protects the teeth, with advertisements focusing on anxiety reduction by showing details of how the toothpaste works on the teeth. Similar approaches have been used for shampoo with the promotion depicting a woman being admired for her beautiful hair in the UK and details of how the shampoo works in Germany. Increasingly, these approaches are being combined within pan-European promotion campaigns which focus on both the details of how the shampoo works on the hair, as well as the shiny hair as a result, e.g. the campaign for Pantene Pro V that started in 1995.

One or different brand names: one advertising format with different executions

Another strategy has been to promote similar products with different brand names using one consistent advertising approach such as comparison, testimonial, or drama, adapting the theme to people, languages and culture. Procter & Gamble uses different brand names but the same promotion message for sanitary towels, detergents and cleaning liquids, e.g. Dreft, Fairy, Ace. Different commercials are made for each country with their implementation reflecting national cultural values. In this way, advertisements in some countries portray large power distance cultures with elders advising younger consumers, while others reflect small power distance cultures showing the opposite situation.

One or different brand names: one platform with different executions

A different approach is to have a common abstract theme, or idea, applied in different ways targeted at local consumer culture, e.g. the campaigns used by Nestlé for KitKat chocolate biscuits, Knorr sauces and Sara Lee/DE coffee. KitKat's campaign is 'have a break, have a KitKat': Knorr's is 'professional cooking' and Sara Lee/DE's theme is 'togetherness, enjoying coffee in the home'. Recognizable elements such as the brand name and package, e.g. the KitKat pay-off, Sara Lee/DE music, or a particular symbol, such as the Knorr professional cook, are common to all the advertisements. Different executions based on the common elements are adapted to each country's culture. The advantage of this strategy is using the combination of local values and a centrally recognizable theme or idea. Actual advertisements may be used globally, regionally or locally depending on the need for cultural adaptation.

Multi-local: act global, think local endorsement

This approach enables the benefits of globalization in production, sourcing, distribution, marketing and the related benefits of economies of scale in production and organization to be achieved. It appreciates that the mental images used in each country cannot be standardized and shows appreciation of local cultural values. These companies build positive relationships and trust with consumers through their promotion. The company's name is used as an endorsement, e.g. Nestlé, Volkswagen and many Japanese companies.

In practice, a combination of approaches is used for international promotion. Local or regional promotion concentrating on one country, or the regions within a country, are extended across borders and, as appropriate, to international geographic coverage. Within international promotion, consideration also has to be made for the advent of regionalism, that is, for targeting regions within countries. Promotion approaches are obliged to support not only national cultures, but also the influence of regional cultures. For example, within a European campaign, they must consider not only the cultures of France, Germany and Spain but also the regional cultures, such as that of the Alsace in France, the Bavarians in Germany and the Basques and Catalonians in Spain. International promotion has to account for these regional differences within a global promotion strategy. This situation is exemplified in the beer sector where international firms such as the Dutch Heineken maintains its global image, as well as its regional interests within its promotion strategy. It promotes the international Heineken brand across Europe and, at the same time, it has regional brands such as El Aguila in Spain which latterly it has re-named Aguila within its Amstel division. Similarly, Guinness of Ireland promotes its global brand names across Europe and beyond.

Obstacles to international promotion implementation

A major consideration when undertaking cross-border promotion is accommodating the regulation in different countries. Such regulation may be controlled by legislation or by general practice, in particular where industry codes of practice act as constraints. For example, a toy or confectionery maker wanting to run a pan-European TV advertising campaign has to consider the different rules and regulations for each country concerned. In Sweden advertising targeted at children is forbidden; some countries require advertisements for sweets to carry a toothbrush symbol, and others have rules intended to curb advertisers from encouraging children to exercise 'pester power'. The same maze of national rules exists when it comes to promoting alcohol, tobacco, pharmaceuticals and financial services. There are diverse regulations on how much of the human body can be revealed, whether prices can be discounted for special offers and the use of free gifts in sales promotion (Summers, 1996).

All these differing rules cause barriers to cross-border trade and make it difficult for consumers to get redress when things go wrong according to the European Commission

(1996) paper covering 'commercial communication', i.e. all forms of advertising, direct marketing, sponsorship, sales promotion and public relations. The paper considers that some national advertising restrictions are a form of disguised protectionism and suggests that a body be set up to encourage standardized promotion campaigns across Europe, chaired by the Commission and made up of representatives of each member state. It would examine national differences in commercial communication within Europe to assess whether national rules related to promotion controls meet the public interest, and it would act to remove any restrictions that were found. In this way, more standardized promotion campaigns could be achieved across Europe, providing benefits of economies of scale for all concerned.

ROLE OF ADVERTISING AGENCY

Promotion activities may be conducted by the firm using internal or external resources. The firm's internal resources may be its own promotion/advertising department with promotion specialists or it may be an advertising co-ordinator whose role is to manage the promotion campaign implemented through advertising agencies. Usually firms undertaking mass media advertising employ the services of advertising agencies which, in turn, take responsibility for producing the promotion to be placed in the media. Such advertising agencies receive commission from media owners for their services of providing 'advertising materials' in a format ready for direct input to media. Traditionally, such commission has been around the 15 per cent level, but the commission levels are subjects of much negotiation.

Table 7.6 shows the world's largest advertising agency organizations, in terms of their billings in 2001. While traditionally the US-based groups have dominated the advertising agency industry, there has been much merger and alliance activity, which confuses the nationality issue. The pressure for agencies to offer a full advertising service for international businesses and to have sufficient scale to be in a strong negotiating position with media owners has led to consolidation within the advertising sector. At the same time, to offer the desirable range of promotion services to clients, advertising agencies have had to become larger with extensive networks of associated agencies. For example, in 1998, Dentsu, Japan's leading advertising agency, took a minority share in the US-based Leo Burnett. It already had a relationship with the US, Young & Rubicam. At the same time, the US Omnicom Group and WPP acquired interests in other Japanese advertising agencies.

SELECTION OF ADVERTISING AGENCY

Many factors come into play when advertisers are choosing an advertising agency. Not surprisingly, clients expect advertising agencies to be creative. A survey in 1994 found that nearly three-quarters of the 117 marketing directors surveyed expect a prospective agency to be committed to creativity with 78 per cent wanting the agency to have original ideas (*Campaign*, 1994). Compatibility of all concerned in the contract is critical. The survey also found that half (51 per cent) of advertisers change their agency if there is a clash of personalities.

189

Table 7.6 The world's top 20 advertising organizations, 2001

Rank	Group	Worldwide gross income (US $m)	Billings (US $m)
1	WPP Group	8,165	75,711
2	Interpublic Group	7,981	66,689
3	Omnicom Group	7,404	58,080
4	Publicis SA Group (including Bcom3 Group)	4,770	52,892
5	Dentsu	2,796	20,848
6	Havas Advertising	2,733	26,269
7	Grey Global Group	1,864	12,106
8	Cordiant Communications Group	1,175	13,388
9	Hakuhodo	874	6,862
10	Asatsu-DK	395	3,501

Source: adapted from Advertising Association (2002b), Table 24.1, p. 232, reprinted from 22.4.2002 issue of *Advertising Age*, Crain Communications Inc.

Choice of advertising agency is influenced by:

- objectives of the promotion campaign;
- resources: budget, staff and time;
- past experience;
- stage of life cycle of product;
- geographic coverage of promotion campaign.

Other sources of information include the advertising agency Ballester Report on pan-European client satisfaction survey, which is undertaken every two years. It details client views of the advertising agency campaign effectiveness, creativity and employees across the advertising agency sector, as well as on individual networks. Agency performance is ranked against that of competitors on subjects ranging from 'understanding of client problems' to how likely an agency is to be put on a client's shortlist during a review. However, the report is expensive (£20,000 in 1998) and has been criticized as being too generalized (Martin, 1998) suggesting that the report is not the full answer to agency assessment.

Advertising agency organization

Advertising agencies undertake to produce and manage the advertising process for their clients. Within the agencies there are various managerial functions, shown in Figure 7.1, that have to be undertaken including:

- account management;
- creativity;

Managing director

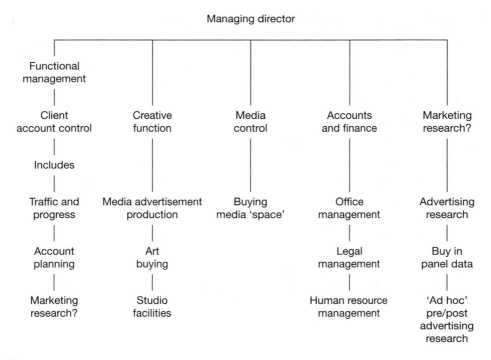

Figure 7.1 Advertising agency functions

- media control;
- accounts and finance administration;
- marketing research.

Account management

Advertisers may use different advertising agencies and account managers for different brands. Account managers (sometimes termed 'planners') are responsible for particular clients within advertising agencies. They liaise between agency clients and the persons undertaking the various functional activities within the agency. The account managers investigate, analyse and define campaigns; they monitor the progress of contracts and act as the intermediaries between clients and agency personnel. They specify the objectives of a campaign before the creative personnel set to work and are responsible for ensuring the creative ideas meet these objectives (Fletcher, 1998). This approach forces the creative people to follow the specified promotional strategy from the start and reassures clients that the agency's creative ideas match the agreed objectives while still engendering and encouraging advertising creativity.

Creative function

The creative function has the role of creating and preparing advertisements for the media and is involved at all stages of the process from defining the advertising objectives to

preparing story-boards and mock-ups of possible advertising designs, through to production of the advertisements for the media. The creative function may be undertaken by using
internal agency staff, or external sources may be used. Increasingly, advertising agencies
employ external groups for the less stimulating projects because talented advertising professionals prefer to work on projects that demand a high level of creativity. In particular, many
creative persons avoid products such as perfume and cars because they find the work unex-
citing (Tylee, 1996).

Media control

A critical role for advertising agencies is to manage the media used for the promotion
campaign. This function requires detailed appreciation of the available media including time
schedules, prices, lead-times for media space placement, together with predicted audience
levels in terms of 'reach' and demographics for TV, press, radio, cinema and so on. Such
information requires constant monitoring and, frequently, is undertaken by specialist media
agencies for the advertising agencies.

Accounts and finance administration

Within advertising agencies, clients' financial accounts are administered in much the same
way as for any other business organization. Advertising agencies are required to provide
their customers with additional legal advice, as part of the client service. As should be appreciated, the promotion programme must fall within the constraints of the legal framework
and general good practice of all the countries covered. Advertising agencies can have internal
specialists and/or they can use external specialist legal advisers.

Marketing research

Advertising agencies use marketing research to support the development of their promotion programmes to ascertain likely, and actual, audience reaction. While some marketing research may be conducted within the advertising agency, more frequently marketing
research is undertaken by marketing research agencies under the guidance of the client.
Advertising agencies are expected to have access to general promotional data such as media
audience characteristics, e.g. the profile of television audiences in terms of sex, age group
and class. But more specific data, such as audience reaction to a particular promotion
campaign is usually obtained from marketing research agencies using both qualitative and
quantitative research methods (see Chapter 4). For example, often group discussions are
used at the creative stage to examine brand image and perception to develop possible themes
and 'stories' for the promotional programme. Surveys could be conducted before, during
and after advertising in the media to determine advertising effectiveness using a combination of street and telephone interviews as well as questions placed in the relevant omnibus
panel. Such assessments of consumer opinion are used to help decision-making throughout
the promotional programme.

BOX 7.1 COCA-COLA'S DECENTRALIZED ADVERTISING

Coca-Cola is pursuing a decentralized advertising strategy and, in 1995, switched agencies for its European advertising from McCann-Erickson to Publicis. Coca-Cola believed McCann's work had become stale and not sufficiently creative (Hatfield, 1995). Coke's strategy is atypical of other major advertisers who have been moving to centralize their advertising with agencies around the world. While Coca-Cola has added advertising agencies such as Wieden & Kennedy, Fallon McElligott, Lowe Howard-Spink, Bartle Bogle Hegarty, Chiat Day and Casadevall Pedreno to its roster, advertisers from Microsoft to Reebok to Mars and IBM have moved to streamline their use of advertising agencies.

Since 1993, Coke has been tailoring commercials to suit different target consumers and has appointed specific agencies to create them. For example, Coke used Wieden & Kennedy to create from scratch the OK cola brand; Fallon McElligott was appointed to run a campaign promoting the shape of the new Coke bottle; Doner was required to make Coke synonymous with Christmas. At the same time, the Lowe Group has tried to give Diet Coke a more emotional sell; Chiat Day launched the new-age drink, Fruitopia; and Bartle Bogle Hegarty reinforced Coke's 'real thing' credentials in the face of the UK assault from own-label cola. Coke is trying to avoid the blandness of much multinational advertising.

INTERNATIONAL BRANDING

As discussed in Chapter 5: International product development, firms may deploy branding strategies in a number of ways which may have global, international or national coverage. Examples of brands that are recognized worldwide include:

- Benetton, the Italian clothes producer and retailer;
- Caterpillar, the industrial earth-moving equipment manufacturer;
- Coca-Cola and Pepsi-Cola, soft drink producers;
- Heinz and Kellogg's, food producers;
- IBM, Hewlett Packard and Compaq, computer manufacturers;
- Microsoft, software producer;
- Kentucky Fried Chicken (KFC) and McDonald's, fast-food providers;
- Kodak and Fuji film;
- Levi's jeans.

Examples of international brands covering a more limited range of countries are Timberland fashion wear and Marks & Spencer, the international clothes and food retailer. National brands include many food and drink producers and retailers such as Jordan, organic cereals, and Sainsbury's; regional brands include Irn Bru, Scottish soft drinks, and Cava, Spanish sparkling wine.

193

BOX 7.2 CAR INDUSTRY PROMOTION

In 1998, car manufacturers spent £3.3bn on consumer advertising in Europe's five largest markets (Burt, 1999). The highest expenditure was in Germany where almost £980m was spent on press broadcast and cinema advertising, which was followed by advertising expenditure reaching £720m in France and £716m in the UK. Italy had the largest increase of 19 per cent in car advertising expenditure to £513m. Advertising expenditure across Europe rose by 8 per cent in 1998, while new car registrations rose by 7 per cent in value terms. In the UK spending rose 8.5 per cent, although car registration expenditure rose by only 3.5 per cent.

In 1998, Ford of the US spent £172 for every car sold in Britain (an increase on the £134 per car spent in 1995), but Cadillac, the General Motors brand, invested £14,883 per car sold. In 1998, Renault spent £382m, more than any other leading car manufacturer, on promoting its product range, General Motors spent £297m, Ford £269m, Peugeot £245m and its associate Citroën spent £206m. In the UK the largest percentage increase in advertising was recorded by Skoda, the Czech arm of the Volkswagen group, with a 700 per cent increase to almost £12m (Burt, 1999).

Combining the Society of Motor Manufacturers and Traders (SMMT) sales figures with those from Register-MEAL reveals that in 1997 the average car manufacturer spent £425 on advertising for every car it sold (Dwek, 1996). The highest spender per car, Alfa Romeo, spent £1,629 per car sold (see Table 7.7). Peugeot 106, Citroën ZX, Volvo 850, Honda Civic and Volkswagen Golf together accounted for £64m of the sector's advertising expenditure in 1995. Yet not one of them was a top-ten seller (see Table 7.8) where the Ford Escort, Ford Fiesta and Ford Mondeo led as car brand sellers.

European case studies

Rijkens (1992) brought together 15 case studies covering European advertising strategies used by major international organizations in the lead-up to the implementation of the Single European Act (1987) aimed to provide a harmonized Single European Market (SEM). These cases range from After Eight (chocolates), Apple Computer, Club Mediterranée (holiday resorts) and Mercedes-Benz (commercial vehicles) to Miele (household electrical goods) and Seiko (watch technology). Those interested in international promotion directed at Europe are recommended to read these cases.

CONCLUSION

The chapter examines the nature of international promotion, the implementation of international promotion strategy in terms of the contribution of each of the promotion mix components, namely advertising, sales promotion, personal selling and public relations. The process of international promotion starts by setting the objectives of the promotion by

Table 7.7 *Advertising expenditure per car sold in the UK, 1995*

Rank	Brand	GB £	US $
1	Alfa Romeo	1,629	989
2	Daewoo	864	525
3	Saab	736	447
4	Hyundai	665	404
5	Volvo	583	354
6	Proton	581	353
7	Kia	563	342
8	Suzuki	536	325
9	Daihatsu	453	275
10	Jaguar	450	273
11	Skoda	444	270
12	Mitsubishi	434	263
13	Audi	405	246
14	Citroën	378	230
15	Seat	360	219
16	Honda	349	212
17	Toyota	346	210
18	Nissan	318	193
19	Porsche	297	180
20	Renault	259	157
21	Fiat	256	155
22	Volkswagen	250	152
23	Mercedes-Benz	243	148
24	Mazda	230	140
25	Lada	227	138
26	Peugeot	224	136
27	Vauxhall	211	128
28	Rover Group	187	114
29	BMW	149	90
30	Ford	134	81

Source: adapted from Burt (1999) and Society for Motor Manufacturers and Traders (SMMT)

Note: Calculations based on US $1 taken as equivalent to £0.607

Table 7.8 Top ten car brand sellers in the UK, 1995

Rank	Brand
1	Ford Escort
2	Ford Fiesta
3	Ford Mondeo
4	Vauxhall Astra
5	Vauxhall Cavalier
6	Vauxhall Corsa
7	Rover 200
8	Peugeot 306
9	Renault Clio
10	Rover 100

Source: adapted from Burt (1999) and Society for Motor Manufacturers and Traders (SMMT)

BOX 7.3 KIWIFRUIT RE-BRANDING PAYS DIVIDENDS FOR ZESPRI

In the early 1970s New Zealand launched kiwifruit on world markets but never bothered to register the name as a trade mark. This led to marketing difficulties as farmers in Chile, France, Iran, Italy and the US began selling the fruit grown from original New Zealand vines in large volumes. In 1997, the Kiwifruit Marketing Board changed its name to Zespri International and announced plans to market the fruit under the Zespri brand name, becoming the butt of New Zealander jokes (Hall, 1998). But within a year, the Board's decision began to pay dividends.

In 1998, in the main selling season in Europe, between June and November the Board achieved 80 per cent market share in New Zealand. Its global market share over the same period was 67 per cent. In 1997, Zespri International sold 99 per cent of all fruit shipped from New Zealand, showing minimal fruit loss. The international marketing success of Zespri kiwifruit using the new brand approach is boosting confidence and improving trading conditions for New Zealand farmers after a long period of severe losses.

Robin Mills, Chief Executive of Zespri International, commented that the Zespri brand gave a marketing opportunity for the fruit that would create a lasting franchise with retailers through differentiating the product by brand-focused promotions and delivering constant, quality product. Zespri International estimated that prime fruit would have returned NZ $5.25 (US $10.8) a tray for the 1997 season, before adjusting for the NZ $50m (US $98m) adverse currency movements. Without the currency problem, the industry would have earned around a dollar a tray more than in 1996. With no complaints from overseas customers and the sales success noted above, Zespri is proving that promoting the fruit by brand, rather than by country of origin, is a major success.

considering the resources available in terms of finance, persons and time and determining the message to be communicated. These decisions influence the selection of the methods of promotion and the appropriate media. Media performance evaluation also contributes to the decision process.

Implementation of international promotion can encounter numerous difficulties due to the complexity of the process. In particular, the role of national culture has to be considered as has the different uses of media across international markets. The promotion mix used in one country, say, France, is not necessarily appropriate for other countries, say, the Argentine or Denmark. The objective of the promotion message to be communicated may be the same for all countries concerned, but the way in which the promotion is implemented is likely to differ. The media selection may be similar but differ according to media usage in each country as shown by a higher share of total promotion expenditure being spent on television and radio in Peru than in the UK, where the press takes the higher share. Details of the message communicated may differ between countries and regions within countries, despite the prime objective of the promotion being the same. In particular, the language used for portraying the same message will change.

The role of the advertising agency in international promotion is examined, especially that related to the preparation of promotion campaigns. The ways in which advertising agencies have expanded internationally, even globally, to service international customers is considered. Advertising agency international expansion has been achieved largely through the acquisition of national agencies which has led to increasing consolidation and associated domination by the larger advertising agencies within the advertising industry. Smaller advertising agencies operate as specialists, with the larger agencies sometimes sub-contracting to them parts of the major contract. Medium-sized advertising agencies are vulnerable to acquisition by the larger agencies.

These advertising agencies work towards promoting international brands. Advertising agencies have close links to the media, which are also increasingly international in their coverage. It is this close relationship between advertising agencies and the media that encourages global firms, especially MNCs, to use their services, especially within the consumer mass market. International firms servicing industrial markets often choose to use their own internal resources for international promotion rather than those of international advertising agencies.

REVIEW QUESTIONS

7.1 A multinational corporation (MNC) wishes to run a global promotion campaign across North America, Europe and the Far East. Suggest ways in which such a campaign could be undertaken. Some of the factors to consider are:

- setting objectives of the promotion programme;
- selection of promotion methods;
- selection of advertising agency(ies);
- monitoring progress of the promotion programme;
- resource implications.

7.2 What are the likely differences in approach for international promotion for industrial and consumer manufacturers? How do these approaches differ from what might be used for the service industry? Discuss with examples.

REFERENCES

Advertising Association (2002a) *European advertising and media forecast*, Henley-on-Thames: NTC.

Advertising Association (2002b) *Advertising statistics yearbook 2002*, 20th edn, Henley-on-Thames: NTC, June.

Advertising Standards Authority (1979) *British code of advertising practice*, London: Advertising Standards Authority.

Broadbent, S. (1997) *Accountable advertising*, Henley-on-Thames: Admap.

Burt, T. (1999) 'Spending on car adverts hits peak', *Financial Times*, 5 July, p. 2.

Business Europe (1996) 'Mail bonding', 28 October, p. 1.

Campaign (1994) 'Survey results (advertising agencies: included articles on choosing an agency)', 23 September, p. C.3 (5).

Cateora, P.R. and Graham, J.L. (1999) *International marketing*, Boston: Irwin McGraw-Hill, Ch. 16, pp. 480–517.

Dwek, R. (1996) 'Are car advertisers wasting money?', *Campaign*, 10 May, p. 34.

Edgecliffe-Johnson, A. (1998) 'Bus shelter ad Titans square up', *Financial Times*, 22 May, p. 10.

European Commission (1996) 'Commercial communication: internal market', European Commission.

Fletcher, W. (1998) 'Spark in the creative process', *Financial Times*, 20 March, p. 29.

Hall, T. (1998) 'Kiwifruit rebranding pays dividends for Zespri', *Financial Times*, 12 March, p. 39.

Hanger, D. (1995) 'International advertising', in Hart, N. (ed.) *The practice of advertising*, 4th edn, Oxford: Butterworth-Heinemann, Ch. 17, pp. 237–48.

Hatfield, S. (1995) 'What's Coke up to?', *Campaign*, 14 July, p. 28 (2).

Kotler, P., Armstrong, G., Saunders, J. and Wong, V. (1999) *Principles of marketing*, 2nd European edn, Upper Saddle River, NJ: Prentice Hall.

Martin, M. (1998) 'Is the Ballester report still a must-see for global agencies? (European client satisfaction survey)', *Campaign,* 27 March, p. 27.

Mooij, M. de (1997) *Global marketing and advertising: understanding cultural paradoxes*, London: Sage.

Rawsthorn, A. (1998) 'Cinemas attract biggest audiences since 1972', *Financial Times*, 30 April, p. 13.

Research (1997) 'India's official TV meter goes into ring with rival', Market Research Society.

Rijkens, R. (1992) *European advertising strategies*, London: Cassell.

Smith, A. (1998) 'The need to play by rules', *Financial Times*, 25 March, p. 29.

Stewart-Allen, A.L. (1998) 'Keys to success in Europe's massive mail-order market', *Marketing News*, 6 January, p. A8.

Summers, D. (1996) 'Campaign sans frontières', *Financial Times*, 16 May, p. 11.

Tylee, J. (1996) 'Do advertisers get the creative team they want?', *Campaign*, 25 October, p. 12 (1).

RECOMMENDED FURTHER READING

Cannon, J., Warner, R. and Odber de Baubeta, P. (eds) (2000) *Advertising and identity in Europe*, Bristol: Intellect.

Chapter 8

International channels of distribution

INTRODUCTION

We live in revolutionary times, no more so than in international channels of distribution. The advent of the Internet and the continuous development of its applications means that an infrastructure is being built up that is likely to effect a change of seminal proportions. It is certain to alter the dynamics of competition, perhaps to differing degrees, across all industries. The speed of transformation to the electronic medium has been accelerated even more by the increasing ease of access to it as computer prices tumble. At the same time, the larger Internet Service Providers (ISPs) are switching from charging on an annual, or monthly basis, to offering their services free, making their profits from a share of the call charges and/or advertising revenue. This is compounded by the explosive growth in Europe of the no-contract, pre-paid cellular phone which promises to give access to millions on tight budgets or who require the convenience of mobile communication. This will provide yet another access point to the net as new ideas being developed by firms like Nokia to connect mobile phones to the Internet become commercial propositions. Innovative approaches to marketing of the new services are creating market segments that did not exist before and are stimulating demand further for products and services through the medium, so providing a fillip to further innovation. This present attempt to describe these changes inevitably will be overtaken by events.

The changing nature of the infrastructure for distribution channels does not mean that existing channels will be wiped out or that earlier studies in channel behaviour are invalidated. Rather, firms, often only recently set up and driven by a radical concept or technical development, will dominate new vehicles for the channels. These vehicles may have to be embraced by traditional providers of products and services just as Rupert Murdoch, the Australian/American newspaper tycoon, has bought over Internet interests to ensure that any decline in the print media is offset by growth in the electronic medium. The freebooting digital economy will of necessity become subject to

200

more stringent regulation, not applied at the moment since it is necessary to allow it to develop. In the meantime, the excitement of the innovations, buy-outs, start-up successes (and failures) and convergence of technologies will slowly define the structure of the new market. It will provide international marketers with challenges that make them examine current channels and practices to determine whether these need to be adapted, or extended, in the light of continuous advance and change.

LEARNING OBJECTIVES

The objectives of this chapter are to:
- examine the nature of international distribution channels;
- identify significant changes in channel infrastructure;
- underscore the importance of relationships in channel management;
- evaluate the contribution of formal agreements to effective channel working.

When you have completed the chapter you should be able to:
- demonstrate familiarity with the effect of electronic communication technology on channels;
- show awareness of channel behaviour;
- apply criteria to the choice of channel and/or its development;
- articulate the skills needed to harness the competencies of other organizations in the channels.

NATURE OF CHANNELS

The reduction of cost and the increase of efficiency brought about by specialization have provided the fillip to organizations to enter trading relations with other organizations. In Chapter 1 the wider reach, whether global or regional, was examined. No longer do companies seek a specialized supplier and negotiate a price each time a need is felt. When two or more organizations acknowledge that it is in their mutual interest to perpetuate a relationship across a national border, this is generally viewed as an indication that a channel of distribution has emerged. The logical outcome of a relationship of two or more organizations that perceive mutual gain from developing, or continuing their relationship, is mutual dependence. Mutual dependence is a basic concept which requires the management of a number of important behaviours (Bowersox *et al.*, 1980).

Co-operation, conflict and dependence

By the act of aligning themselves with other organizations in a relationship of dependence, organizations commit themselves to co-operative activities. Such co-operation takes the

201

form of fulfilling a negotiated role in the channel of distribution which may include the functions to be undertaken for agreed rewards. It is a code of conduct which lays down the contribution of channel members as expected by other channel members. Since an adequate channel performance is crucial to the maintenance of harmonious relationships within the channel, failure to achieve adequate performance can lead to frustration and conflict. When channel members are located in different countries, with differing cultural, linguistic and ideological backgrounds, insensitive behaviour by one channel member from the view-point of another culture can spark a conflict which would be otherwise avoidable.

Example

A Mexican agent who had succeeded in effecting the sale of a major item of equipment felt discriminated against when his UK principal insisted on applying the terms of his own agreement with his credit insurers. Under this, the principal was required to hold a lien on the agent's commission to ensure the agent's commitment to the payment of long-term credit instalments. The agent would only receive his commission on the payment of instalments by the buyer, contrary to the custom of the country whereby the agent had to make payment for services rendered to persons instrumental in having the order placed. His/her outgoings would not begin to be recovered until receipt of the third instalment of ten, which was eighteen months after delivery. The two perceptions of the situation were different. 'Facts' are likely to be interpreted in the light of prior experience which will be coloured by the cultural practices that have emerged. Co-operation of necessity includes the handling of conflict as the supplier is dependent on the agent for his success in a market and the agent on the supplier for his. Channel members enter into a relationship because they are unable on their own to perform efficiently all the functions which must be completed to accomplish their goals.

Power

In a channel of distribution those members perceived to possess a relative power advantage may assume a position of channel leadership. Inter-organizational relations are more likely to be characterized by unequal rather than equal power, enabling one party to a relationship to enjoy a relative power advantage. In Germany wholesalers came together horizontally before manufacturers could integrate vertically, allowing them to exert greater influence than those in other European countries over the decisions and behaviours of other channel members.

A firm's tolerance of this imbalance is related to its dependence on other channel members. German manufacturers accepted the situation of wholesaler channel leadership provided there was something in it for themselves, which, in their case, was freedom from competition from foreign manufacturers. There are still challenges in attempting to enter the German market through a distributorship agreement. The alternative of buying into the market is also problematic. Much of the wholesale business is held by family-owned, medium-sized companies (the *Mittelstand*) resistant to buy-outs and hostile bids. The US-based retailer, Wal-Mart, made two acquisitions in 1997 and 1998 to make it Germany's fourth largest hypermarket chain with 10 per cent of the market. However, it misjudged corporate culture, planning and social regulations, market demand and, critically, disregarded the structure of distribution in German food retailing, using its US model of controlling distribution to stores itself rather than leaving it to the suppliers. By 2000, despite some refurbishment of the 95 stores, it was losing about US $200m–$300m per annum. Wal-Mart found it challenging to pursue its usual policy of building up market size and achieving critical mass by acquisition of established retailers and retracted from the German market (Benoit, 2000). On the other hand, Wal-Mart's entry to the UK in 1999, where buying and selling of whole companies is viewed, certainly by the financial markets, as a legitimate activity, has been much more successful. Wal-Mart acquired ASDA, one of the 'Big Five' supermarket chains with the hub of its activities in northern England where smaller independents are particularly vulnerable to the entry of a low price competitor like Wal-Mart. In 2003 the EU Competition Commission stepped in over concern that market leaders Wal-Mart (ASDA), Tesco and Sainsbury's bidding for the Safeway group might become too dominant. Ultimately, it decided in favour of the original bidder, the Morrison group which has been obliged to sell some of the Safeway outlets to meet with the strict anti-competition rules relating to the UK food and household retail market.

CHANNEL ALTERNATIVES

International market entry methods were introduced in Chapter 2: Framework for international marketing, pp. 39–40. The principal traditional channels are further illustrated in Figure 8.1, showing that the higher the level of commitment of resources, the more the cost and the greater the control that can be exerted. The principal collaborative channels of distribution will be discussed below.

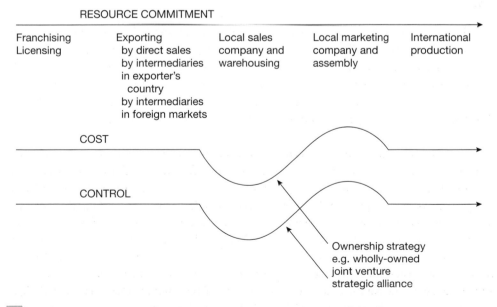

Figure 8.1 Choosing channels for international market entry or revised distribution (adapted from Robock and Simmons, 1984)

Franchising

This is a form of market approach by which a company, the franchisor, grants another independent organization the right to do business in a particular way. This right can involve the selling of the franchisor's product, or service, using its name, production and marketing techniques or general business approach, or a combination of these. The franchisee shares the benefits of the company's advertising. The fast food industry typically uses franchising for its expansion, e.g. KFC, McDonald's and Pizza Hut. Companies franchising others in this way do so often for reasons of market potential, particularly where domestic markets are saturated, and sometimes to counter competitor action in a foreign market. The major elements of a franchise comprise a common trade name and an on-going relationship with the parent company, usually spelt out in the contract. The agreement usually ties the franchisee to supplies from the franchisor. Quality is a prime concern reflected in training, often on a continuing basis, by the franchisor's staff, and is supported by procedural manuals. A one-off franchising fee and on-going royalties are payable by the franchisee who, in effect provides the capital for the expansion activities of the franchisor, although the latter may finance stocks. Franchising agreements are tight with no scope for negotiation. The franchisee is in a situation where he/she accepts the agreement or does not.

The franchising approach appeals to the individual aspiring to his/her own business or the small company. It provides expertise that would not otherwise be available. In the EU, recognition of franchising as one of the fastest ways of growing a business has been given legal backing to improve competition. It has been excluded from the strictures of Article 85 (1) of the Treaty of Rome and the general prohibition on restrictive agreements likely to distort free competition. The scope of the ruling does not extend to industrial franchising where a manufacturing process or technology, such as the manufacture of up-and-over garage doors, is involved. This area is covered by separate regulations which provide exemption from competition restrictions on know-how licensing agreements and by an existing rule giving clearance for patent licences.

Licensing

Licensing agreements concern the sale of knowledge, access to that knowledge and the means to exploit it. As many countries look to develop their economies and MNCs look for markets, or market segments, into which to expand, or to overcome protective trade barriers, the potential host countries seek more of the value-adding activity for themselves. Licensing-in becomes an attractive alternative to them. It is also a short-cut to competitiveness where that has been lost or has not existed. The licensor can grant to the licensee patent rights or know-how rights. This access to intellectual property is attractive to many would-be licensees. The licence can relate to the right to:

- make a product for sale or to use particular know-how or both;
- to bottle, fill or package for sale the subject product, usually in the food, chemical or pharmaceutical industries;
- to use without manufacture or sale;

204

- to assemble and sell parts of a patented product, as with the automotive, electrical and appliance industries;
- to distribute and sell only the patented product.

Similarly, licences can be granted for trademarks and brands.

EXPORTING

Within the exporting category, a company may have its own export department, or division, and engage in direct exporting. It and its customers will negotiate agreements of purchase and sale. Where expert discussion is required, company personnel may travel round the world visiting various markets. Often the people visiting these markets are nationals of the country, or speak the language fluently. Most exporting organizations will have some form of foreign representation which may have to be supported by direct negotiations between members of the buying and selling organizations.

An alternative within this category is where an export merchant buys products in the country of origin and sells abroad at his own risk. A similar situation exists where a foreign customer has a buying office, or is represented in the country of origin. Either way, the *Irrelevant* resultant contract is equivalent to a domestic transaction and does not give rise to the same problems as in inter-country transactions. It can expose the foreign buyer to the laws of the supplier country. Another alternative is the use of a foreign-based intermediary who can be either an agent or a distributor, giving rise to (often exclusive) distributor and agency agreements. A large proportion of sales to companies, other than affiliated companies, is handled through such intermediaries.

Other modes of exporting include consortium agreements and group representation which involve the co-operative action of a number of manufacturers of associated equipment and products/services who can jointly obtain business which individually they could not achieve. These represent a small proportion of total export sales. *would be set as large consortium ...?*

Agents and distributors

Legal perspectives distinguish between agents and distributors. An agent acts for a named principal who then enters into an agreement with the agent's customer. A distributor acts on his own behalf and carries the economic risk of the transactions into which he enters. In return for his/her efforts, an agent receives a commission on sales, or where circumstances justify it a retainer and reduced commission. The latter is frequently used where sales are of large value, but infrequent. Usually, the agent also receives territorial exclusivity. Distributors receive exclusive, or limited distribution, in addition to the profits accruing from their efficiency in purchasing, from their estimates of their own markets, the price the product is sold at, and their effectiveness in managing their administrative costs. In return, they are expected to exert their best efforts in the sale of the supplier products. Some countries go further and distinguish an agent acting on behalf of an undisclosed principal. In Belgium and Italy, this kind of agent is known as a *commissaire* or *comisario*.

A supplier of goods or services does not usually have the choice of using an agent or a distributor. Rather the nature of the offering determines the type of intermediary selected. Normally, producers of consumer goods, consumer durables, industrial consumables as well as low-cost capital equipment and products will use a distributor. Normally, raw materials and high-cost capital equipment are marketed through an agent, where not sold direct to the end-user. In practice, the distinctions are not so clear. An agent may act as such for his/her principal's products, but as a distributor for spares and consumables. A distributor may act as such for his supplier but may be paid commission when required to service accounts of competing distributors being supplied by the same maker. Indeed, 34 different types of agent/distributor have been identified (MacMillan and Paulden, 1989). In the provision of services, agents are often used because the intangibility of many services precludes the transference of ownership, as in the case of travel agents and insurance brokers.

Joint ventures

Joint ventures are distinguished from agency/distributorship and licensing agreements by their greater complexity and greater power in the system. The concept of joint venture has been applied to every kind of economic activity undertaken jointly by two or more organizations. It may take almost any form. It may be horizontal, vertical, or conglomerate and it may be owned by firms which are unrelated in business interests or created for marketing, production or research. Chiefly, it is used in connection with a legally independent entity under the joint control of the participants. The term is also used to connote other undertakings which have no legal status and in which the participants are controlled by means of a committee or management team with delegated power to make decisions. Joint venture is a convenient concept, being used when a purely contractual arrangement is insufficient and where the drastic irreversible solution of the merger is more than is required to achieve the desired objectives. The participants are willing to co-operate as independent operators. The venture is only workable as long as all participants agree and there is mutual understanding between them.

Foreign government restrictions on ownership of joint ventures have intensified in recent years, often specifying maximum foreign participation at 50 per cent or less, forcing sophisticated management to examine means of ensuring efficiency and control. The burden of giving effect to these, or achieving an equitable compromise, falls squarely on the shoulders of the negotiators. There are laws in many countries against agreements and practices which are in restraint of trade. In developed, industrialized countries these usually refer to restrictions on competition between independent companies. In developing countries frequently they are viewed as limitations imposed on a locally based company by a foreign parent company.

Joint ventures in the EU

The essential factors in the consideration of a joint venture are its objects and effects. Where the restrictive clauses are may have a significant effect on competition, e.g. by bringing about a change in the market structure or affecting trade between member states, exemption will depend on the economic context within which it occurs. Non-competition clauses may be accepted and exemption granted to enable a joint venture to get started but, invariably, they will be limited in their duration to ensure that such restriction is confined to the minimum time that is considered indispensable.

Strategic alliances

As indicated in Chapter 1, increasingly organizations embrace a strategy of globalization and core competence. Globalization forces companies to sell their products in as many different places as possible, a practice which frequently requires other people and other organizations to help them. The preference of firms to stick to what they do best, or their core competencies, means they must let others outside the organization, often abroad, help them with everything else. In this way, the best practice can be called upon irrespective of source in all aspects of the company's market offering.

Strategic alliances come in a variety of forms. The joint venture discussed above, in which companies either hold a proportion of their partner's equity or set up a joint company, is the most rigid form of strategic alliance. The most fluid form is where there is no formal agreement to fall back on and the participants rely on a common vision and considerable trust. The latter type is characterized by McDonald's (of the 'Big Mac') and Coca-Cola, although most of McDonald's alliances are of the more formal kind, e.g. a ten-year alliance with Disney. Most strategic alliances fall somewhere between the two extremes and can be fairly vague. Their open-endedness is part of their appeal. When they have served their purpose, which may be sooner rather than later, there is no legal requirement for them to continue until resolved by lawyers, making them self-regulating. New alliances can be a form of faster, cheaper growth than other more formal arrangements. However, while alliances can be relatively inexpensive to set up, they need to be well managed, using good communication and negotiation skills as well as the older skills of diplomacy and a high tolerance of uncertainty. The trust implicit in informal agreements comes from the parties taking slight risks in divulging information about themselves and releasing more when this is not used to exploit them. It is an incremental, and delicate, process.

By bringing together different firms with unique skills and capabilities, alliances can create powerful learning opportunities. As alliances become more common, exploiting the learning potential of alliances will become more important.

CHOOSING DISTRIBUTION CHANNELS

Choosing from available channels to enter a new market, or develop an existing one, is confined to the above alternatives as shown in Figure 8.1. The increased commitment of resources requires increased outlay and provides increased control when moving from franchising and licensing through exporting to foreign direct investment alternatives. Establishing strategic alliances, as in the airline business, is a low cost strategy aimed at expanding the market as a means to access a wider public. Such alliances operate in parallel with other means, e.g. traditional intermediaries like travel agents with latter-day electronic websites inviting 'e-bookers' to take advantage of the services offered. Like alliances, ownership

BOX 8.1 INTERNATIONAL AIRLINES AND ALLIANCES

International mergers have been frustrated for years in the airline business where there are in excess of 200 national carriers conveying passengers across the world. Bans on foreign ownership and lingering government control over routes, flights and slots at major airports prevent international mergers and limit the ability of airlines to enter new markets. The incentive for mergers is to grow revenue and reduce costs to become even more competitive by reducing fares. This frustration has to a certain extent been overcome by super-alliances between national carriers operating out of international 'hubs' like Amsterdam, Buenos Aires, Chicago, Copenhagen, Hong Kong, London, Paris, Rome and Tokyo. Major airlines have grouped together with names like One World, Star, Delta and KLM/NW to sell tickets to a wider range of destinations without flying to more. They also draw on the 'spokes' of each member airline's associated companies operating out of other airports in the member's country to the hub. Partners in an alliance sell each other's flights, and even book blocks of seats on each other's aircraft. Many airline alliances share codes so that customers do not readily know which member company undertakes the transportation. One such alliance is Opodo, which was created by Aer Lingus, Air France, Alitalia, Austrian Airlines, British Airways, Finnair, Iberia, KLM and Lufthansa. Booking is by the alliance's web site www.opodo.com. It claims to be the first pan-European travel service set up to address the real needs of today's travellers, offering access to over 400 airlines, 30,000 hotels and a fleet of 750,000 hire cars worldwide. Some alliances have frequent-flier programmes to buy the loyalty of passengers, and a growing number are reducing costs by sharing services such as catering, training, maintenance and aircraft buying. Until regulations preventing full-scale mergers are relaxed, airlines will continue to live in the twilight world of shifting alliances.

strategies also affect costs and control. If a joint venture is set up in preference to, say, a wholly owned subsidiary, being shared reduces the cost, but the amount of control exercised will be reduced too.

Determinants of choice

The factors which determine choice of a channel, or channels, of distribution are both external and internal to the organization. These factors show how the options open to organizations are restricted. For example, small companies may not have the resource or expertise to become involved in foreign direct investment; markets with low break-even sales volumes favour low-cost channels such as licensing or exporting. If a new market is found to have a high sensitivity to price, e.g. by removal of inhibiting regulations or tariffs, volumes may increase spectacularly, making a chosen channel, which was appropriate at an early stage in the development of the market, unsuitable at a later stage. This underscores the need for accurate information to identify an appropriate channel from the outset. Traditional decision-making techniques can be applied to such decisions. In Figure 8.2, there

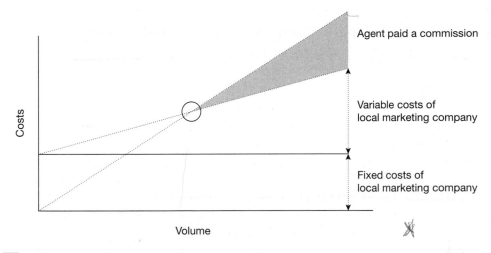

Figure 8.2 *Using break-even analysis to choose a specific channel*

is an example of how break-even analysis can be applied to the question of specific channel choice. There is a point beyond which it becomes more profitable to have direct invest-ment in a foreign selling company than to operate through an agent. The shaded area represents the cost savings.

External influences on choice

Market size is a primary consideration, together with trends in the market like segmenta-tion and the estimated share of the market that can be achieved in view of the competition. The existing distribution methods will determine whether single or multiple channels are developed. Host country policies are important since any special standards, import quotas or duties will increase the cost to the consumer and disadvantage foreign suppliers in rela-tion to domestic ones. If a company wants to hold on to its technology, there is little point in trying to enter a market by means of a foreign direct investment (FDI) where there is insistence on its transfer. Market structure is important in that the number of competing intermediaries may contain organizations with affiliations to competitors either locally or from outside the market. The economic infrastructure becomes critical when specialized expertise is required or the services are needed for the competent financing, manufacture and distribution of a company's output. Production costs are critical where these consti-tute a high proportion of the total costs of a product.

Organizational influences on choice

Factors relating to the organization have a bearing on the channel decision. International experience and commitment normally will be necessary before undertaking expensive foreign investment, as will training for those entering the international market for the first time. Company policy, e.g. defending its designs or know-how, may exclude countries

209

where there is little protection for them. The product, or the technology, may be a deciding factor in the channel decision; a bulky product transportable across borders only at great cost may be more profitably manufactured under licence in the customer country. It should go without saying that finance, including appropriate cash flows, should be available for the channel project. In many organizations, there is a dominant coalition which, for differing reasons of the individuals concerned, may decide to enter a market or revise its channel approach. Finally, a company has, or should have, a long-term strategy which can influence the channel decision; if it wishes in the long term to exploit a particular market, then it will not license its product or process in that market.

PREPARING TO NEGOTIATE CHANNEL AGREEMENTS

The vast majority of channel co-operation arrangements are the subject of written agreements whereby, apart from the vaguer agreements of alliances, the details and conditions of how the parties are going to work together are spelt out. The best agreements will address the possibility of conflict and the means of resolution to be adopted should that contingency occur. This could cover the law under which the agreement is to be interpreted, the language version of the agreement which is to be the definitive one, as well as the place and body which will arbitrate in the case of disputes. The duration of the agreement is critical. The shorter the period, the simpler it is to have a review of arrangements, as long as it is consistent with the confidence of the partners to invest in the arrangement, e.g. building up stocks or taking on personnel to implement the agreement. Revisions included in a new agreement should take account of changes in the relationship that arises. The self-determination of the parties that exists at the time an original agreement is made is complicated by factors of performance and commitment to the joint activity once it has been put into operation. The original objectivity is clouded by the history of the growing relationship and the subsequent negotiations that take place within the original agreement.

Power in the negotiation situation

If there is a preponderant dependence of one party on another, that party is in a position of relative weakness *vis-à-vis* the other party. That dependence can change due to changes taking place in the environment. Such changes can come from an extension of competition through such factors as new or substitutable products, changing market structures, new selling support activities, changing exchange rates, new perspectives on payment terms, or changes in consumer preferences. That dependence can change for better, or for worse, as a result of actions in the negotiation situation. If a salesman finds out from, say, an engineer in the buying organization that his/her quotation is the only one that meets the buyer's specification, his/her power is greatly increased. Conversely, when a purchaser establishes that a supplier is short of work, the purchaser's position is strengthened. When reputable agents are in short supply, such scarcity gives the apparently weaker agent a strong negotiating base. If a distributor, or agent, has a special relationship with key customers, or has special facilities or capabilities, and brings this out in the course of interacting with the supplier's representative, that too strengthens his/her bargaining power.

A licensor's, distributor's or potential joint venture partner's hand is strengthened if the product is patented, or incorporates copyright or a trade mark. The credibility of the company will be another factor. Any presentation which can highlight this in terms of heavy users or significant sales will reinforce this credibility. The credibility of the negotiators themselves, and their effect on each other in terms of creating a climate of confidence, can also affect the relative power situation.

Building in power

When a small US supplier quoted a large European electrical company in euros, the Eurozone currency, but was asked in negotiations to agree to payment in dollars, he did so with alacrity. What the US supplier did not know was that the European company was in possession of currency fluctuation projections which indicated that over the period between agreement and payment there would be a considerable weakening of the dollar in relation to the European currency. Had the US company known this, it might not have agreed to the terms when the agreement was made. Information is power and, through its collection and analysis, strengthens the negotiator's armoury.

When a supplier has created alternative sources of action such as other candidates for a distributorship, and can subtly make this known, he/she creates a more powerful negotiating position for him/herself. In the same way, if distributors or agents can indicate competition for their services, they are performing a similar function.

Unless such alternatives are consciously made, no effective balance of power will be available to the negotiating parties. Power so held must be real. Bluffing is often used as a tactic in sales situations to obtain the best possible settlement. It can include such ploys as holding to a strong position which is not tenable in reality or telling a downright lie with conviction. In negotiating agency/distributorship or licensing agreements, it can be costly. The expectation that a negotiator has of his opposite number is that he is acting in good faith, as both will be involved in operating any resulting arrangement over an extended period.

The joint venture has so much power floating around in it that each party has the potential to move the other a considerable way from its initial bargaining point. Furthermore, in any joint venture negotiating situation there is the potential to harness the power of other institutions. For example, if one possible partner is a company from an industrialized country while the other is a company within a less developed country, then the latter might seek to strengthen its hand if it can create alternatives and show these alternatives to be active. The government of India has in the past invited companies interested in an oil venture to indicate their degree of interest and visibly has entered into, and continued negotiations with, more than one company.

When an international organization is considering a joint venture, its efforts regarding information gathering and creating appropriate perspectives can be enhanced by developing local affiliations, such as enlisting the support of other companies. This is an approach adopted by the Japanese when seeking joint ventures in Malaysia where the situation is delicate as the commercial strength and business acumen of the large Chinese minority is challenged by laws setting equity targets for Malaysian and other companies. These require

211

Malaysian non-Bumiputra companies, i.e. Chinese non-native Malaysian, to hold no more than 40 per cent of a company's shareholding and foreign companies to hold no more than 30 per cent.

CULTURE AND NEGOTIATION

From time to time issues can be coloured by the transference to them of the values of one's own culture, termed the 'self-reference criterion'. Conflict can arise on ethical issues. This is particularly evident in the subject of corruption. It can arise worldwide, but when put into a cross-cultural context, corruption can be interpreted very differently in different countries.

In many parts of Latin America, black Africa, parts of Asia and in the Arab countries, the use of family and friendship ties is widespread, being a necessary and important means of doing business. The use of agents and distributors raises the question of commission and bribery. This has been well put by Muna:

> To the Arab business mind, using personal ties and connections, because of their reciprocal nature, means using up old 'credits' or accumulating new 'liabilities' depending on one's 'balance sheet' of reciprocal transactions. Either way, there is usually a value attached to the use of personal connections which is not always an economic value. When a foreign organisation employs an agent on its behalf, the agent/middleman will incur several costs, one of which might be the cost of his/her capital and his/her personal 'ties/connections' capital. For these services the agent feels entitled to a commission. Thus, while there is one line between commission and bribery for a Westerner doing business in the Arab world, the dividing line may be drawn differently for the Arab businessman. The line of demarcation for the Arab is a clear one. He may, or may not, use a proportion of his commission for bribery, as a Westerner might style it; that for him represents a commission for services rendered.
>
> (Muna, 1980)

NEGOTIATING MARKETING AGREEMENTS

Marketing agreements, as illustrated above, cover a range of activities from sales to FDI agreements. With the exception of franchising, they are all subject to negotiation.

Agreements of purchase and sale

Most of the areas of concern in the negotiation of these agreements are concerned with the marketing mix. Products need to be modified to meet the needs of the intermediary's customers or a promotional thrust requires a change to meet a revised strategy. Price is the focal point in that, when discount structures are revised, or terms of payment changed, or modifications made to the product, or amended distribution or communication arrangements introduced, it is seen as the total value placed on the package.

BOX 8.2 AN ARAB BUSINESSMAN'S VIEW OF THE DIFFERENCE BETWEEN CORRUPTION AND COMMISSION

If one offers money to a government to influence it, that is corruption. But if someone receives money for services rendered afterwards, that is a commission . . . If one-sided or greatly unequal in value or given with the purpose of inducing favourable treatment, then such gifts become bribery . . . While some Arab executives may regard with disfavour the use of personal ties and connections, it is often the only viable alternative. Both the society's values and its institutions encourage the use of these means for doing business.

The assertiveness which can be a strength in uncovering problematic issues in the negotiating of joint venture agreements between parties of Western origin can be a positive drawback when interacting with nationalities who do not respond to these approaches. Scandinavians, who have a much quieter style than Americans, Germans and even British, and in any case are very much concerned with working as a team and making team decisions, will find it difficult to establish relationships with individuals exhibiting assertiveness. Many East Asians will view it as aberrant behaviour and find it difficult to connect. Australians will tend to interpret it as overbearing and react accordingly.

Differing perceptions of a basic situation will have different cultural responses. An insight into the Japanese concept of time in a negotiating situation is given in Box 8.3.

(Adapted from Muna, 1980)

BOX 8.3 NEGOTIATING JOINT VENTURES WITH THE JAPANESE: THE TIME SCALE OF PATIENCE

The Japanese prefer to resolve difficulties through discussion, and the US partner should respect the Japanese wishes. Should conflicts arise, these are usually discussed in lengthy sessions. Both sides will wish to reach amicable conclusions that will be mutually beneficial. In the process, various trade-offs will be made. In short, both partners have to learn to give and take. In Japan, issues are always resolved through negotiations. The chairman of one large US company, Sperry, stated emphatically that it is important for foreign businessmen to realize that:

in dealing with Asia, matters are not resolved through votes. In Japan and Asia in general, if I have three votes on the board and someone else has four, it does not mean the other partner will win on the issues. All our business in Japan has been handled through lengthy discussions, from middle management all the way up to top management.

Usually the chairman of Sperry and the vice-presidents of the various divisions are actively involved in the negotiations. 'These issues are resolved through many, many meetings, which could be very lengthy. Through the numerous lengthy sessions we finally arrived at a form of company that is mutually beneficial to the parties.' According to Omata (Japanese-American in charge of the joint venture) the company, fortunately, has never been confronted with an issue that could not be negotiated; both sides have always been able to resolve their differences. Large companies like Mitsui or Mitsubishi are cosmopolitan in their outlook and, consequently, very accommodating to differing perspectives.

From the Japanese standpoint, if a difficulty cannot be resolved, both parties will continue to negotiate until common ground is reached and the differences are ironed out. An example of a problem that would require negotiations between the two parties is how to respond to the product needs of the Japanese market. Recently there arose a need in Japan to produce computers capable of processing Japanese characters (*kanji*). To operate as a native industry, the joint venture company had to develop a '*kanji*' processor. The US partner had to understand that and work with them. As a result NUK developed a processor with '*kanji*' capability. This development was only possible after innumerable meetings between Sperry development people and those of NUK, the joint venture.

Another type of problem that requires negotiation is that of quality. The Japanese are obsessed with quality; the zero-defect movement is strong in Japan. Sperry has to work with NUK's technical people constantly to respond to consumer specifications. To resolve such issues, both sides must engage in long discussion sessions lasting over a year or longer.

The Sperry chairman noted that in a joint venture some issues might be unresolvable: 'If the issue cannot be resolved, and we arrive at a confrontation point, we will sell out or we will buy them out.' Even here, both parties would go through a long discussion period until it became obvious to one side there was no solution. At that point, the venture disintegrates. Some US–Japanese ventures have, unfortunately, arrived at this stage. The Japanese process of conflict resolution is time-consuming and more drawn out than in the US, where both parties bring in their attorneys and begin suing each other. That is unlikely to happen in Japan. The Sperry chairman believes that:

> the Japanese system works better where there is a possibility for solution because once you arrive at a decision, then you obtain total support from the two sides. But in a confrontation process where there is really no solution, the Western way is much better. Where there is a way to work out the difference, the Japanese system is better. We could use the analogy of a divorce. In America you might get a divorce that you really did not have to.

(Adapted from Tung, 1984)

Licensing agreements

A licensing agreement will have clauses covering whether an agreement is exclusive or non-exclusive, how long it will last, the area it is to cover, the applicable law and where arbitration will take place. Usually, the price is the royalty paid as well as any initial down payments. It may include geographic restrictions to confine licensees to their agreed areas, but this can be a pious hope to prevent competition from their own product in third markets from would-be licensees desperate to export their licensed product. Sometimes, minimum quantities are stipulated to encourage the licensee to meet target sales. Grant-back provisions deal with improvements that are made to a patented product by the licensee. Often, licensors give their licensees the right to sell any improvements they make to the other licensees provided they receive for 'free' the full details of the improvements.

Negotiation/renegotiation of the agency/distributorship agreement

If a supplier tries to negotiate hard about commission, in the case of agents, and discount arrangements, in the case of distributors, particularly when holding the whip hand in relation to the power balance between them, then that action can be counter-productive. An agreement perceived to be unfair in operation by the intermediaries will have a de-motivating effect. Clearly, mutual benefit in an agreement which is presumed to have a long-term duration must be desirable. Before a contract is signed, agreement must be reached on:

- products/brands included in the agency/distributorship;
- territory covered by the agreement and whether agreement is exclusive or non-exclusive. Some markets are so small exclusive agreements are needed to ensure adequate return for effort;
- duration of the agreement;
- prices and currency of quotations and invoices and trade discounts to distributor;
- percentage agency commission, when and how it is to be paid to the agent;
- place and body of arbitration;
- law of the agreement.

The environment can change either dramatically as in the case of the devaluation of the currency of one of the parties to the agreement, or insidiously as in the case of imperceptible long-term changes like the strengthening over time of particular interest groups. Smaller retailers banded together under symbol groups with names like Spar (from the Dutch word meaning to save) and Mace, set up by the wholesalers as a counter-balance to the powerful retailers grown large by merger and acquisition with a strong position to negotiate substantial discounts. The object was to benefit from the advertising of the symbol group and to get better prices as a result of their much greater buying capability. In the mid-1980s Cadbury refused to give Spar, already organizing on a European basis, similar discounts for similar quantities given to the large and growing supermarket groups. It was only when Spar threatened to boycott Cadbury's products in 11,000 Western European outlets that the chairman went post-haste to Amsterdam and conceded the point at issue.

The symbol groups were to be treated as an entity and not a collection of small buyers as Cadbury had contended. As retail groups grew even larger and fewer in the 1990s, and negotiated even better discounts, so Spar responded by further extending its membership. Today, manufacturers have to take account of an even greater accumulation of power in the case of Spar International which has several hundred wholesaler members and over 40,000 small retailers in Western Europe. Currently, its negotiation power is considerable and the lower prices they are able to agree go a long way to making more equal the price they can charge *vis-à-vis* their big supermarket brothers with maximum discounts, economies of scale and vast promotion budgets.

Negotiating joint venture agreements

Joint venture agreements are characterized by greater complexity as well as greater power in the system mentioned earlier. Where the joint venture is set up under local law, as most are under equity participation arrangements, it is advisable for the parties to go beyond the financial arrangements to anticipate, where possible, the conflicts that will inevitably arise. These include:

- quality of performance of the partners in the joint venture;
- policies and objectives of the new company;
- contributions of the parties, their rights and obligations;
- rights of the partners to sell their shares;
- procedures for recruiting and dismissing;
- responsibilities for the import of components and the export of finished goods;
- training and experience to provide cross-cultural coping strategies to staff of both organizations.

IMPACT OF THE INTERNET

For the time being there is little or no regulation of the Internet, which allows the medium to develop as the market dictates. It is a classic approach. As governments get more and more knowledge of its impact, it will be used to generate influence and power to counter the anarchic quality of present use and the possible threat to competition from its domination by the big players.

Where the industry approximates the classic structure of perfect competition, contracts are not often used (Galbraith, 1975). Supply responds readily to changes in market prices, and since there is a goodly number of sellers, it is not necessary to make special middle- or long-term arrangements with each one. This could be construed as 'free-flow' distribution. Transactions taking place under this practice may, or may not, have a degree of permanence. They have not yet reached the stage where long-term, written agreements are considered necessary. With globalization, a worldwide market and international channels replace the local nature of traditional channels. Its geographic extent is encouraging new electronic MNCs to determine the nature of new channels and to buy up successful start-up companies that match their mission objectives.

Some Internet developments

Overheads are considerably less for e-commerce intermediaries than for traditional ones. They do not require the conventional investment in warehouses, demonstration shops and associated equipment and staff. In the US, an organization like FurnitureFind.com is eroding away the idea that certain kinds of products cannot be sold on-line. New entrants to web markets are more likely to be in the laggard categories like clothing and art than the established staples like CDs and books where competition is heavy. Even perishable groceries and car parts are becoming available on the net. The so-called 'look and feel' issues are being addressed as entrepreneurial companies spend to overcome the objections of buyers, e.g. by providing high resolution pictures of items they cannot touch and the value of art objects is being assured by endorsement by reputable experts.

The US leisure catalogue company, Lands' End, already established in Europe, has developed a 'swim suit finder' feature to mollify women who do not want to buy beachwear they cannot try on. It allows women to pick their body type from an array of choices and recommends suits likely to fit. This, together with a noticeable increase in the proportion of women logging on, is expanding the market for such items. Companies like eBay, an electronic auction house, are taking away classified advertisement business from newspapers, and on-line news services similarly are nibbling away at the editorial side. The classified advertisement business particularly is important for regional newspapers in the UK where it is estimated to amount to about 50 per cent of revenues. If the trend is continued, smaller newspapers may take their classified advertisements to the web providers as one way of retaining the business. It remains to be seen what will follow.

The rapidly emerging new class of middlemen is offering real value and attacking inefficiencies in the price and cost structure of business. It would appear that not only are traditional retailers looking to undertake Internet operations as a hedge against electronic developments but they are looking to integrate shopping, combining stores, the Internet, catalogues, the telephone and eventually television. It is a seductive concept which is making electronic channels consider investing in 'bricks and mortar' retailers. The advantage of the bricks and mortar organizations is that they do what the vast majority of the electronic IT companies have failed to do so far. They make a profit. Association with these traditional retailers by acquisition, or merger, assures a base for further investment.

North European challenge

The largest users of the Internet, even larger than the US as a proportion of the population, are the Scandinavian countries. It is to be expected that considerable entrepreneurial thrust will come from there. And it does. The Finnish brokerage company, eQ Online, is preparing to offer trading in shares in Germany having established itself some months earlier at home, entering what is expected to be an exceedingly fast growing European market. It is setting up a system for trading shares using mobile phones with a German language version for export. The Swedish company, Boxman, is already Europe's leading on-line CD seller and is moving into local markets in the larger European country markets with websites designed for the purpose. The Stockholm-based company, Icon Medialab, has offices in

LEARNING OBJECTIVES

The objectives of this chapter are to:
- show the relationship between the elements of the marketing plan;
- highlight the critical role of marketing planning to successful international marketing;
- identify the major influences on the effective implementation of international marketing plans;
- highlight the challenges faced in implementing marketing plans.

When you have completed the chapter you should:
- be aware of the contribution of marketing theory to international marketing planning;
- understand the process of international marketing planning;
- be able to put together the structure of an international marketing plan;
- appreciate how international marketing planning should be implemented.

NATURE OF INTERNATIONAL MARKETING PLANNING

The student should appreciate that the determination of the organization's strategic goals is complex and largely follows rules that have been worked out from experience of military warfare. The ways in which strategic goals are determined are discussed in depth within the strategic management literature, e.g. Johnson and Scholes (2002); Hooley *et al.* (1998). For the purposes of this chapter, the student should recognize the close linkage between an organization's corporate strategic goals and the implementation of marketing plans to attain the goals. The international marketing plan, like the national marketing plans, should outline the process whereby the organization's strategy is fulfilled.

Usually the marketing plan will aim for growth, in which case, in terms of international market expansion, the firm may undertake 'initial entry', 'local market expansion' or, at a much later stage, 'global rationalization' (Douglas and Craig (1989) and see Chapter 2, pp. 29–31). The international marketing plan should incorporate these phases of expansion (as will be discussed on pp. 223–5) emphasizing the methods expected to be used to achieve the desired growth. For example, initial entry might require establishing appropriate channels of distribution, such as agents and distributors, to support export activity. Local market expansion might need marketing to focus on promoting a particular message using 'above the line' media such as television and the press as well as 'below the line' sponsorship and public relations. Global rationalization could be undertaken by concentrating on cost cutting throughout the operations to achieve more competitive prices.

Whatever the level of international expansion, an international marketing plan has to be prepared. The marketing plan is a document that details the methods and tactics for attaining the strategic goals of the organization. It shows the actions needed to achieve the strategic objectives. Strategic plans usually have long-term vision, providing direction for the organization for upwards of two, three, four or five years ahead. Marketing plans most commonly run on a one-year time scale with provisional guidelines for the subsequent years two and three. Usually marketing plans are prepared on an annual cycle that fits the firm's financial accounting year. Typically, the annual tax year (from 6 April to 5 April in the UK) is used; some firms choose the year-end (31 December). Normally, the selected cut-off date is maintained for subsequent planning rounds.

MARKETING PLAN

A marketing plan sets out to provide a framework for the proposed marketing to take place. It identifies the objectives of the plan together with the methods and resources to implement it. Typically, it covers some, or all, of the topics shown in Figure 9.1.

Further details of the market planning process are provided in McDonald (1995) and simplified illustrations are shown in McDonald and Morris (1987). Cooper and Lane (1997) also consider practical marketing planning issues. McDonald and Payne (1996) concentrate on applying market planning within the service sector. Aaker (1998) identifies some of the problems associated with implementing formal planning systems and provides insights in to how they can be overcome.

International marketing plan

For international marketing planning, firms extend the traditional marketing plan to the international arena. Such plans start by defining the firm's business mission and strategic objectives showing the strategic direction in which the firm wishes to move. The plan proceeds to analyse the environment in which the firm operates, showing the external influences on the firm, as discussed in Chapter 1. The environmental analysis examines the political (and legal), the economic, social and technological influences on the firm's activities. At this time competitor activity within the market is assessed and the firm's competitive position is ascertained relative to the competitors examined.

The firm's business mission, strategic objectives, the environmental analysis and the firm's competitive position provide the framework for assessing the firm's strengths, weaknesses, opportunities and threats (SWOT analysis) within the market. The resource constraints are also considered, including the finance, human resources and time available to reach the defined goals. The plan provides an assessment of the firm's internal strengths and weaknesses as well as those of its competitors. Internal strengths and weaknesses relate to internal operational and organizational factors such as product characteristics, management expertise, research capability as well as financial position. External strengths and weaknesses concern the firm's performance relative to its competitors.

The plan should also consider the internal and external opportunities and threats facing the firm. Opportunities may relate to issues ranging from new product developments and new markets to mergers and acquisitions. Threats can include an assessment of the firm's vulnerability to over-extending resources through too extensive geographical coverage, dependence on importing agents, lack of transferability of products and service to new markets, etc.

223

Business mission:	Mission statement encompassing the whole organization, often following a general goal, e.g. 'to be the market leader'.
Corporate objective:	Specifics of business mission statement. Objectives are usually given in quantifiable terms, e.g. to achieve 'X' turnover and 'Y' profit, or 'Z' increase on previous year's performance; supporting qualitative objectives may also be used, e.g. to increase product quality profile among customers.
Environmental audit:	Market environment in which the firm operates in terms of political (including legal), economic, social and technological (PEST) environmental issues.
Marketing audit:	Analyses competitor activity, providing relative position of the organization within the total market. It assesses: – firm's internal strengths and weaknesses. – firm's external opportunities and threats.
Market analysis:	Assessment of market size, trends and segments; regional and local market characteristics; seasonal variations in sales, etc.
Marketing objectives and major strategies:	Definition of objectives indicates achievement forecasts in terms of increased sales, customer awareness, channel coverage for the product or service, etc. Corporate strategies relate to the analyses of environmental and marketing audits discussed above.
Marketing programmes and tactics:	Implementation of marketing tactics to achieve the strategic objectives through the marketing mix.
Market information analysis:	Discovery of market gaps, new markets/segments, customer characteristics, etc. It incorporates Marketing Information System (MIS), marketing research methodology and implementation including selection of marketing research agency if appropriate.
Marketing mix:	Favoured combination of product, price, promotion and channels of distribution approaches.
Product:	Assessment of product characteristics, range, features; sales trends, performance history and planned developments. Competitive analysis and advantage.
Pricing:	Assessment of positioning strategy, customer perceived values. Competitive analysis and advantage.
Promotion:	Assessment of media advertising, direct mail, special promotions, exhibitions, public relations and measurement of communication effectiveness. Competitive analysis and advantage.
Channels of distribution (covered by the term 'place'):	Assessment of channel strategy, channel selection; selling strategy, sales plan and sales force organization. Competitive analysis and advantage.
Resources:	Constraints within which plan has to operate.
Finance:	Marketing budget, revenue and gross margin forecast, target marketing ratios and cash flow projection.
Time:	Scheduling of proposed marketing activities within the plan (often using a Gantt chart).
Human resources:	Personnel requirements for plan.

Figure 9.1 Structure and contents of a typical marketing plan

The marketing plan identifies areas where the firm has strengths and weaknesses, and seeks to show where opportunities for expansion occur as well as any threats that may be encountered by these tactics. Awareness of these issues provides a framework for management to implement an action plan to optimize the opportunities and minimize the associated risks.

Traditionally, international marketing plans have followed the theoretical framework of a firm's international growth taking place in incremental steps. Initial plans detailed proposed marketing operations in one country. As expansion occurred, they were extended to encompass the other countries involved (Douglas and Craig, 1989). Typically, international marketing plans for smaller firms have shown this type of incremental growth. The plan set out to establish marketing in one country. Gradually, according to the firm's resources, marketing was extended across borders to encompass more and more countries. However, many firms, especially the larger organizations, have established international, even global, operations. In these cases the international marketing plan is much more extensive, often being a combination of national plans that fit the corporate strategy. These large firms have passed the initial market entry stages of the newcomer and have established marketing operations in the countries concerned.

In the situation of the large firm, usually management operating within each country, or territory, prepares its own marketing plan. The plans have to fit the corporate strategic plan and have to be agreed with central, head office management. Considerable negotiation between all parties concerned may be required before the plans are accepted. The mission, the strategic goals and objectives, will be common for all concerned, but the method of implementing the goals may differ. For example, in the case of the global detergent supplier Unilever, the marketing plan used in Chile or Canada, while similar, is likely to differ in detail from the marketing plan used in Hong Kong or the UK. But the country plans will fit into the overall corporate plan.

A further complication in international planning is the potential for rapid international expansion using IT. With the support of IT, especially the increased use of the Internet and its associated services, firms can internationalize their operations almost instantaneously, should they so desire. Firms starting to market their products and services can reach many customers directly through the Internet. Since most of the developed world and many parts of the less developed economies have access to the Internet, there is the potential for global coverage at the early stages of international expansion. The major constraint, apart from access to the Internet, is the limitation of logistics support for the product or service to reach the consumer, as is evident at peak demand periods such as Christmas when demand cannot always be met within the time constraints. In this way, increasingly, international marketing planning incorporates extensive use of the Internet as a communication channel alongside conventional international expansion approaches. Indeed, some firms concentrate entirely on using the Internet, almost to the exclusion of the conventional marketing mix. Firms such as Amazon.com and easyJet.com develop their marketing mix in terms of the product/service, promotion and pricing tactics in response to customer demand as evident through their use of websites within the Internet channel. In this way, the market planning process is increasingly used to consider cross-border international expansion on a shorter and more extensive scale than had previously been practicable.

International Marketing Information System (MIS)

The International Marketing Information System (MIS) including marketing research (discussed in Chapter 4) plays a crucial role in assessing the market to determine potential opportunities and threats. The MIS is used in marketing decision-making to ensure successful international expansion by identifying markets to target for expansion and the entry methods favoured by the potential consumers. The MIS can help to identify the favoured marketing mix, that is, the characteristics of the products or services that should be offered as well as the pricing, promotion and channels of distribution tactics that are most likely to ensure success.

The fundamental approach to formulating a MIS for international marketing is the same as for the domestic situation although, obviously, the MIS used will be more complex and difficult to develop than that used for domestic marketing. For the established international group, or MNC, the complexity of marketing planning reflects the group's international activities. In the same way as for the firm expanding from a domestic base to international operations, the established international group is required to fulfil its strategic objectives to ensure that each country's management meets the goals that have been set. The MIS, together with marketing research undertaken for both domestic and international markets, plays a critical role in the marketing decision process necessary to achieve the strategic objectives. These, in turn, influence the implementation of the marketing mix both within, and across, countries. The large MNC endeavours to set up a global MIS, usually by assimilating smaller MISs dedicated to individual countries, product or service groups. The corporate MIS is likely to be an amalgam of the MISs developed nationally, and even in regions of countries, as for Europe covering the EU, the Pacific rim for countries in the Far East and even Australasia, North and South America, etc. Over time, the MNC will try to rationalize the systems, encouraging common approaches in their development. For the smaller organization, the corporate MIS will, similarly, comprise MISs developed within individual countries. They will be expanded to match management's requirements.

Problems to be overcome with international MISs include those associated with assimilating the different systems developed within individual countries across national borders. Apart from the obvious problems of considering the distinct cultures of the different countries and regions within countries, differences occur at the operational level of collecting data which is assimilated within the MIS. There are different methods of collecting data, e.g. face-to-face interviews with women may be appropriate within Western Europe but could be more difficult to undertake in some Middle Eastern markets. There are different languages used with different alphabets and so on. Over and above these cultural issues, further challenges to achieving a cohesive MIS for global planning purposes can be posed by the different software and hardware used to process the data, e.g. some parts of the organization may use IBM compatible PCs, others AppleMacs or other computing equipment. These problems can be accentuated when organizations expand internationally through mergers and acquisitions that have their own information systems, hardware and culture that differ from those of the dominant organization. Nevertheless, an all-embracing

MIS for the international, or multinational, organization has to be developed to keep the corporate management informed. While challenging, and often costly to implement, this can be achieved by assimilating the data from the various MISs in a consolidated format, using the individual country MISs, that can be fed into the international market planning process. The potential help provided by such planning encourages management to find ways to evolve the most appropriate plans.

Product

The nature of international product development is discussed in Chapter 5. The international marketing plan has to determine the characteristics of the products, or services, that are to be marketed. It will consider the range and features of the products using tools such as sales trend analysis, product performance history and forecasts of product developments. These attributes should be compared with competitor offerings to ascertain the firm's product performance. This procedure is termed competitive analysis and is used to indicate advantages, or disadvantages, faced by the product in association with its competitors.

Pricing

The nature of international pricing is discussed in Chapter 6. In particular, positioning strategy and customer perceived values are considered. Their inter-relationship plays a critical part in defining the firm's product or service range within the market. Product prices are compared with the prices of competing goods, or services, and any advantage, or disadvantage, identified. Close monitoring of a firm's pricing strategy compared with competitors and the sales achieved is required to enable effective international marketing planning.

Promotion

The nature of international promotion is discussed in Chapter 7. The promotion strategy and its proposed implementation have to be encompassed within the international marketing plan. The promotion mix is determined to match the characteristics of the product or service being marketed. It can incorporate a range of promotion methods including conventional 'above the line' media advertising and direct mail as well as 'below the line' sponsorship, special promotions and exhibitions, etc. Firms are advised to invest in public relations support which acts as a catalyst to the whole promotion process. Assessment of competitive analysis and any advantage, or disadvantage, are required to measure the effectiveness of the proposed communications (see Chapter 7). For example, the proposed international promotion plan might contain forecasts of cost effectiveness in terms of advertising expenditure compared to forecast sales in different countries. These ratios should be compared with the equivalent for the major competitors within the firm's international markets. The processes of comparing the firm's proposed promotion plan with that of competitors acts as a gauge to monitor performance and will help in future planning.

Channels of distribution (covered by the term 'place')

The nature of international channels of distribution, as discussed in Chapter 8, includes determining channel strategy and channel selection for the product or service being marketed. It covers the firm's proposed selling strategy and sales plan for the sales force. Once again, the firm is recommended to undertake competitor analysis to determine whether the proposed channels of distribution strategy and its implementation can provide competitor advantage at an international level. It is useful to establish whether the firm's proposed channels of distribution plan matches the expectations of channel members, including intermediaries such as importing agents, franchisers, wholesalers and retailers. If the plan differs, it can meet with resistance from those involved, preventing its successful implementation. Care has to be taken when planning changes to the traditional channels of distribution approach, even more so at an international level when misunderstandings can so easily be made due to different cultural interpretations of behaviour.

Resource implications

At the same time as the plan for the marketing mix is being assimilated, the financial, human and time resources for international growth have to be considered. Resource implications affect the tools available to implement all stages of international expansion. The amount of finance available will determine the scale of expansion that can be undertaken. Many firms have failed in their bid to establish international operations because of misjudgements of the real costs involved. Furthermore, financial resources affect the level of support that can be given to product development, to different pricing approaches, to promotion campaigns and to intermediaries within the channels of distribution to stimulate demand within the international markets. Access to the appropriate human resource expertise is critical to the successful outcome of the expansion. The time available to implement the proposed expansion also plays a crucial role. It is to be expected that as physical distance from the administrative headquarters, manufacturing and operational activities and the customer increases, the time for the goods and services to pass through the value chain is also likely to increase. Certainly, the value chain is likely to become more complex.

   The international marketing plan is usually depicted through a flowchart, termed a Gantt chart, which depicts the start and finish of each activity along the value chain. This enables management to determine the order and timing of the various activities, helping in the implementation of the plan.

Human resource constraints

As well as finance, the availability of appropriate human resources has to be incorporated within the international marketing plan. Proposed international expansion projects have often been constrained, and even shelved, because of lack of available trained managerial expertise to oversee the expansion within the proposed time schedule. Since the early 1990s, many European firms have had to curtail their international expansion to Eastern Europe due to reticence on the part of European national managerial staff to re-locate to Poland,

Hungary and the Czech Republic. For example, Tesco, the UK-based food retailer, found that the process of international expansion took longer to implement than was originally envisaged partly due to the need to train local nationals to undertake retail management and local suppliers to service logistics support. The number of European nationals prepared to re-locate was limited.

IMPLEMENTATION OF INTERNATIONAL MARKETING PLAN

As discussed above on p. 223, international marketing plans form part of the strategic planning activity, usually undertaken on an annual cycle. The plan is a guideline that is agreed by all parties concerned, i.e. the strategic corporate planners at central head office and the operational managers within the organizational divisions. Theoretically, the plan can be revised, or modified, in agreement with all concerned, but such changes have to be justified. The annual plan provides goals, budgets and outline methods whereby these should be achieved, with those for the first few months usually being more detailed than for the later period. Indeed, it is often expected that as the planning year progresses new evidence will become available (such as sales performance) that favours modification of the original plan. Some flexibility is required to encompass the latest market information (probably provided through the MIS). However, the fundamental strategic approach as projected within the plan should remain. The strategic direction of international operations is usually maintained, although the details of the methods used to implement the strategy may be modified to suit local conditions.

All concerned in the marketing operation are expected to work to the agreed plan. The methods used as identified by the proposed marketing mix and the resources made available should match the plan. During the planning cycle, usually at monthly intervals, the actual performance is compared with predictions made in the plan. Any discrepancies are monitored and minor adjustments made to the plan to ensure the goals are achieved. Towards the end of the planning cycle, a review panel often assesses how well actual performance matches the plan. Lessons learnt from this analysis should be carried forward to the next year's international marketing plan.

CONCLUSION

This chapter considers the nature and role of the international marketing plan. It discusses how the plan is prepared and used within international marketing. International marketing plans are tools to implement corporate strategy, being a formal proposal of the marketing tactics required to achieve the goals of the organization. They should reflect the theoretical process of international expansion, traditionally taken to be growth by incremental steps. They should also encompass IT developments that can help marketing implementation.

Typically, international marketing plans set out the organization's strategies, mission statement and objectives. They analyse the market conditions that exist in terms of the environment and competitor activity. They consider firms' strategic and marketing options and select the preferred marketing approaches for the organization concerned. International MISs are used to provide the data for marketing decision-making.

The international marketing plan aims to provide a framework for implementing marketing tactics, covering approaches to product development, pricing, promotion and distribution. The plan identifies the financial, human and time-scheduling resource implications of the recommended actions.

Usually, international marketing plans are derived through a process of combining individual national (and even regional) marketing plans into a corporate plan. Such plans have to be agreed by all the parties concerned to be effective, a process that can take considerable management skill to effect. It is this skill that is necessary for the successful implementation of international marketing across national borders.

REVIEW QUESTION

9.1 In 1999, as part of its international expansion programme, the US retailer, Wal-Mart, acquired UK's ASDA. Consider ways in which an international marketing plan might have helped Wal-Mart to assimilate the UK retail group ASDA into its European marketing operation.

REFERENCES

Aaker, D.A. (1998) *Strategic market management*, 5th edn, Chichester: John Wiley, Ch. 15, pp. 277–93; Ch. 16, pp. 294–305.

Cooper, J. and Lane, P. (1997) *Practical marketing planning*, Basingstoke: Macmillan.

Douglas, S.P. and Craig, C.S. (1989) 'Evolution of global marketing strategy: scale, scope and synergy', *Columbia Journal of World Business*, Vol. 24, No. 3, Fall, pp. 47–59.

Hooley, G.J., Saunders, J.A. and Piercy, N.F. (1998) *Marketing strategy and competitive positioning*, 2nd edn, Harlow: Financial Times/Prentice Hall.

Johnson, G. and Scholes, K. (2002) *Exploring corporate strategy: text and cases*, 6th edn, Harlow: Financial Times/Prentice Hall.

McDonald, M. (1995) *Marketing plans*, 3rd edn, Oxford: Butterworth-Heinemann.

McDonald, M. and Morris P. (1987) *The marketing plan*, Oxford: Heinemann.

McDonald, M. and Payne, A. (1996) *Marketing planning for services*, Oxford: Butterworth-Heinemann.

Appendix: Answer guide to review questions

CHAPTER 1 INTRODUCTION TO INTERNATIONAL MARKETING

1.1 The comparative sizes of the different economies are only a general indication of the extent of their associated markets. Distribution of income among that population is often difficult to establish although research by Amartya Sen (1998), Nobel prizewinner, indicates that a reasonable proxy of how widely the benefits of GNP, including income, are spread among a population, is the life expectancy of its inhabitants at birth. The longer the expectancy, the wider is the distribution. If any two of the countries in the statistics are being compared, it is useful to remember that GDP is a measure of the total flow of goods and services produced by an economy over a specified time period, normally a year. GNP is GDP plus income accruing to domestic residents from investments abroad less income earned in the domestic market accruing to foreign residents. GDP is obtained by valuing output of goods at market prices and then aggregating them and applying PPS or PPP. Only goods used for final consumption are included irrespective of the value added elsewhere. It can happen that a country attracts final assembly through making that attractive by low corporate taxes or tax breaks. It can be that greater value is added in another country (where the market can be) but that is not reflected in GDP and hence the GNP data. Also, transfer prices can skew the figures. A high population growth and a static GDP/GNP per capita can conceal a vibrant country working hard just to stand still while one with a falling population can give a higher figure.

1.2a The following factors will give the bargaining power to countries: the size of the country in economic, demographic and geographic terms; the technological infrastructure available; the specific skills of the work force; level of inducements given; desirability of the market; availability of materials and other supplies; the number of feasible alternative countries and political stability.

1.2b The following factors will give bargaining power to companies: the size of the company, its reach and financial strength; distinctive competencies available for transfer; the number and influence of local allies the company has; the reputation of the company in the host country; the number of competing companies for the contract in a given country; the level of support from the home country.

1.3 There is little doubt that many companies are moving to transnational mode. However, it does not necessarily follow that all companies will go down that route. Companies with multi-domestic products may wish to exploit the different markets by adapting as necessary to the environment in which they find themselves and remain multinational as a consequence. Where the expertise and technical or natural resources remain in one country, that industry is likely to maintain an export orientation. Where the highest quality is required or speed of production is a key factor or cost is crucial to performance, production will go to where the critical factor is best met and the organization will be global. It is clear, however, that the transnational organization is the most rapidly growing organizational form in the global market with its emphasis on resources and capabilities, national responsiveness and worldwide innovation and learning.

1.4 Ability to identify cultural differences is a key starting skill in cross-cultural interactions. For example, if you have struggled to speak school French in France and the Frenchman breaks into your own language, you come to realize that the typical Frenchman does not like to hear his language murdered. If you have been to the US and find that irony, understatement or wit do not endear you to the listener, you are on the way to finding that these savour covertness in a society that prizes openness, sincerity and candour.

Nature's way of handling the uncertainty inherent in these situations is to stereotype. That is all right as long as you realize that there must be a constant refining of these stereotypes in an attempt eventually to communicate with your foreign counterpart in a way that reflects that person's individuality. This comes from a process of learning that starts with a knowledge of one's own culture that enables people to avoid the *self-reference criterion* or *projective cognitive similarity* whereby they erroneously bring behaviours and perceptions induced by their own culture to their interpretation of another culture.

1.5 If this chapter had been written 10 years ago, only academics and military men would have known and perhaps used the Internet. Since then it has become part of the business infrastructure with an increasing number of applications. The US interactive share trading company Charles Schwab is the first company to trade in shares in Europe using the Internet. We can expect competitors to appear on a regular basis. New servers have appeared giving free access to the Internet, like hotmail.com and btclick.com. Companies can source products from websites advertising what their owners have on offer and more and more electronic intermediaries are using the medium. The Internet has the possibility of completely transforming the way we do business, not just providing another medium. Some analysts go as far as to suggest that those organizations that are too late in taking it up could go out of business.

1.6 You should be able to summarize the arguments on both sides. *The Economist* view of 'aid not trade' (years ago it was advocating just the opposite) could be challenged as well as the view that free trade is beneficial in all circumstances. The subject of ethics can give rise to long and serious debate.

CHAPTER 2 FRAMEWORK FOR INTERNATIONAL MARKETING

2.1   International marketing theory has evolved from a combination of sources, including the study of economic trade, strategy theory, marketing surveys and case studies covering both manufacturing and service industries. Until the 1990s, most theorists considered international marketing within the context of the organization's strategy with expansion being implemented by incremental growth. The international expansion of firms usually started in a limited number of countries with coverage increasingly moving towards a global goal. Few firms actually achieved global coverage.

    Some marketing theorists explained international expansion by using models that illustrated the implementation process of international marketing. In particular, Douglas and Craig (1983 and 1989) analysed the process of selecting markets, establishing in those countries and the subsequent movement towards further international expansion in other markets. They highlighted the decision process that management had to follow to achieve this expansion. Other theorists such as Harrell and Kiefer (1981) and Goodnow (1985) extended the analyses of marketing research for the selection of international markets and methods of entry to include setting quantifiable marketing objectives, such as return-on-investment and market share targets.

    Initially, international marketing theorists concentrated on the experiences of starting up in international markets. More recently, international marketing theory has considered firms with established international businesses. In particular, strategic issues as well as the organizational and cultural challenges posed by international marketing on multinational corporations (MNCs) have been examined. Consumer behaviour studies have been extended to encompass an international dimension by comparing consumers across different countries. Similarities between customers are leading to market segmentation classifications becoming more international in their coverage, although they still attempt to maintain the obvious nationality distinctions. It is appreciated, for example, that the European teenager consumes in similar ways across Europe despite national boundaries. International marketers are developing brands that consider the international similarities as well as the national characteristics of consumers.

    International marketing theory reflects changes in international business approaches. As yet, there is limited theoretical coverage of the role of the Internet and associated information technology (IT) in the theoretical models that have been developed. Future theorists will have to extend marketing theory to recognize the role of IT in international expansion, in particular the potential for expanding globally much more quickly than traditional theory has recommended. It remains to be seen how the international marketing of the 1990s will be interpreted within the current theoretical framework but it will require recognition of the potential of the Internet for e-commerce. International marketing theory is required to reflect the dynamic changes taking place in the approaches to marketing at the present time.

2.2   Traditionally, international expansion in business has been seen as a gradual process with growth occurring incrementally from national to international geographical coverage. Expansion has been achieved by firms becoming established in one country and then extending their geographical coverage across borders, gaining expertise in the newer countries and progressively gaining more international coverage with the goal of global coverage. Marketing theorists described this process in terms of the decisions that were required. These often focused on marketing research to help to select the more appropriate markets, methods of entry and marketing mix to ensure successful international expansion.

Commerce involves exchanging products and services for economic benefit and has always been dependent on sound communication taking place between all the parties concerned. IT plays a critical role in this communication, especially when business extends its coverage across national borders. The increasing sophistication of IT is enabling ever more intensive and less costly communications on a near-global level. Tools such as the traditional telephone have extended their usage from personal communication between two individuals in fixed locations to allow mobile flexible communication. Persons can make telephone contact much more readily with relatively lower costs. Systems have been introduced to add services to the humble telephone and the telephone cable carrier. Management Information Systems and Marketing Information Systems (MISs) make use of the cables to transport data collected from within and outside the organization to those who require it for management decision-making. Video conferencing has been introduced to enable personal communication nationally and across continents, reducing the apparent physical distance between individuals.

From the 1990s, e-mail using the Internet has enhanced the potential for instantaneous communication both within and external to the organization. This can benefit the speed and effectiveness of the collection, assimilation, analysis and interpretation as well as the dissemination of marketing information throughout the organization. Within the MIS the Internet can be used to collect data from internal sources in the organization, for marketing intelligence and for marketing research. The data can be processed and analysed using computer systems and transmitted to management. For example, the Internet is used for international surveys of staff, actual and potential consumers providing responses much more quickly than traditional personal face-to-face, telephone or postal methods. Progress in IT has given firms the potential to transmit this database, almost instantaneously, across national borders minimizing disadvantages of geographical distance.

It is appreciated that there are problems associated with using IT for international communications. The potential to communicate more effectively is dependent on a number of issues including the individuals concerned having access to personal computers, comparability of data obtained from within and outside the organization as well as adequate security control. Nevertheless, IT is providing the potential for developing and using increasingly dynamic MISs and is used to the benefit of consumers and business. Products and services are being developed, priced, promoted and distributed to satisfy consumer demand more effectively and efficiently both within countries and across borders on an international scale. Developments in IT are encouraging the potential for instantaneous global coverage provision in international marketing.

Thus, IT is changing the traditionally accepted route to international expansion. While the international expansion of firms has been constrained by resource considerations, e-commerce is enabling firms to achieve instantaneous international and, even, global coverage. E-commerce is forecast to increase substantially. Many firms are continuing to maintain the traditional organization and structures for their international expansion systems but, at the same time, they are introducing methods using e-commerce to support and extend traditional practices. For example, eToys, the leading US Internet retailer of toys and children's products, launched its UK retail website in late 1999 as a first step towards its geographic expansion. The UK site http://www. etoys.com features more than 5,000 products and is divided into four virtual shops: toys, videos, computer software and console games. The toy section includes some specifically British toys including Noddy, as well as a range of international brands such as Lego. In this way, eToys is using IT to expand internationally from its US base far more quickly than would previously have been considered feasible. International businesses like toy producers, using traditional marketing practices, especially traditional channels of distribution, are facing increased competition from IT-related developments that will change the traditional international expansion theory and practice. IT provides the potential for instantaneous global coverage provision that has been much more difficult to implement using traditional international expansion approaches.

CHAPTER 3 EUROPEAN MARKETING

3.1 The challenges faced in implementing the enlargement of the EU from 15 to 25 members in May 2004 are formidable. This is evident by the considerable political effort that was made in the Barcelona (2002), Copenhagen (2002) and the Thessaloniki (2003) summits, and it continues to cause concern. While there is strong political will to bring into the EU the countries from Central and Eastern Europe (CEE), that is, the Czech Republic, Estonia, Hungary, Latvia, Lithuania, Poland, the Slovak Republic and Slovenia, together with Cyprus and Malta, it is appreciated that this will be costly. However, it is considered that over time the enlargement should evolve to become a 'common market' that will benefit the standards of living and national security across Europe. The EU principles of encouraging the 'freedom of movement of people, goods and services' across Europe is expected to have repercussions on the migration of people from CEE to Western Europe, at least in the short-term. There is concern that this migration and the associated influx of labour will have adverse effects on employment levels and pay of persons in the established EU. Other worries relate to the Common Agricultural Policy (CAP) and the level of subsidy that will be required to bring agriculture in the CEE to the level of Western Europe. With a finite level of financial support available, it is likely that the current farming subsidies will be reduced to compensate for the increase in expenditure in the CEE, which worries the farming communities, especially those in France, Germany and Ireland. Security associated with the increasing ease of illegal entry to Europe is also taxing the authorities.

The enlargement of the EU is expected to increase competition at all levels, reducing manufacturing costs as Western European production is transferred to the

235

lower cost countries. This process has already begun with MNCs setting up in the CEE to seek more competitive prices. However, such moves involve substantial investment in capital, work force training and education as well as in the development of support infrastructure, so there are associated compensating costs involved.

On the more positive side, the proposed enlarged EU will give access to a further 124 million people, taking the total Single European Market (SEM) to around 570 million people. Already the major European retailers are taking advantage of this increased market with firms such as the French Carrefour, Geant, Leclerc and Auchan, Germany's Metro as well as the UK Tesco moving to Poland and Hungary. It is anticipated that with the limited growth available within the existing EU countries more retailers will look to increasing investment in the new member countries, at the same time helping to bring cohesion across Europe.

In summary, the challenges of the enlargement of the EU are substantial. However, since the change in political structure in CEE since 1989, the inequalities of the CEE economies compared to those to the traditional EU are being addressed through the proposed enlarged EU. There are marketing opportunities available to those prepared to work with these developing economies as evidenced by the rush to expand into CEE. It is expected that in the long term the enlarged EU will be beneficial to all concerned.

In this respect, students are advised to read the quality and financial press to keep abreast of developments related to the enlargement of the EU.

3.2   As the CEE countries have been liberalized so they have been replacing their traditional markets with the Soviet Union and other socialist countries by the developed markets from Western Europe and North America. The poor infrastructure throughout much of the CEE countries has limited the penetration of foreign products to the capital cities. However, over the last five years, there have been great improvements, which have encouraged Western producers and retailers to enter the CEE markets.

Traditionally, 'Western' firms used direct exporting approaches through approved government bodies to enter most CEE country markets, although exceptionally, for Poland, Hungary and even Romania, some joint venture agreements were made. However, with the increasing liberalization since 1989 associated with the change from Communism, it has become possible to undertake direct investment, licensing, franchising, contract manufacturing and the management methods commonly used in international marketing. Nevertheless, many firms still favour the traditional approach of exporting as it reduces risk.

Encouragingly, as firms have become more confident and familiar with the market, some of these traditional exporters are expanding their operations in the CEE countries using other market development strategies. With the lower costs of labour, firms are setting up manufacturing and processing bases in CEE. Typically, German firms have moved production to the former East Germany and across national borders especially into the Czech Republic and to Hungary. Other examples include the brewing industry where the leading European brewer Heineken and others have invested heavily in Poland and the Czech Republic in particular. Service providers, including those from the banking and insurance sector, have entered the market, e.g. Swiss Allianz operating in Poland. Within logistics service provision, the UK Tibbett and Britten has become proficient in operating within the Hungarian market.

At the same time, European retailers have used a range of routes to become established in the area, although for the most part they have set up 'new build' operations following similar retail operations to those practised in Western Europe. Over the last ten years UK-based Tesco acquired the local retailer Hit in Poland, using the Hit brand alongside its own. French-based Carrefour, Leclerc and Auchan also operate in Poland. Among consumer goods retailers, especially fashion clothing retailers, franchise arrangements are commonly used, e.g. the Swedish company H&M uses this method for its expansion to Warsaw in Poland.

Nevertheless, firms are hesitant to become involved in high-risk investment and continue to be wary of the unfamiliar and the possible association with 'mafia' type organizations in parts of CEE. Consequently, they are more cautious in their expansion to CEE than might be the case for similar expansion within Western Europe. At present, most of the investment is concentrated in the capital cities with the concentration of population such as Warsaw and Prague. There is little evidence of the large European supermarket food chains expanding across Poland and elsewhere at present, although this may come in due course. Furthermore, the retail operations being used are less sophisticated than those in Western Europe, e.g. in 2003, Tesco in Warsaw has not yet introduced any form of 'loyalty' bonus card like that in the UK.

In essence, similar methods to those used in Western Europe are being used for market entry and expansion in the CEE countries. But the methods are being introduced in a cautious manner. Market entry has progressed from direct exporting to some forms of production and assembly, acquisition and franchising with close control being kept by the incoming firm. Some forms of joint venture activity are used, but there is concern regarding obtaining suitable partners able, and willing, to match the Western European contribution. As experience and confidence increases it is likely that more investment in the potentially attractive CEE markets will occur.

3.3 The objective of the Single European Market (SEM) (or Single Market Programme (SMP) is to have an harmonious 'open' market with the same economic conditions throughout so that consumers are offered the same product or service at the same price and quality. The European Commission of the EU influences marketing practice related to product development, pricing, promotion and the channels of distribution used as well as the Marketing Information System (MIS) used to implement marketing practice. These issues are discussed in the text.

For example, regarding product or service quality, the European Commission has introduced regulation at various levels to control waste disposal throughout the supply chain. It imposes regulations on manufacturing processes, monitoring effluent that is put into the air and water such as car exhaust and factory chimney emission as well as chemical waste into the sea, rivers and landfill. While these controls have been initiated at local and national authority level, the EU regulation is much more strident and effective. The EU 'Blue Flag' award for a clean beach is highly prized and necessitates close control of manufacturing and agricultural practice. Other EU controls on product development include the introduction of EU patents and quality standards to name but a few.

In relation to pricing, the European Commission is increasingly influential in working towards the standardization of European pricing approaches. For example, the car pricing strategy of MNCs has been closely examined together with their approaches to tied dealership distribution. When surveys of car prices in Europe showed that the highest car prices were in the UK, Ford and others MNCs explained that this was due to UK cars unusually needing right-hand drive accessories. But the European Commission did not accept this situation and obliged the MNCs to introduce lower prices. It has also highlighted concerns regarding restrictive practices associated with car dealerships which have had to be changed. European Commission proposals to harmonize taxation across Europe have been more difficult to implement.

The European Commission also oversees mergers and acquisition activity. In 2003 it raised the issue of unfair government subsidies hindering competition related to the proposed French government support for Ahlstrom, a major engineering firm manufacturing high-speed trains as well as other capital goods. While a compromise agreement was made to ensure that Ahlstrom did not go into receivership, the EU prevented unfair support for the group.

The EU is increasingly influential over marketing messages that are presented to the public in the form of promotional messages. While traditionally national bodies such as the UK Advertising Standards Authority for press publications have undertaken controls, the EU can override national decisions. For example, in the name of personal safety, car advertisers can no longer emphasize excess speed in their advertising. It is likely that the EU will become even more influential in this area in due course. Proposals to support the banning of cigarette and alcohol advertising are becoming effective, as evidenced by the adverse consequences for sports funding. For example, over the next few years, European Formula 1 racing will move to countries such as Brazil to receive tobacco sponsorship.

In this way, the EU has become a 'super authority' obliging national and local governments to consider a higher level of control than they might initially have wished to impose. While it is appreciated that fish stocks in the waters around the EU have to be protected, national governments find it politically difficult to fully impose the correcting solution. The European Commission of the EU considers the matter from a higher level with much more authority. The Spanish firm marketing frozen fish will have to accommodate the influence of the EU on sizes of fishing catches and fish market prices, the production process, the promotional communication and the channels of distribution, including logistical support, needed for the fish to reach the end consumer. No longer is it appropriate to simply accommodate the regulation of national authorities, the rules of the EU must also be considered.

3.4   Increasingly, MNCs view Europe as a trading 'bloc' within the global market and organize their marketing management to suit that approach. While it is appreciated that each member state has its own culture and may require specific marketing approaches to match consumer demand, yet there is much similarity between the demand within each EU country. It is becoming less necessary to consider that each country should have its own individual marketing approach. There can be some cross-over in approaches with Europe segmented geographically, into Mediterranean and Northern countries, or by income, population density, language or other criteria, rather than as a collection of individual countries with separate marketing approaches. Generally, MNCs control their marketing through a headquarters centre located within the densely populated area of Europe, that is, within the 'Banana belt' in the Benelux (Belgium, Netherlands and Luxembourg) countries, in northern France or in southern England.

Cities frequently used for European marketing headquarters are Amsterdam in the Netherlands, Brussels in Belgium, Paris in France and London in the UK. Many US MNCs first located their European operations in London due to the advantage of a common anglophile culture but, more recently, many firms have looked to a mainland European base within the Eurozone. From the central headquarters, European marketing can be organized by bringing together countries with similar cultures, often those in geographical proximity to one another. Typically, groupings such as Scandinavia (Norway, Sweden and Denmark) and Finland, Spain and Portugal, countries of the Iberian peninsula, as well as Germany, Austria and Switzerland may be linked.

MNCs operating in FMCG markets use marketing service organizations such as advertising and marketing research agencies to support their marketing operations. Traditionally, these agencies have located their European headquarters in major centres such as London and Paris. They have been supported by national and regional subsidiaries, say in Madrid, Frankfurt, Milan and Zurich. The MNC with its headquarters in Amsterdam, Brussels, Paris or London or elsewhere usually organizes its promotional campaigns and associated marketing research through these advertising and marketing research agencies. Advertising is placed in the national and regional media through the advertising agency network (see Chapter 7: International promotion). Marketing research is conducted by the marketing research agency through its national and regional subsidiaries and associates (see Chapter 4: International Marketing Information Systems: marketing research for further discussion). Sales force management is likely to be organized in accord with the European country regions used by the marketing research agency, A.C. Nielsen, as this helps sales monitoring. A.C. Nielsen collects sales data related to country regions which can be used to ascertain a firm's sales performance.

While MNCs frequently locate their headquarters for European marketing at major cities in northern continental Europe, production and logistics distribution centres will not necessarily be at the same location. Increasingly, production is being located outside Europe in low-cost production centres which are supported by European logistics distribution centres. Until recently, often these logistics distribution centres have been nationally located but, more and more, they are located in accord with logistical need, rather than to match different cultural requirements.

Ideally, the marketing function should be organized to support market segmentation criteria, e.g. according to age and incomes. However, in practice, within Europe, culture and language often override the ideal. It is unusual for a Swedish national sales manager to oversee a sales force in Greece, Spain or France, although it would be technically possible within the rules of the EU. More commonly, local nationals oversee national marketing, although this practice is changing. While it is difficult to imagine, theoretically, a Spanish national could manage a MNC's sales force operating across Spain and Portugal as well as across France and Belgium if that were appropriate.

3.5 International firms targeting European mass markets can consider various options. These can range from exporting direct to the end-user using an intermediary such as an agent, a wholesaler and/or a dedicated distributor. It may be appropriate to set up a sales force. Retail outlets may be used to reach the mass market consumer. The firm may own these, or they may be part of a franchise arrangement. Other issues to consider relate to the location of the manufacture and/or assembly of the product being marketed. This may be in the home country, in a low-cost country, or in the country were the product is to be sold. Details of methods of selection of the appropriate channels of distribution are discussed in Chapter 8: International channels of distribution.

Within Europe, the issues relate to the characteristics of the product or service being considered. For mass products in the form of perishable goods such as foodstuffs it might be appropriate to consider locating the source of the production as close as practical to the end-consumer. In this way, beer and water producers might consider having a number of local production units each located within the more densely populated areas of Europe, in the Benelux countries, southern England and Milan. On the other hand, if the produce has a long life, as for example, batteries, it would be more appropriate to locate all the production at one manufacturing plant in Europe (or even at a low-cost site in CEE or the Far East). The goods could be transported from the plant to each of the European markets.

In terms of distribution, it may be possible to go direct to the end-user as in the case of Internet marketing. Consumers can order direct from the Internet through sites such as amazon.com and have the goods sent through the conventional post and other express delivery services. An agent could be used, but that is less common for mass markets across Europe. While cosmetics and some household goods are distributed by door-to-door in the UK and elsewhere in Europe, e.g. Avon, these do not operate across Europe.

The more commonly used approach is to distribute through retailers, in particular, for foodstuffs and household goods. Retailers such as Carrefour and Auchan operate across most of continental Europe (see Chapter 8 for details).

Regarding the process of achieving logistics distribution across Europe, while there has been a reduction in the barriers to movement of goods and services across national borders with the removal of border controls, yet there is not free movement of goods. Some countries have introduced no Sunday travel for commercial vehicles, notably France, Germany and Austria, which leads to additional costs for international hauliers. Some countries charge commercial vehicles a 'vignette' tax for using 'toll-free' motorways for trans-shipment of goods, again hindering the free movement of goods across continental Europe. Such extra costs have to be considered when deciding on the most appropriate market entry and channels of distribution routes to use to market products across Europe. Certainly, when considering mass markets, these extra costs can prove sizeable and will influence decisions related to the selection of channels of distribution.

CHAPTER 4 INTERNATIONAL MARKETING INFORMATION SYSTEMS: MARKETING RESEARCH

4.1   The critical elements of an international Marketing Information System (MIS) should be explained, namely the nature of internal reporting, marketing intelligence and marketing research. In the text an MIS is defined as being 'people, equipment and procedures to gather, sort, analyze, evaluate and distribute needed, timely and accurate information to marketing decision makers' (Kotler *et al.*, 1999 – see Chapter 4 reference section for details). Within this framework internal reporting relates to the data that can be gathered from within the organization which could include management reports such as sales analysis and production records. Other secondary sources of data available in the public domain, in particular, through the Internet could also be used including an extensive range of government and trade association publications, etc. Marketing intelligence involves the gathering of information through networking and similar activities. Examples of this process include attending trade exhibitions and seminars, professional conferences to keep abreast of market developments. Marketing research concerns much more formalized research seeking to obtain primary data to assess market conditions. An international MIS sets out to systematically assimilate these three types of market data and to analyse them to monitor demand across the selected international countries.

The three sources of data are used to assess the market concerned. Usually secondary sources of information are less expensive to obtain. However, often they may not fully address the issue under investigation. They may well only provide part of the answer. It is the gaps in these secondary sources that more formalized marketing research using primary sources seeks to answer. This field research is likely to be more costly and time consuming to conduct but will target the specific issues raised, for example, the favoured demand characteristics of a new car model to be introduced for the European market.

An international MIS seeks to formalize the process of collecting market data across national borders, analysing secondary data sources that are readily available together with appropriate primary sources. Challenges can occur in obtaining data from different countries that can be assimilated, although increasingly analytical tools can help to reduce these difficulties, which are considered in the text.

4.2   The text explains the nature of qualitative and quantitative marketing research. Qualitative research seeks to provide 'insight' into consumer behaviour using one-to-one personal interviews and group discussions. Quantitative research sets out to

241

measure this behaviour through some form of survey and collecting data that can be shown in numerical terms. These survey methods frequently include questionnaire completion using face-to-face, telephone, postal and Internet communication. Both qualitative and quantitative research have their roles in marketing research, qualitative research being used to investigate the reasons and ways in which consumers behave, whereas quantitative techniques attempt to quantify the behaviour. Issues to consider when undertaking international marketing research using both qualitative and quantitative research methods particularly relate to cultural differences that occur between nationalities. These are considered in depth in the text, as is the influence of geography and climate. It should be appreciated that such differences between peoples in different countries do not preclude undertaking cross-border marketing research. Rather, research methods have to be adapted to assimilate the distinctive differences. Furthermore, with the trend towards increased 'commonality' between many peoples and the move towards mass marketing, the apparent differences are not always so evident. Products such as Mr Muscle cleaning polish are becoming commonplace across the world, certainly across Europe, from the UK to Poland, suggesting that supporting marketing research is also likely to be fundamentally similar, despite the use of different languages and the different geographical and climate conditions and the like.

4.3 Personal interviewing whether in the form of face-to-face, telephone or Internet 'chat' interviewing has its particular challenges in the domestic market. In particular interviewer bias may be cause for concern. Once the geographical coverage is extended across national borders these challenges are necessarily increased. The process of setting up the interviews can pose difficulties with some countries having more widely disposed populations, differences in access to databases and directories and so on. At the time of the interview there can be differences in language and culture to address. Communications may be difficult, leading to misinterpretation of responses. In essence, the process of interviewing becomes more complex as it is extended into the international arena.

4.4 A consumer panel is a 'permanent representative sample maintained by a market research agency from which information is obtained on more than one occasion either for continuous research or for 'ad hoc' projects. They are used to monitor market trends such as consumption over time and to examine issues including brand switching, repeat buying and media audiences. Typically a consumer panel has operated in only one country but, more recently, they have been developed to cover more than one country in Europe. In particular children, youths and their parents are covered in the Carrick James Market Research (CJMR) consumer panels covering Western as well as some Central and Eastern Europe (CEE) countries. These panels could enable studies of proposed advertising concepts related to new products to children across national borders. As youth become more and more similar across Europe and even globally, wearing similar clothing, watching the same films (e.g. *Harry Potter and the Prisoner of Azkaban*) in the cinemas and programmes on television, so it becomes important that their demand is researched in markets that extend across national borders.

Answers should also discuss the growing importance of access panels which marketing research agencies have developed to overcome the problems of low response rates of other forms of quantitative marketing research. These provide access to consumers willing to participate regularly in marketing research and cover Europe, the US and Canada, providing an international dimension that is helpful in global marketing.

4.5 In order to encourage export behaviour many governments actively encourage international marketing research. There is little direct encouragement for the importers. Government support is required to fall within the rules of international trade and may not provide undue financial support that is detrimental to competition in the global market. The text cites the example of government support given to exporters in the UK by Trade Partners (see details at the website http://www.tradepartners.gov.uk). Reference is made to the Trade Partners UK Information Centre which brings together extensive library resources providing international market data in the form of trade statistics as well as associated services to support the exporter in assessing market conditions in the relevant countries. Other government-backed support includes export insurance provision through the Export Credits Guarantee Department (ECGD) and international promotional activities such as trade missions, overseas trade fairs and store promotions. There is also financial support for the Export Marketing Research Scheme (EMRS) to support international marketing research. Other services include the Country Help Desks which provide support for the smaller firm setting out to start exporting.

The services discussed above are typical of those provided by most developed economy countries to encourage export activity. Sometimes they are provided by government bodies (as in the case of the UK – although even these are being moved to the private sector where it is practical to do so). Sometimes, these services are provided in conjunction with industry trade bodies, such as the Chambers of Commerce, which are financially supported by the local trade and industry. Indeed, in France, the Chambers of Commerce are closely aligned to many business schools. In this case the promotion of international trade while primarily supported by private enterprise often links into government support.

CHAPTER 5 INTERNATIONAL PRODUCT DEVELOPMENT

5.1 Earlier studies in the late 1970s and early 1980s emphasized the importance of global products and brands as the key to global markets. Later commentators saw this underlying philosophy as resting on the growing homogeneity of markets, on a universal preference for low price at acceptable quality and on scale economies of production and marketing, all of which they strongly challenged. We have seen that there are forces that push organizations in the direction of standardization and forces which encourage adaptation, both approaches having their benefits. Increasingly, it is possible to provide both groups of benefits by mass customization. Where this is not possible, the selection of niche markets or market segmentation is a well tried approach. Even here, there often has to be a degree of adjustment to markets.

Where the brand is significant in relation to the product, the global brand is essential if the client is working on a global basis. It is usually necessary with technological products. Even if a product is global, it does not follow that the brand is. There are numerous examples of identical products operating under different brand names due to cultural and other factors. Cultural factors also determine whether a brand is multi-domestic and has to be adapted to separate countries, e.g. in the case of brands associated with food and financial services.

5.2   We saw that there were restrictions imposed by governments on what might be supplied as products by a company if it wants to market its products in a particular country. Equally, there are laws aimed at creating rules for keeping order in the market such as how the various elements of intellectual property are applied. This is where the product can be matched to the legal environment as where these laws in relation to patents, trade marks and copyright are harnessed to augment the value of the product in the eyes of a user or intermediary. Other attributes are the packaging and how it can add value; the warranty which is given in respect of the product can also be important. The final enhancement of the product is through an item or related items of service which set the product apart from that of competing suppliers. For example, Direct Line was the first company to offer life insurance cover by way of a telephone discussion of the customer's specific needs.

5.3   Brands perform a security function by reducing search costs, risks, etc. to customers. For suppliers they perform a function of facilitating new product introductions, segmentation, etc. They are symbols around which relationships are built. Brands also have an associative function in the customer's mind. The combinations of various signals and symbols result in associations which may have a positive or negative meaning for the customers about the products they intend to buy. Brands have an economic function in that they make the decision process easier. They can also be used to express a particular lifestyle or status or seek to identify with a particular group. In Business-to-Business situations brands have a continuity function, i.e. the brand name, reputation and image of the supplier guarantees the delivery of these services in the future and hence the continuity of the customer firm. They also have a differentiation function for the supplier in that they may change a commoditized product into an identifiable and instantly recognizable offering.

Global brands are hard to achieve, the more so because some products do not lend themselves to the global approach for reasons of government regulations, product use embedded in a culture or failure to match brand and stage of economic development. The so-called quasi-contract between the product and the consumer is not made. When, in several countries, groups of buyers appear sensitive to the same advantages and expect the same features, there is an opportunity for a global brand connecting the above functions. Globalism expresses a corporate view, whereas at the level of the consumer in each country, in spite of so-called similar needs, their choice is individualistic.

5.4   The European Commission has ruled that it will no longer be possible for manufacturers to refuse warranty obligations for their products irrespective of the channels through which they have reached the market. Companies making purchases from parallel importers have now the same rights as purchasers buying direct from manufacturers or through their accredited representatives in a given territory. Advice to top management must make this clear as a legal obligation, contravention of which is likely to incur severe penalties.

5.5   Prescriptive matching to a market is a function of good up-to-date information on the source of regulations unique to a market. This can include requirements to show country of origin, precautions that must be taken to prevent infestation, regulations to protect operatives, restrictions in relation to food additives or genetically modified ingredients and specifications in respect of pharmaceutical compounds. It is part of a company's market intelligence gathering and should become generally known throughout the organization.

Discretionary factors stem from the organization's capacity to incorporate within the offering features meeting the needs of users in a way that reflects an intimate knowledge of the user and the market. It is not something imposed as in the case of prescriptive factors. Examples include the provision by IKEA, the Swedish furniture retailer, which identified a need for well designed products at substantially lower prices and for the customer to take on key tasks to achieve this, tasks like assembling the product and undertaking the transporting of the product home. SKF, the ball-bearing manufacturer, can supply software called 'CADalog' to customers so that they can watch a demonstration on their PCs of a three-dimensional rotating bearing, observe the details of how it functions inside different kinds of products and how it can best be installed, cared for and repaired. These discretionary activities are regularly reviewed and renewed to provide a competitive advantage.

5.6   Test marketing is used to provide an indication of likely success that a product or service may have when it is introduced to the market commercially. It can be used to develop the proposed product or service concept, as in the case of product clinics used within the car industry (see the Ford Fiesta case in Chapter 4: International Marketing Information Systems: marketing research). Product clinics can be held at various locations across the world to determine national and global demand. In the case of the Ford Fiesta, product clinics were held in Switzerland and representatives of the European country markets being investigated were flown in to participate in the product clinic. Similar product clinics were undertaken in the US and elsewhere to determine the most favoured characteristics of the proposed car design suitable for the global market.

Traditional test marketing involves testing a product or service that is close to its final format on a sample of the target market. Tests may take place using flagship retail outlets, test towns, commercial television catchment areas and similar locations. Theoretically, test markets can determine whether or not to proceed to full market coverage with the proposed product or service. In practice, the investment in new product development is so high that it is unlikely that marketing of the product would be halted at this stage. It is more likely that minor adjustments would be made.

For international marketing, it may be that a limited test area would suffice or, as often happens, a whole country could be used, before rolling out the marketing campaign across borders to other countries as appropriate. Test markets are relatively expensive to undertake, involving setting up a miniature scaled marketing operation without the benefits of economies of scale. There are the substantial costs involved in developing and producing the new product. For the test, there can be high costs associated with selecting a test location (retail outlet, town or commercial television catchment area), persuading representative retailers to trial the product on their limited shelf space and setting up a supporting sales force (and even a merchandising team). Apart from these costs there are also those involved in developing the appropriate promotional campaign which has to reflect a national (or international) campaign. It may not even be possible to downsize the campaign to the level of the test area. Commercial television catchment areas are unlikely to match the needs of the selected town, or towns, so different promotional methods may need to be considered.

A major criticism of conventional test marketing is the lack of data that will provide evidence for decision-making. The product being tested may not be readily differentiated from other similar 'me-too' products, e.g. one chocolate bar or a biscuit is very similar to another. Thus, with the relatively high costs involved, compounded by giving competitors advance warning of the impending new product, many firms have introduced their new products and services with the minimum of test marketing, on a roll-out basis. The product is tested and, once the appropriate support is ready in the form of production, logistics and marketing, its geographical coverage is extended across regions and borders. Close monitoring of sales figures provides evidence as to the success of the launch and the product's progress along its life cycle. In this way, traditional test marketing has become less critical, but close market assessment through marketing research has become ever more important for mass-market products. For more expensive consumer durables, including cars, product clinics play their role in new product development, once again making conventional test marketing less critical. In essence, alternative methods of gauging potential demand have evolved to supplant traditional test marketing.

CHAPTER 6 INTERNATIONAL PRICING

6.1a Quotations in GB pounds

If the value of the pound falls against the bolivar, the distributor will be able to buy more pounds and therefore pay less in bolivars for a given amount of STEADY. As the brand is at the top end of the market (price inelastic) there will be no pressure on the distributors to reduce the price to retailers. In effect, this will mean that, unless MacBeth's takes positive action, the distributors will increase their profits from existing business. There is no indication that the distributors are dissatisfied with their usual margins. MacBeth's should therefore increase its price to the distributors so that, in terms of the bolivar, it is as it was before. MacBeth's get the advantage of the increased margin between costs and revenue resulting from the relative movement in the currencies. This it can use as it wants to increase dividends, invest in updated equipment, or, as is more likely, further to promote STEADY in the Venezuelan market. The temptation is to let the additional revenue go to the distributor by default.

GLEN RIVER, on the other hand, is a 'cash cow'. Macbeth's is relying on it to generate cash to further develop the market for STEADY. The pricing strategy for GLEN RIVER is therefore to let the distributor of that brand have the benefit of the strengthening of the bolivar in relation to the pound. No action need be taken except the positive decision not to take action. The distributor is encouraged through the greater margin on GLEN RIVER to reduce the price and increase sales in the more price elastic market. Control can be exercised through monitoring the distributor's sales volumes, which should be growing.

If the value of the pound rises in relation to the bolivar, less STEADY and GLEN RIVER can be purchased for a given value of bolivars. Exports are more expensive. Competition is likely to be from the drinks of competing countries whose currency has not risen in relation to the bolivar, or has not risen so much. Co-operative advertising might be a good tactic in the circumstances.

6.1b Quotations in US dollars

With the pound strengthening against the dollar, whisky exports will become more expensive since a given number of dollars, when realized in pounds, will be less. The dollar price will need to be raised to match its fall in relation to the pound. Since the strengthening of the pound will affect all Scotch whiskies, MacBeth's is unlikely to be disadvantaged in price against other brands of Scotch, except in the short term when some exporters may be tardy in increasing their dollar prices. Competition may well come from competing drinks of other countries and strategies will need to be devised to contain this, e.g. co-operative advertising.

In the event of the pound falling steadily in relation to the dollar, MacBeth's needs take no action as payment in dollars is more advantageous than in pounds. But for the adverse terms of trade which Venezuela has with the UK, there might be pressure for prices and payment in pounds. There might be some merit in reducing the dollar price of GLEN RIVER to the distributor to match any fall in the value of the pound against the dollar, as the objective in selling GLEN RIVER is to generate cash to provide support for STEADY.

6.1c As and when the UK joins the European Monetary Union (EMU) the problem brought about by exchange rate variations will disappear. To quote and invoice in euros will be normal and exchange risk will have disappeared. Irish whiskey will be well placed in the meantime to take advantage of the new stability (and the cost advantages therein) as Ireland is a founder member of the EMU. Most of the business with the EU will be conducted in euros by MacBeth's but while the UK remains outside there will still be exchange risk, but with one currency instead of eleven. There are minor advantages in this in that the cost of changing euros into pounds rather than into a host of other currencies is reduced.

When doing business with those countries left outside the EMU, there will remain the need to change these separate currencies into pounds. In view of the referendum 'no' decisions, it is unlikely that Denmark or Sweden will enter the Eurozone in the forseeable future. Indeed the UK's entry is also questionable. However, as Denmark's currency is linked to the euro and Sweden is shadowing it, there is little need to hedge.

6.2a

Table A.1 *Answer to question 6.2(a)*

Proposed DDP PRICE in US $ delivered to customer's factory	$766,960
Equivalent in GB pounds	£479,350
less: charges Hilo and costs to customer's factory	£2,200
CIF duty paid price	£477,150
less: duty paid to US Customs in Hilo 12.5% on CIF price (1/9th)	£53,016
CIF price Hilo	£424,134
less: insurance and freight to Hilo	£14,200
FOB price British port	£409,934
less: transport and insurance from works to FOB point port of shipment	£1,800
Ex Works price	£408,134
less: agent's commission (12.5% on ex works price)	£51,016
Net ex works price	£357,118
less: estimated costs	£300,500
Gross profit	£56,618

Margin on sales $\dfrac{£56,618}{£408,134} \times \dfrac{100}{1} = 13.8\%$

i.e. margin on sales in excess of the 10% policy limitation.

6.2b One risk in extending credit to the customer for three years lies in the extra time for payment during which exchange rates can vary considerably. While these can go up or down, involving the possibility of gains as well as losses, a loss on a large contract can threaten the very existence of a company. Even if order books are healthy, failure to generate the necessary cash flows to cover current expenses can kill off a company. It is therefore necessary to ensure some form of hedging whether by selling forward or holding sufficient of the foreign currency to cover the amount at risk, or by any other form.

Another risk is that of inflation which, although apparently mastered by European countries, remains real for some others. Contract price adjustment clauses are a fair way of handling this. Should the threat of deflation, induced by insufficient demand to employ idle capacity and highlighted by the economist, Paul Krugman, come to haunt us, buyers will obtain a reduction of final price under contract price adjustment clauses.

The final risk is the normal commercial one of inability to pay through bankruptcy, acts of God and wars. If they have not already done so, the British company should insure the credit with ECGD. Banks usually insist on this credit being made available before providing finance for such transactions.

CHAPTER 7 INTERNATIONAL PROMOTION

7.1 Consider the example of the US MNC Procter & Gamble promoting its dishwashing liquid globally. The group's board of directors would agree the group's strategic objective which could be to maintain the MNC's current leadership position with a growth in turnover of 5 per cent per annum in real terms. The promotion objective would be required to fit this strategic objective. The objective of the promotion campaign might be to achieve a 5 per cent increase in current sales volume, together with a 7 per cent increase in profit within the countries targeted. An increase in market share may be required to obtain the desired sales volume and profit. An associated objective might be to achieve higher awareness of the dishwashing liquid brand Fairy within the countries in which it is used.

Procter & Gamble's head office marketing staff would consider the promotion tactics required to achieve the promotion objective globally, regionally and nationally. Past performance and associated promotion performance would be examined to determine sales targets and associated profits for each country concerned. National management would then be directed to implement the global promotion within each country. For example, in the UK, marketing staff at Procter & Gamble UK would direct the promotion campaign; French-based staff would manage the campaign in France and Chilean-based staff the equivalent for Chile.

The promotion methods used in the UK might be to concentrate advertising expenditure on 'above the line' media, predominantly using television, but also using press and cinema media to target mass consumers. This expenditure would be supported by some sales promotion expenditure in the form of discount coupons to encourage point-of-sale awareness.

Procter & Gamble's head office marketing staff decisions would strongly influence the selection of advertising agencies that would be used at national, or regional, level. Most likely, head office staff would select a major global agency that country management would be expected to use. In this way, the MNC ensures that the same broad message is promoted worldwide, although the precise way in which the message is promoted may differ from country to country to match the cultural requirements of each country. Not only can the message differ, the selection of media will probably differ from country to country in line with the general practice in each country.

The resource implications of the proposed promotion would be scrutinized throughout the promotion process, both at national and global levels. The advertising expenditure would be closely monitored at all stages, that is, at the beginning when advertising agencies quote for the promotion contract, during and after the campaign, to ensure that the quotes are maintained. Expenditure would be compared with the results achieved which in this case would be the sales, profit and awareness levels of the Fairy brand concerned. The effectiveness of the promotion programme would be monitored both globally and nationally. Sales achieved in each market would be assessed by retail outlets, by region within each country and would be compared with the sales achieved by competitors. Staffing costs would also be considered, as would the efficiency with which time scheduling was maintained.

7.2   Industrial manufacturers usually target a small number of customers, whereas consumer manufacturers target a large number. For example, Cleco, an UK-based manufacturer of forklift trucks would target organizations using sophisticated warehousing systems, numbering less than 500 across Europe. On the other hand, Mars, selling confectionery, could target 600 million or more European consumers. The promotional approach used by the industrial firm would be likely to concentrate on communication with organizational decision buyer groups. It might use 'above the line' promotion through the technical press (perhaps including the specialist *Logistics Europe* in the case of Cleco), attendance at international trade exhibitions (Hanover Trade Fair) and a sales force comprising specialist engineers with expertise in forklift design. The sum spent on this promotion would be low compared to the expenditure by the consumer manufacturer, Mars. In that case, Mars would be likely to spend many millions of GB pounds (or euros) across Europe on 'above the line' media, concentrating on media likely to reach the mass market, that is, television, press and cinema. This expenditure would be supported by 'below the line' promotion through sponsorship of high-profile events such as sports competitions as well as by redemption coupons, '3 for 2' type discounts and point of sale materials.

Industrial manufacturers are likely to undertake their promotion campaign primarily by using their own staff and bringing in external support as appropriate. Consumer manufacturers would almost certainly primarily use the services of international advertising agencies, although they would be managed by the firm's internal promotion division within the marketing remit.

Service industry's approach to international promotion depends on the type of service concerned. Services that most closely reflect those of industrial manufacturing, for example, logistics services, industrial consultants and computer software providers, are likely to follow similar promotion approaches. Services that are more similar to consumer manufacturers, for example, those of airlines, household insurance, hotels and restaurants, are more likely to use mass-market promotion methods. McDonald's fast food outlets spend much more on international promotion than would Nippon Express, Deutsche Post or Tibbett & Britten in promoting their logistics service provision. McDonald's would use international advertising agencies to implement its promotion through the media; Nippon Express, Deutsche Post or

Tibbett & Britten might use international advertising agencies but would be more likely to undertake their promotion using their own internal staff resource.

In conclusion, industrial manufacturers would communicate with their customers (and potential customers) using appropriate methods that are likely to be more targeted than those used by consumer manufacturers. Industrial manufacturers will have small numbers of customers to target, each of whom is likely to have the potential to spend large sums; consumer manufacturers will be targeting large numbers of customers each spending relatively low amounts. Promotion methods have to be adapted to reach the types of customers targeted. The methods used influence the ways in which promotion is implemented.

CHAPTER 8 INTERNATIONAL CHANNELS OF DISTRIBUTION

8.1a The two situations are connected in that Casa Avila's position as supplier of a line of complementary equipment will be affected in the long term if it cannot obtain sales rights in Mexico from the new company for the glass-lined vessels. Klinger Kahn could make this contingent on Casa Avila reducing commission during the period before local manufacture. Because the relationship has been successful and Casa Avila has shown itself to be a good import agent, it might be able to call on the precedent of the relationship to mitigate the severity of the cut in commission.

Given a satisfactory conclusion to the commission issue, Casa Avila can show it is extremely well connected in terms of providing finance and general support for the customers. Its reputation in this respect must carry some weight, but it may need to demonstrate this before it can influence Klinger Kahn. If the German company cannot perceive these abilities, then no power will be exerted by Casa Avila as a result. For its part, Klinger Kahn can exercise power if it is aware that Casa Avila needs its products to complete its line of product offerings to the customers; it gives them leverage.

While the two parties may be aware of the power they exert, they should also realize that they are mutually dependent, particularly in the light of the projected growth of the market, which fact also gives them combined power in terms of their potential. Also, it will be difficult for Klinger Kahn to disregard the market knowledge of Casa Avila in the light of its experience and connections in the industry. It is important that Klinger Kahn is seen to make an equal sacrifice rather than an equal percentage reduction in its margin.

8.1b Exchange rate variations are usually the first factors that spring to mind when possible changes in the environment threaten the harmony in the relationship between a principal and an agent based abroad, but this has been eliminated as a result of the decision to manufacture in Mexico. The misunderstandings that arise from the differences in culture will be reduced as the management of the new company comes to understand the Mexican way. If any parts need to be imported, that will be the responsibility of the new company, whereas import of goods exported from Germany would have been the responsibility of the agent under the earlier arrangement. Any spares would have been the responsibility of the agent to stock and supply under the previous agreement, with perhaps the agent needing to buy the spares as part of the agreement. Under the new agreement, as sales agent, Casa Avila cannot expect to receive the same amount of commission as when buying and stocking spares and undertaking the duties involved in arranging for customs clearance of shipments received on behalf of customers.

8.2a Exclusive agreements are made with an agent when that agent is seen to specialize in the market which includes a principal's supply. To retain the agent's efforts on his behalf, a principal gives the agent exclusivity in the market. It is a strong incentive to promote the principal's product and learn more about its application as a result of the wider experience of the whole market, making the agent more effective in his dealings with customers and potential customers.

8.2b Some markets are not big enough to give the agent a return which justifies the effort expected of him by a manufacturer. In the circumstances, it may be desirable to give the agent another territory or territories. Machinery manufacturers for the construction industry may find that a French-speaking agent in the Ivory Coast has not a business sufficiently lucrative in his own country where the industry is small. However, when his country is combined with that in countries like Senegal, Mali and Burkina Faso, they may provide a return commensurate with the effort normally expected of him. A similar situation might exist for the sale of machinery to the sugar industry in Kenya, Uganda, Zambia and Zimbabwe.

8.3 This question seeks to distinguish between the criteria for selection that depend on scientific or other analytical ascertainment on the one hand and those that depend on opinion and consensus on the other. The former is illustrated by market size which can be measured or established by inquiry like industry structure; the latter is demonstrated by company strategy or dominant coalition. Strategy can be a matter for debate within the decision-making caucus of an organization. A dominant coalition can be a joint decision by those in influential positions to take a certain course of action among alternatives instead of another, based on their own perceptions and preferences, for example, when a group of people decide to expand into new countries rather than develop further their existing markets because of their common interest or ability in foreign languages.

8.4 This question is aimed at increasing your awareness of developments in the use of the Internet insofar as they affect distribution channels. For example, at the time of writing these were very new:

■ E-Crossnet is a network run by a new company of that name set up by Merrill Lynch Mercury and Barclays Global Investors. It is financed by nineteen of the largest UK-based fund managers to enable them to bypass the London Stock Exchange and continental bourses. At European level, a single stock market planned by traditional bourses is set to face competition from Posit, a cross-border electronic trading system aimed at bypassing it altogether.

■ I-Resource is an Icelandic company which has devised software to enable mobile telephones to be used to connect to the Internet so that users can contact websites of their choice to transact business direct or through an intermediary. It is this system that Nokia and Ericsson are developing to extend access.

Can you identify new entrants to existing electronic channels or new ideas that have emerged in the recent past as in the above examples?

CHAPTER 9 INTERNATIONAL MARKETING PLANNING AND IMPLEMENTATION

9.1 European food retailing presents a much more fragmented picture than its equivalent in the US. There is no Continent-wide chain of supermarkets but instead a proliferation of food retailers with international interests including the French Carrefour, the Dutch Aldi and the British Tesco. Europeans do not even have the same shopping habits. In the Netherlands, 'basket' shopping at small supermarkets is still common, a pattern which has largely died out in the UK where large edge-of town superstores have taken an increasing market share. Europe has different languages, tastes and cultures, particularly in the food market. For example, sausage, defined as being 'finely minced meat, usually pork or beef, mixed with fat, cereal or bread and packed into a tube-shaped animal intestine or synthetic casing' differs between regions and countries. German Bratwurst is not the same as Italian salami; French saucisson is very different from the British sausage.

It would be difficult to prepare a European marketing plan for Wal-Mart that could generalize across all European countries. Rather it would be appropriate to assimilate national marketing plans within the overall European plan. This will be considered below, using the ASDA marketing plan as typical of what could be considered for a European national plan.

Outline of Wal-Mart's European marketing plan

Wal-Mart's international marketing plan would cover the basic framework outlined in Table 9.1. It should indicate the group's business mission and associated corporate objectives. Thus, the Wal-Mart business mission could be assumed to be: to maintain continued growth in the US and to extend domination internationally in targeted markets, including the Americas and Continental Europe.

Its corporate objective is to achieve 'an annual growth above the average gained by the food retail industry in general, and above the average annual growth rate achieved by Wal-Mart over the last three years'. An annual turnover growth rate of 5 per cent above inflation with profits of 7 per cent might be set. Additional objectives (or targets) might be to increase customer loyalty as measured by customer repeat shopping visits to Wal-Mart outlets.

253

The plan should include an environmental audit covering the political (including legal), economic, social and technological (PEST) climate in which the retail industry is operating. Examples of social issues might include the trend towards longer hours, even 24 hours, retail outlet opening; technological factors might include Electronic Point of Sale (EPOS) developments. The plan would progress to undertake a marketing audit for the market being considered. It would indicate the market size and trends, the characteristics of targeted consumers and the competitors to be considered. Consumers can be defined in terms of their geo-demographic characteristics including their age, sex, income and regional distribution within the market. Competitors may be assessed in terms of their turnover, profitability and market share. Such analyses should enable market segments to be identified and the relative performance of the firm concerned (ASDA) to be gauged.

The plan should consider the firm's internal strengths and weaknesses within the market and establish the opportunities and threats presented. These will indicate the marketing tactics that might be used by Wal-Mart management to achieve the strategic objectives and goals set for ASDA in the UK, as well as for the projected expansion to other European countries.

The Marketing Information System (MIS) should provide data for management decision-making. It would encompass the MIS previously set up for the UK-based ASDA acquisition. It will cover the UK market and may also encompass parts of Continental Europe, even countries within CEE. For the UK, internal data sources would relate to sales achieved within ASDA retail outlets as shown by customer point of sales scanning. External sources might include data provided by A.C. Nielsen national retail audits and Taylor Nelson Sofres (TNS) consumer panels. Marketing intelligence could be obtained from intermediaries within the value chain, such as food producers, wholesalers and logistics service providers.

The plan should proceed to indicate the type of product and service that the retailer expects to provide, that is, the product range. There will be details of the expected combination of products brands (own brands and private brands) together with past and forecast sales (and profit) performance and new product proposals. Pricing and promotional strategies should be given, as should those for channels of distribution provision.

Thus, the plan should indicate the type and volume of products forecast to be sold at different times in the annual planning cycle. For example, it may be that Heinz mayonnaise will be expected to sell heavily in the summer between May and August. ASDA's own brand of mayonnaise will similarly have peak sales in the summer but the plan might (or might not) set its sales to the same level as those for Heinz, depending on data gathered from the MIS. Price levels and supporting 'below the line' sales promotion should similarly be shown.

Throughout the marketing plan, consideration has to be made for the resource implications associated with the proposals. For example, it is important to ascertain the likely cash flows associated with buying stock for fluctuations in sales due to holidays such as Easter and Christmas. Consideration should be made for financial provision to support the need for extra staffing at holiday times or for training staff to use new information technology and so on. At the same time, the plan has to high-light the time-scheduling implications associated with the marketing proposals. For example, should management decide to promote the benefits of shopping at ASDA within the media, preparations should be made to accommodate any consequent increase in consumers.

Thus, the US retailer Wal-Mart would use a variety of sources to undertake inter-national marketing planning. Its European marketing plan would be required to fit into its global mission and corporate plan. It should be assimilated from individual country plans such as that outlined for Wal-Mart's UK acquisition, ASDA. The country plans should consider each European country's particular market conditions and methods of marketing, using appropriate MISs. These country plans can be brought together to provide a comprehensive viable European marketing plan that considers the complexities of international marketing.

Index

Page numbers in italic type indicate figures, tables or boxes.